Educating the Muslims of America

Educating the

Muslims of America

EDITED BY

YVONNE Y. HADDAD, FARID SENZAI,

AND JANE I. SMITH

OXFORD
UNIVERSITY PRESS

2009

OXFORD
UNIVERSITY PRESS

Oxford University Press, Inc., publishes works that further
Oxford University's objective of excellence
in research, scholarship, and education.

Oxford New York
Auckland Cape Town Dar es Salaam Hong Kong Karachi
Kuala Lumpur Madrid Melbourne Mexico City Nairobi
New Delhi Shanghai Taipei Toronto

With offices in
Argentina Austria Brazil Chile Czech Republic France Greece
Guatemala Hungary Italy Japan Poland Portugal Singapore
South Korea Switzerland Thailand Turkey Ukraine Vietnam

Published by Oxford University Press, Inc.
198 Madison Avenue, New York, New York 10016

www.oup.com

Oxford is a registered trademark of Oxford University Press

Library of Congress Cataloging-in-Publication Data
Educating the Muslims of America / edited by Yvonne Y. Haddad,
Farid Senzai, and Jane I. Smith.
p. cm.
Includes bibliographical references and index.
ISBN 978-0-19-537520-6
1. Islamic education—United States. 2. Islamic education—Canada. I. Haddad,
Yvonne Yazbeck, 1935– II. Senzai, Farid. III. Smith, Jane I.
LC913.U6E38 2009
371.077—dc22   2008026397

9 8 7 6 5 4 3 2
Printed in the United States of America
on acid-free paper

Preface

Shortly after September 11, 2001, the American Muslim community was stunned when it was reported by the *New York Times* and other high-profile newspapers that textbooks in Islamic schools were promoting anti-American and anti-Semitic views. Americans began asking whether Islamic schools in America could be breeding grounds for homegrown terrorists, like the so-called *madrassas* (Arabic for "schools") of Pakistan that received much post-9/11 media coverage.

Since that tragic day, there continues to be considerable media coverage and insistence by some policy-makers that Islamic schools are part of a "fifth column" and thus should be placed under surveillance. This heightened attention reflects an effort by some to link Islamic schools to extremism, thus suggesting that they may be a growing threat to national security. In the post-9/11 environment Muslims are under increasing scrutiny, particularly by those who fear that Islamic schools are producing radical youth.

Meanwhile, many American Muslim parents have started asking whether it would be safer to send their children to Islamic schools so as to avoid an anti-Muslim backlash in public and parochial school systems. As a result of 9/11 Muslim parents have been challenged to reflect on their own family identities. Those who want to reinforce the Islamic values of their families may decide to place their children in Islamic schools.

As attention on Islamic education intensifies in the media, the need to examine the state of Islamic education in North America becomes more urgent. The growth in the number of Islamic schools and homeschools across the country, reflecting growth in the American Muslim population, deserves a closer review.

Islamic education in the United States is an increasingly salient issue for the Muslim community, yet a relatively new topic of research for the academic community. Very little empirical research exists on the subject to date. Although scholars, educators, administrators, and practitioners in the field are now organizing conferences and presenting their preliminary findings on the state of this nascent field, much more remains to be done.

This book is an effort to fill that gap. It is a result of a conference on Islamic education held on April 6, 2006, at Georgetown University, hosted by the Institute for Social Policy and Understanding and the Prince Alwaleed Bin Talal Center for Muslim-Christian Understanding. The conference attracted researchers, scholars, and educators from around the country for a full day of presentations, discussion, and exchange of ideas pertaining to the status of Islamic education in North America.

In addition to outlining key areas pertaining to Islamic education, this volume, like the conference that preceded it, attempts to highlight the many challenges facing educators, parents, and religious leaders in their efforts to address the education needs of their communities. Islamic schools in particular have faced many challenges, including their ongoing development and sustainability.

As the number of Islamic schools increases throughout the country, scholars and practitioners are beginning to understand the difficulties faced by these fledgling institutions. They have also begun to propose ways in which to provide sound religious education in a pluralist society. The late Shareefa Al-Khatib, who was a leading pioneer for Islamic education and the president of the Muslim Education Council, reflected that many of these schools still "have a lot of growing to do." But as the contributors to this volume point out, as with any new community, there are difficulties associated with trying to mobilize, organize, and institutionalize new schools. Like so many other earlier religious groups, the Muslim community has not been spared from the trials of finding its niche in American public life. We hope that this volume helps us better understand the growing pains faced by educators and offers insight into addressing these ongoing challenges.

—*Farid Senzai*

Acknowledgments

This project was initially conceived by Mohamed Nimer of American University. In collaboration with Yvonne Haddad of Georgetown University, Sulayman Nyang of Howard University, and Zahid Bukhari of Georgetown University, he assembled a team of experts—including scholars, activists, and practitioners—to elaborate on the key topics in the field of Islamic education. This group included Susan Douglass and Munir Sheik, Council on Islamic Education; Karen Keyworth and Judi Amri, Islamic Schools League of America; Samuel Shareef and Shomraka Omar Keita, Sister Clara Muhammad School, Washington, D.C.; Zaheer Arastu, Alhuda School, College Park, Maryland; Mahboobeh Ayat, Muslim Community Schools, Potomac, Maryland; A. Rahman Khan and Khurrum Zaman, Al-Rahmah School, Baltimore, Maryland; Ahmed Al-Alawani, Graduate School of Islamic Social Sciences, Ashburn, Virginia; Afeefa Syeed, Al-Fatih Academy, Herndon, Virginia; and Emily Smith, a homeschool educator.

A conference on Islamic education, cosponsored by the Institute for Social Policy and Understanding (ISPU) and Prince Alwaleed Bin Talal Center for Muslim-Christian Understanding (ACMCU), was held on April 6, 2006, at Georgetown University. A select number of papers from the conference were assembled for this book, along with some additional studies commissioned specifically for the volume. A project of this scale would not have been possible without the assistance and financial contribution of numerous individuals and organizations. We would like to especially thank ISPU and ACMCU for their generous financial support. Additional financial contributions were provided by the Berkley Center for Religion, Peace and World Affairs, Georgetown University; the Center for Contemporary Arab Studies, Georgetown University; the National Resource Center on the Middle East, Georgetown University; the Office of the Muslim Chaplain, Georgetown University; and the Division of United States Studies, Woodrow Wilson International Center for Scholars. We would also like to thank ISPU's board members, Mazen Asbahi and Muzammil Ahmed, for their assistance and support, as well as Zareena Grewal, a member of the ISPU research team and faculty at Yale University, for her review of the papers submitted for the conference. We are also most grateful for the support and management skills of ISPU staff members Afshan Siddiqi and Huma Alam and ACMCU staff members Huma Malik and Denisse Bonilla-Chaoui.

Contents

Contributors

MONA ABO-ZENA is a doctoral student in the Eliot-Pearson Department of Child Development at Tufts University, with research interests in religion and identity development. She earned her B.A. in sociology from the University of Chicago and her Ed.M. from Harvard University's Graduate School of Education. Abo-Zena has over ten years of teaching and administrative experience in public and Islamic schools. Her efforts to support learning and teaching about Islam include organizing events for children and adults in a range of venues, including schools, religious institutions, and the Boston Children's Museum.

ANNA BOWERS is a filmmaker living in Brooklyn, New York. She holds a B.A. in film and anthropology. Her study began as a project for a seminar on Islam in America. The interviews she conducted have encouraged Bowers to focus her work in journalism and documentary film on human rights, education, and public policy. She would like to dedicate her chapter to prison imams, whose compassion and commitment inspire and transform those they counsel.

LOUIS CRISTILLO is a research assistant professor at Teachers College Columbia University in the Department of International and Transcultural Studies. He teaches courses on education and development in the Middle East and the Muslim world as well as Islamic education in the United States. He is the principal investigator of the Muslim Youth in New York City Public Schools Study, a three-year research project funded by the Ford Foundation that examines the impact of post-9/11 school climate on the religiosity, identity, and civic belonging of Muslim American adolescents. Cristillo coauthored a chapter in *A Community of Many Worlds: Arab Americans in New York City,* and has written entries on schools and higher education in the *Encyclopedia of Islam in the United States.*

SUSAN L. DOUGLASS, who has an M.A. in Arab studies from Georgetown University and a B.A. in history from the University of Rochester, was a senior researcher for the United Nations Alliance of Civilizations initiative and is an affiliated scholar for the Institute on Religion and Civic Values. Her publications include *World Eras: Rise and Spread of Islam, 622–1500* (2002) and *Teaching about Religion in National and State Social Studies Standards* (2000), copublished by the Freedom Forum First Amendment Center. She creates teaching resources for the Council on Islamic Education, the National Center for History in the Schools, IslamProject.org, and the San Diego State University curriculum project World History for Us All. Douglass is currently a student in the doctoral program in history at George Mason University.

YVONNE Y. HADDAD is a professor of the history of Islam and Christian-Muslim relations at the Prince Alwaleed Bin Talal Center for Muslim-Christian Understanding at Georgetown University. She is a past president of the Middle East Studies Association and a former editor of *Muslim World.* Her published works include *Contemporary Islam and the Challenge of History; Islam, Gender, and Social Change* (with J. Esposito); *Not Quite American?, Islamic Values in the United States* (with A. Lummis); *The Muslims of America; Christian-Muslim Encounters* (with W. Haddad); and *Muslim Women in America* (with J. Smith and K. Moore).

KAREN KEYWORTH is a cofounder and the director of education for the Islamic Schools League of America (established 1998), a national organization dedicated to the development and growth of quality education in full-time K–12 Islamic schools throughout North America. An educator for over 20 years, she holds a B.A. in linguistics and an M.A. in English; has taught English as a second language, developmental writing, and developmental reading; and was the founding principal of the Greater Lansing Islamic School (established 1996). Keyworth has also published on K–12 Islamic education and postsecondary curricula and has done education consulting for public and private schools and businesses.

NADIA INJI KHAN is a graduate of Georgetown University. She majored in Arabic and studio arts (with a painting concentration). She has a certificate in Muslim-Christian understanding; she is also a calligraphy student under the tutelage of Muhammad Zakariya. Khan is currently studying Arabic in Oman and Qatar and hopes to study Islamic law and how it deals with the arts in graduate school.

PRISCILLA MARTINEZ is a homeschooling mother of six children in metropolitan Washington, D.C. She was elected to the board of directors of the Organization of Virginia Homeschoolers in 2004 and also served as the chair of the board's Public Relations Committee. Martinez is the founder of the Ashburn-Sterling Homeschoolers group and is an active volunteer for the National Capital Area Council of the Boy Scouts of America, the Girl Scouts Council of the Nation's Capital, the Interfaith Council of Metropolitan Washington, the All Dulles Area Muslim Society, the Ashburn Soccer Club, and Dulles Little League. She frequently delivers seminars and workshops designed to help parents new to homeschooling.

SHABANA MIR is an assistant professor at Oklahoma State University's College of Education. She received her Ph.D. in education policy studies at Indiana University, and she has an M.Phil. in school development from Cambridge University and an M.A. in English literature from Punjab University (Lahore). She has taught education at Eastern Illinois University and Indiana University and English at the International Islamic University. She was a visiting researcher at Georgetown University and a research affiliate at Harvard University's Pluralism Project. Mir has contributed chapters to *Comparative Education: The Dialectic of the Global and the Local*, *Nurturing Child and Adolescent Spirituality*, and *The Encyclopedia of Islam in America*.

YASMIN MOLL is a doctoral student in sociocultural anthropology at New York University. Her main research interests relate to the intersections of neoliberal globalization, transnational media, and Islamic piety in Egypt. She is also interested in Muslim-American narratives of belonging and diasporic media. She has an M.A. in Near and Middle East studies from the School of Oriental and African Studies in the United Kingdom.

BARBARA SAHLI provides educational outreach on understanding Islam and Muslims, working particularly with students and teachers. She designs and coordinates educational encounters between Muslim and non-Muslim students at several Islamic schools and serves as a resource for teachers seeking accurate information about Islam. Sahli has collaborated with Boston Children's Museum on creating interactive events showcasing Islamic culture; she has also taught reading/language arts to middle school students at the Islamic Academy of New England in Massachusetts. She has a B.A. in psychology from Clark University in Worcester, Massachusetts.

FARID SENZAI is an assistant professor in the Political Science Department at Santa Clara University. He is also a fellow and the director of research at the Institute for Social Policy and Understanding, focused on researching the Muslim community in the United States. Senzai has been a research associate at the Brookings Institution, where he studied U.S. foreign policy toward the Middle East, and a research analyst at the Council of Foreign Relations, working on the Muslim Politics project. He has also served as a coordinator for Oxford Analytica and the World Bank. Senzai received his M.A. in international affairs from Columbia University and his Ph.D. in political science and international relations from Oxford University.

JANE I. SMITH, recently a professor of Islamic studies and codirector of the Macdonald Center for Christian-Muslim Relations at Hartford Seminary, is now the associate dean for faculty and academic affairs at Harvard Divinity School. She teaches in the areas of Islam in America, interfaith dialogue, and history of religions. Smith is the author of *Muslims, Christians and the Challenge of Interfaith Dialogue* (2007); *Muslim Women in America* (coauthored with Yvonne Haddad, 2006); *Becoming American: Immigration and Religious Life in the United States* (coedited with Yvonne Haddad and John Esposito, 2004); and *Islam in America* (1999).

CHRISTINA SAFIYA TOBIAS-NAHI is the director of public affairs for Islamic Relief in Washington, D.C. She has taught comparative religion and religion and politics at Tufts University, where she participated in setting up an interfaith youth program, and she has worked with the Islamic Legal Studies Program at Harvard University. Tobias-Nahi received an M.A. in international relations from the Boston University–Paris Overseas Graduate Center and an M.Ed. from Harvard University's Graduate School of Education. She conducted a national study on Muslim women converts funded by the Harvard Pluralism Project and has written for the media on Muslim responses to 9/11. Teacher certified, she helped found an Islamic school in the Boston area.

JASMIN ZINE is an assistant professor in the Department of Sociology at Wilfrid Laurier University. She teaches in the fields of education and social justice and critical race and ethnic studies. Her publications include coauthored books on race and education and inclusive schooling, along with articles on Muslims and education in the Canadian Diaspora and on Muslim women's studies. Zine has worked on educational initiatives and curricula to promote anti-Islamophobia education. Her forthcoming book on Islamic schooling in Canada is entitled *Staying on the Straight Path: Unraveling the Politics of Gender, Faith, Identity, and Knowledge in Canadian Islamic Schools.*

Educating the Muslims
of America

Introduction: The Challenge of Islamic Education in North America

Yvonne Y. Haddad and Jane I. Smith

Since 9/11 Islamic education in the United States has come under heavy scrutiny, as have many Muslim institutions, fueled by fears that American schools, mosques, and other organizations may be producing radical young Muslims. In a 2005 *New York Sun* article entitled "What Are Islamic Schools Teaching?" for example, the vigilant journalist Daniel Pipes insisted that a number of Islamic schools, which he identified by name, are promoting anti-Semitic views and what he called other aspects of the Islamist agenda. He went on to assert that when Muslim leaders profess themselves to be shocked by such revelations but do not act to make any changes, it is evidence that "Islamic schools, the mosques, and other Muslim organizations . . . will continue their cat-and-mouse game so long as it works."[1] Pipes also raised dire concerns about the establishment of a new school for teaching Arab culture, the Khalil Gibran International Academy, in New York City.[2]

Increasingly, Muslims are facing attacks rising out of public fears about terrorism. Online articles critiquing Islamic forms of education abound, with such titles as "American Saudi Schools: Home Grown Sleeper-Cells" and "U.S. Islamic Schools Teaching Homegrown Hate."[3] On March 15, 2007, an online petition requesting that Islamic schools be banned entirely was circulated, charging that such institutions are imposing religion and backward traditions on children under the age of 16, encouraging "discrimination, inequality, revulsion, segregation and isolation right from childhood."[4] The challenge for Muslims as they face the task of educating their youth and other members of the community is thus threefold: (a) they must continue to improve the quality of education they provide about the faith and practice of Islam to Muslims themselves, (b) they must be vigilant to ensure that the fears of Pipes and others about Muslim institutions in post-9/11 America are not valid, and (c) they must intensify efforts to educate the American public—who may know about Islam only through the often distorted lens of the media—about the elements of their religion that are consistent with the message of the Qur'an and the teachings of Prophet Muhammad.

The importance of education to Muslims from the earliest days of Islam to the present can scarcely be overstated. That importance, if anything, has been raised to new levels in post-9/11 America. Local and national conferences and conventions of Muslims from various schools and branches of Islam place the importance of education at the top of the list of priorities for the attention of the community. This volume is presented as an examination of the breadth of the issue of Islamic education in America, showing some of the ways in which education in its many facets is occupying the attention of students and scholars, Muslim organizations and families, as they struggle to determine what it means to be Muslim in a pluralistic America.

Quality academic education about Islamic history, Qur'an, law, social movements, anthropological studies, contemporary politics, and other important areas since the middle of the 20th century has been available in about a dozen colleges and universities of the United States, and academic attention to Islam in all its aspects has increased markedly since 9/11. The percentage of Muslims who are formally teaching about their own religion and history has also grown noticeably, and Muslims are increasingly participating in and taking charge of sections on Islam in major academic association meetings. A small number of Christian seminaries and theological schools now have Muslims as regular or adjunct members of their faculties. The importance of the academic study of Islam at the university and graduate level cannot be overstated, and in many cases Muslim students themselves are learning not only from their professors but from each other through conversation and classroom dialogue.

Religious education of Muslims, however, generally has been the province of the private realm of individual communities and families across the country as they have struggled to discern the best ways for both children and adults to learn and maintain the faith and practice of Islam. Muslims live as a small but highly visible minority within a majority America that is both secular in ideology—by virtue of the First Amendment of the Constitution's separation of state and religion—and majority Christian in practice. How can they present their faith honestly and persuasively to a non-Muslim American public who continues to cast a skeptical eye toward Islam? How can they educate the members of their own communities about how to distinguish the essentials of Islamic faith from the cultural accretions that represent the variety of cultures from which many of their families originate? How can they both educate their children religiously and at the same time protect them from what many Muslim parents perceive to be the temptations of an often immoral American society? While these efforts to teach about Islam reach across the spectrum from children to adults and even from Muslims to those who are not Muslim, it is with the Islamic education of children and the inculcating of Islamic norms and values that Muslims have been most immediately concerned.

Islamic education in America now takes place in a variety of venues, including homes, Sunday/weekend schools, summer camps, and *halaqas* or study circles, as well as at conventions and through annual symposia. All of these different educational contexts supplement (or, in some cases, replace) the public school, which by definition does not and cannot provide sufficient religious training. K–8 or K–12 Islamic schools provide alternative education for character development; protect children from stereotyping and taunting; offer Islamic alternatives to such social ills as premarital sex, drugs, and violence; and allow children to avoid public school curricula that may in some way be prejudiced against Islam.

A Brief History of Islamic Education in America

As numerous historians of religion in America have observed, Muslim immigrants have come to this country in waves from over 80 nations.[5] Small numbers arrived in the late 19th century, with more coming after the first and second world wars. For the most part these Muslims enrolled their children either in public schools or, if they could afford it, in private institutions, with a preference for Christian parochial schools where their children could gain an ethical foundation. They had very limited means and resources and were too few in number to be able to afford their own schools. Many of them tried their best to blend into American society and would not have wanted to be distinguished by having parochial schools with Muslim identity. They were, however, concerned about maintaining their children in the faith and did establish the equivalent of Christian Sunday schools to teach them Islam and Qur'an.

By the second decade of the 20th century several groups began to work seriously to offer religious education to Muslims. Ahmadiyya missionaries had been providing translations of the Qur'an and other Islamic materials for their American converts, mainly African Americans. The Nation of Islam (NOI), headed by Elijah Muhammad from the 1930s until his death in 1975, started an educational institution called the University of Islam (UOI) in Detroit. Initially set up in the home of Clara and Elijah Muhammad, it was moved to Chicago when the NOI set up national offices there.[6] While bearing the title "university," the UOI was really an elementary and secondary school, one that claimed a universal curriculum. The main function of the UOI was to educate blacks to "know self," "love self," and "do for self."[7] This philosophy was foundational to the NOI, which, although Islamic in name, also espoused certain doctrines considered extremely heterodox by other Muslims.[8] It was out of the UOI that the Sister Clara Muhammad schools developed.

The NOI moved to build more schools in the coming decades, so that by the time Elijah Muhammad died, the UOI network boasted 41 private parochial schools across the United States. They were mainly preschool and early primary but with secondary programs in some of the larger cities. When Elijah's son Wallace, soon to take the name Warith Deen, took over the leadership of the Nation of Islam, he proceeded to educate his followers away from the heterodox beliefs of his father to orthodox Sunni Islam. The UOI system also changed and was then renamed after Sister Clara Muhammad. While students continued to be taught about their African heritage, the religious content of their education became orthodox. When, in 1978, Louis Farrakhan broke with Warith Deen, the rupture affected the running of the Sister Clara Muhammad schools, and many of them were forced to close or reduce their programs.[9]

The new Muslim immigrants who came after 1965 were initially from the professional and more well-to-do classes and therefore were socially mobile, convinced of the importance of education, and wealthier, although some were asylum seekers. They arrived from nations that were more conscious of the need for the specifically Islamic religious education of their children and began to address this need by starting Islamic schools. Immigrant Muslims in America began to turn their attention to the question of Islamic education for their youth, as will be illustrated by the essays to follow, and African American Muslims continued to talk and write about the importance of curriculum and identity. When in 1989 the Islamic Society of North America (ISNA) conducted the first study of Muslim schools in the United States, there were 49 schools in existence. Only three years later the number had grown to 80, of which 34 were Sister Clara Muhammad schools.[10]

By 2000, the development of independent private Islamic schools had become an important part of the picture of Muslim education in America. ISNA initiated annual education forums to provide meeting places for Muslims to gather, reflect, and share their perspectives on the challenges they face in their various teaching venues and to discuss issues such as curriculum, methodology, and educational resources. Financial issues continue to be major in the development of Muslim schools in general as teachers suffer from poor pay and lack of benefits, and the institutions often lack the resources to provide a creative and beneficial learning environment. Such constraints have particularly hindered the Sister Clara Muhammad institutions. The Muslim Teachers College, established in 1991, has suffered from meager financial resources on the part of the African American community as well as lack of financial support from Muslim countries and from immigrant American Muslims.[11]

Muslim efforts to provide Islamic schools in one way mirror the efforts to provide parochial education established earlier by Protestants, Roman Catholics, and Jews in the United States. Islamic schools, of course, are certainly not an American invention. They have existed for years in the Arab world and the Indian Subcontinent, for example, as parallels to public education and to Christian missionary schools. Islamic education had always been associated with the mosques. The Azhar school network in Egypt, the Maqasid in Syria and Lebanon, the Pesantran in Indonesia, the Deobandi school system in India and Pakistan, and the Gulen in Turkey, Bosnia, and elsewhere were developed in reaction to British, Dutch, and French colonial and missionary schools as well as in the effort to provide Islamically grounded moral instruction. They were parochial schools using modern systems of education. Islamic schools in Egypt, Jordan, and other Middle East countries, as well as in Southeast Asia, today provide both the state curriculum and Islamic education. All schools, whether secular or religious, are called *madrassas,* which technically means "places for studying."

Unfortunately, since 9/11, for many Americans the word *madrassa* erroneously has come to connote a place for the training of future terrorists, a perception that American Muslims are trying hard to counter. There is only one old-fashioned-style boarding madrassa in North America, located in Buffalo, New York. Islamic day schools cater to both Sunnis (some of which are Salafi in orientation) and Shiites. (A network of Shiite schools is located in several states, including Michigan, Maryland, and California.) The Muslim American Society (MAS) has established a large number of such institutions.[12] Youth and working adults wishing to obtain advanced knowledge in Islamic studies may enroll in the Islamic American University (online), which grew out of the work of the MAS.

Many public schools are actively trying to use the opportunity of having Muslim students in class to help non-Muslim students know more about Islam. On major Islamic holidays, parents of Muslim children are sometimes invited to class to explain what the holidays are about and why their children look forward to them rather than to Christmas, Hanukkah, or Easter celebrations. Such opportunities for doing educational *da'wah* (here meaning "educating about Islam") are very important to many in the Muslim community, not only as a sign of respect but as a sign that they are an acknowledged part of American pluralism.

In the Orange Crescent Muslim Elementary School in Garden Grove, California, longtime Islamic educator Zakiyyah Muhammad initiated a unique experiment in Islamic training. From December 2001 to June 2002, she worked with the director of education at the University of California, Irvine Extension, to bring a certification course to her teachers at Orange Crescent. The first of its kind, the Teaching Certificate in Islamic Education gives Muslim teachers exposure to teaching methodologies and assistance in working through new curricula. Thus the teachers have attempted to integrate the secular and religious coherently so as to define the proper role of Islam in American public life.[13]

Educating Islamically in America

Most Muslim children attend public schools in the United States, and their parents are neither economically able nor ideologically inclined to send them elsewhere. Nonetheless, the fact that American public schools, particularly those in urban areas, often are embroiled in problems of discipline, disorder, and decline in the quality of education is a concern to all parents. Some Muslim families who can afford it decide to send children to non-Muslim private schools, many of which have a Christian denominational heritage. For more conservative Muslim families, however, a number of hard realities emerge as they deliberate how to best provide a faith-based Islamic education to their children:

1. Within the curricula of many public schools, especially high schools, certain subjects provide problems for conservative Muslim parents. Many object to the teaching of sex education in mixed classes, to advocacy of protected sex rather than abstinence, or to having their girls forced to participate in physical education or other activities in which they are not allowed to wear appropriate Islamic covering. The Council on American-Islamic Relations (CAIR) also has found numerous illustrations of discrimination against Muslims in school curricula, as well as illustrations of Islamophobia in some of the teachers themselves.
2. Given the negative publicity about Islam consequent to the 9/11 bombings, and reinforced when other acts of terrorism around the world are attributed to Muslim causes, Muslim children enrolled in public schools have faced teasing and sometimes even cruelty from their classmates.

3. Although some efforts are being made to present accurate information about Islam in public school textbooks, many still contain errors and misrepresentations of the religion and its adherents. Even well-intended instructors find themselves inadvertently perpetuating old stereotypes forged out of centuries of imperialist Western views of Islam.[14] CAIR has been working with school administrators to remove both errors in the presentation of the religion and bias in teaching.

Such realities present strong arguments for Muslim parents to try to provide alternative education to public schools for their children. On the other hand, many parents worry that if they isolate children in Islamic schools or try to train them at home, they will not gain the knowledge and experience necessary for participation in a multicultural, multireligious, and often aggressively secular society that they will need in order to survive as adults in the United States.

Muslim parents whose children are enrolled in public schools may decide that it is important also to provide them a specifically Islamic education. Some offer this in the home environment, with one or both parents helping their children to learn the fundamentals of Islamic faith and practice. Many children attend after-school classes offered by mosques or Islamic centers or by members of the Muslim community in their homes. Mosques usually run some kind of Sunday or weekend educational programs, sometimes for both children and adults. Some parents feel that even these opportunities for their children to learn about the faith are not sufficient. They may ultimately want to remove their children from the public school and have them educated in the kind of Islamic environment offered by Muslim schools.

Given the prevailing reality in the United States, in which anti-Muslim prejudice continues to rise, the role of the Islamic school is not only to inculcate information about Islam but also to fashion a new generation of American Muslims that now has the task of being bridge builders to the larger community. The Noor-Ul-Iman School in Monmouth Junction, New Jersey, for example, formed a Media and Public Affairs Committee that includes teachers and students in order to interact with the local media. Teachers are recruited who speak with an American accent and are well versed in world affairs, especially in what pertains to American Muslim interests. According to Fakhruddin Ahmed, teachers today must be "American media-savvy."[15] Part of the training for students is the preparation of media kits containing information on current topics such as Islam and terrorism; countries of the world such as Palestine, Iraq, Kashmir, and Chechnya; and women in Islam and Islam in America.

Concern for youth led some parents to organize the Muslim Youth of North America (MYNA), begun in 1985 as an organization for Muslim youth in middle school and high school living in the United States and Canada. As its Web site advertises, MYNA serves as a platform for organizing activities, discussing issues, and promoting leadership training and skills. As time has passed and the needs of the Muslim community have changed, MYNA has evolved into a larger organization with more emphasis on local community institutions working with and helping educate youth about the religion of Islam and its social dimensions. It now approaches youth work in an organic manner, with youth empowered through involvement in local communities and with the development of a new range of products and services.

One of MYNA's most successful projects—and providing another kind of Islamic education for youth—is the production of five albums of Islamic songs written by Muslim youth from the United States called MYNA Raps.[16] Among its four available albums are *The Straight Track, The Inner Struggle, The Next Level,* and the latest release, *For the Cause of Allah.* Countering the image of a sterile Islam in which music is not allowed, MYNA Raps provides energetic, Islamically acceptable ways in which to celebrate the fun of being Muslim, increase God-consciousness (*taqwa*), and, says the Web site, come closer to Allah. The brothers who featured on the MYNA Raps albums signed with the Mountain of Light/Jamal Records label associated with Yusuf Islam (Cat Stevens) and now form the group Native Deen. In a recent track the group expresses these sentiments about education:

> Remember the days when we were young
> Trying to be cool trying to have fun.
> Oh, we were cool because we had the black sunglasses
> Cool because we making A's in all our classes.
> Thought we'd have some fun we went to high school
> But then you go to college where everyone likes you.
> But in the end when the truth comes to light
> You learn what you did wrong and what you did right.
> As a son of a crescent, I'm not an adolescent.
> I've done a lot of growing, I consider it a blessing.
> Hmmm, I think about my situation.
> I need to increase my Islamic education.
> But Shaitan, he's the master of temptation.
> His goal is to destroy the entire nation.
> 'Cause every single day and every time we pray
> There is something that the Muslim say:
> La'llaha ilallah, Muhammadur Rasulilah.
> La'llaha ilallah, Muhammadur Rasulilah.

The song goes on to reflect that growing up Muslim in public school, with Islamic school on the weekend, does not prevent young Muslims from falling into temptation. Each chorus ends with a warning of hellfire for those who come to the judgment day with their books in their left hands, that is, those who have not lived Islamically acceptable lives. Islamic education in America indeed takes many different forms.

Muslims are committed to provide their children with educational opportunities and see higher education as a means of social mobility and integration. They are extremely eager that their children receive the best education possible and want to make sure that Muslim schools have high educational standards. While some schools boast about the test results of their students and the scholarships their graduates receive to go on to top-notch colleges, the quality of education provided by Muslim schools in America remains a continuing concern for the community.

Islamic Schools in the United States and Canada

Exact numbers of Islamic schools in America have not been easy to ascertain, as the essay by Karen Keyworth in this volume reveals. Figures range somewhere over 200, with some estimates reaching as high as 60,000 children receiving parochial Islamic education in a given year. SoundVision estimates that over $350 million is spent each year educating these students.[17] As we have seen, numerous factors impinge on parents' decision on whether or not to give their children this kind of training, including cost, distance, the quality of education provided, and what context parents feel will provide their children the best opportunity to learn about Islam, to appreciate their faith, and to prepare for their adult lives.

There is no question that the demand for Muslim schools is rising, at the same time that attention is increasingly being drawn to the difficulties in attracting and keeping good teachers, the high cost of parochial school education, and the difficulties many schools have in providing adequate physical facilities for the training of children. Their appeal is that teachers serve not only as instructors but as moral and ethical guides. The schools differ in style and ambiance, crafted by members of numerous American Muslim ethnic and cultural communities. "But the educational structure these schools have forged," says one commentator, "—prayer, discipline and American-style teaching—has an appeal that cuts across lines of national origin and background."[18]

For the past several decades Muslims in America have been struggling to distinguish religion from culture, to determine what unites them as Muslims as well as what particular characteristics and contributions they bring from their personal backgrounds. The task of developing and growing Islamic schools is one interesting facet of this struggle. Some schools are trying to import and integrate texts from other cultures into the required academic curricula, while others are deciding that it is important for American Muslims to write their own texts appropriate to the context in which they now live. Organizations such as the Muslim American Society Council of Islamic Schools are working to help schools in developing curricula that will both meet the academic requirements of Muslim students living in North America and provide the Islamic materials that will help them prepare to become Muslim leaders ready to "contribute to the betterment of American society."[19]

Most Islamic schools adopt the standards set by the state within which they are located and follow the basic curriculum that prepares students for standardized tests. Islamic parochial schools attempt to help students understand and preserve their Muslim identity by providing regular prayer, encouraging Islamic dress, providing halal meals, and integrating Islamic religious knowledge into the academic curriculum.

While many of the essays in this volume deal in one way or another with Islamic day schools, several are specifically focused on this topic. Karen Keyworth, the founder and current director of the Islamic Schools League of America, provides basic and much-needed information about the complex process of establishing and keeping current an accurate list of such schools. She determines that 235 is currently the best estimate for the number of Islamic schools in the United States and U.S. Virgin Islands, acknowledging that because some small schools are not yet identified and new ones are in the process of being established, the count must always be in flux. Most Islamic schools, she finds, are still very young and have not yet been in existence long enough that they can adequately be assessed as to the quality of education provided. Keyworth concludes her essay with a set of specific recommendations for Islamic educational institutions to improve their standards, raise their level of professionalism, eliminate negative stereotypes, grow, and provide bridges to the non-Muslim community.

Are Islamic schools in Canada "safe havens or religious 'ghettos'?" asks Jasmin Zine, addressing the debates surrounding the advantages and limitations of Islamic schooling in Canada. Immigrant parents see Islamic schools as a way to preserve culture and resist total assimilation, and at the same time schools are intended to be safe spaces protecting their children from drugs, gangs, violence, and racial and religious discrimination. Many of the students Zine interviewed validated these concerns, saying that while in public school they felt the need to conceal their cultural and religious identities for fear of being labeled "weird." Some described feeling a sense of family and community in the Islamic school, as well as faith-based social cohesion under a wide range of ethnicities. At the same time, critics say that by secluding Muslim students from their non-Muslim peers, Islamic schools create an unhealthy ghettoized insularity. Some argue that the lack of religious pluralism inhibits the spirit of free debate and tolerance that are at the heart of a liberal democracy. Zine herself counters these critics by challenging the idea that public schools seriously promote knowledge of different cultures, charging that the propagation of Eurocentric knowledge represents the hegemonic way of learning typical of public school curricula.

One of the most important ways in which Muslim public education can be carried out is through the direct involvement of Muslims of all ages in the larger social contexts in which they live. Louis Cristillo, for example, argues that Muslim schools are not cultural and institutional ghettos but, rather, are at the nexus of overlapping social networks that empower Muslim youth and adults toward greater involvement in the larger society. Using ethnographic research of Muslim schools based in New York City, Cristillo examines how the school interacts with a group of institutions, including the mosque, the local business sector, and the local community in general. The inclusion of interfaith education and volunteer opportunities in Muslim schools, he says, is helping students acquire skills in citizenship and civic engagement. The founding and operation of full-time Muslim schools produce networks of social relations and structures that provide ways for people to learn about public issues and take part in civic and political engagement.

Susan Douglass offers helpful data comparing private with public school curricula by locating the development of teaching about Islam in both contexts within the broader trajectory of education about world religions and world history. Douglass explores how efforts since the 1970s and 1980s have focused on correcting errors in the presentation of Islam. She then examines the constitutional issues related to education about religion and the ramifications of the separation of church and state to teaching about religion. Specific guidelines have emerged that shape the form of education about religion in public schools, including not promoting or denigrating any religion and avoiding truth claims. Education about Islam in both public and private schools often comes through teaching world history and geography. Douglass examines the efforts to restore history to the center of K–12 education and the rise of the world history paradigm. Her comprehensive study concludes with a description of the work of the Council on Islamic Education, which has recently been absorbed into a new and broader organization, the Institute on Religion and Civic Values. She argues that it is not possible to draw sharp boundary lines between the Islamic educational dimension and the public dimension. Both strive to educate students to pursue a spirit of inquiry, to make sound individual life choices, and to learn so as to serve society as well-informed citizens.

For parents who want to explore a more personal and focused approach and provide an environment for critical thinking, the alternative of homeschool is always open. In addition, homeschooling provides an alternative for those who have concerns about the quality of the public school system, costs of private schools, and quality of private schools. While relatively few parents actually take advantage of this option, Muslims families are said to provide the fastest-growing component of homeschooled children in America. Priscilla Martinez, who is herself an active homeschooler, details why teaching children in the context of the home is a very appealing possibility for some Islamic families. She reviews various curricular approaches and ways in which parents comply with the requirements of state-approved curricula, sharing educational philosophies that undergird the positive nature of this personalized approach to educating children. Flexibility, of course, is one of the important arguments for home education, giving parents the chance to weave learning opportunities into the regular rhythm of the home and allowing for time to take advantage of experiences offered through museums, libraries, and other local institutions. Children can follow their own bodily rhythms and learn how the disciplines of working, eating, and resting are part of Islamic life. Responding to the argument that homeschooled children forfeit the opportunity to socialize, Martinez argues for the opposite. Interactions with other children can be based on common interests rather than classroom necessities, and home education can be enhanced by participation in community services, youth groups, sports, and mosque activities. Finally, she says, the homeschooling experience is constantly being enhanced with new information available on the Internet.

Islamic Institutions

Are religious educational institutions actually serving to "inoculate" young Sunni Muslims as they face the challenges of forming identities that will serve them as adult Americans? This is the question that engages Nadia Inji Khan in her study of recent Islamic institutions devoted to raising the religious literacy of young Muslims. Khan considers the various forms of education available to children and young adults, such as Sunday schools, Muslim full-time schools, halaqas (which she sees as the Muslim equivalents to Bible study groups), cyberspace as an educational venue, and access to the various programs put on by the Muslim Students Association (MSA). Then she describes from firsthand experience four specific programs that have been mounted for Muslim youth. The first is the Al-Maghreb Institute, started in 2003, which now features 13 "tribes" in the United States and two in Canada. The second is the American Learning Institute for Muslims (ALIM), first held in 1999. ALIM, the most academic of the four, offers instruction in the Islamic sciences, fosters critical thinking, and develops Islamic literacy. Rihla (Journey) provides a third educational experience, based in a very traditional setting such as Dar al Islam in Abiquiu, New Mexico. Many of the instructors at both ALIM and Rihla are white and African American converts. Finally, Khan describes the Zaytuna Institute, begun in 1996 to revive the tradition of sound Islamic teaching. One of Zaytuna's founders is Shaykh Hamza Yusuf. Khan also talks about various opportunities for Islamic learning now available to young Americans in overseas venues.

Parents who wish to provide Islamically oriented programming for their younger children are well served by the rapidly increasing production of Islamic children's media in the United States. Yasmin Moll argues that video programs and animated pictures are actually used by media companies to construct a Muslim American identity as an alternative to mainstream U.S. culture and discourse. Children are entertained at home at the same time that they are learning Islamic values and being presented with a positive image of Muslims. Children's media, she says, range over a number of themes including Muslim diversity and unity, the greatness of the Islamic past and the accomplishments of Muslims throughout history, taqwa (God-consciousness) and the importance of the example of the Prophet, and the importance of the Muslim family, with respect for parents and the significant roles played by women. Secular justifications for good behavior are replaced with "Islamizing" values. The bad behavior of non-Muslim villains is defined precisely as that which Muslims would not do. Moll says that she is still uncertain as to whether such media presentations end up advocating isolationism or ultimately assimilation into Western culture.

Among the different nonclassroom venues in which Islamic education is being propagated are the prisons of America. According to Anna Bowers in her essay here, Department of Health and Human Services statistics reveal that prisons are in a state of crisis. The situation is particularly difficult for Muslim inmates, for whom Islamic programming is underfunded, and there is a serious shortage of Muslim chaplains. Bowers argues that a greater emphasis on education for rehabilitation would do much to arrest the high rate of recidivism. Religious programs are desperately needed to provide both spiritual guidance and education and to advocate for other inmate services. Without a Muslim chaplain to educate new converts about correct Islamic doctrine, she says, inmates become self-appointed religious leaders and the chances are greater of exposure to more extremist views of Islam. Bowers recommends that prison staff be educated about Islam, that more Muslim chaplains be recruited, that funding be provided for outreach and reentry programs for inmates, and that research be done on the possible connection between involvement in a Muslim community upon release and the decreased likelihood of recidivism.

At the current time no accredited Muslim institution in America provides training for imams to serve in prisons or to fill other institutional needs. The one program that does offer accredited study in Islamic leadership is the chaplain training program at Hartford Seminary in Connecticut. Purposely designed to offer instruction to both Muslim men and women (thus it is not called imam training), the Hartford program combines M.A.-level academic training in the study of Islam with supervised field education in the areas of prison, hospital, university, and military chaplaincy. The program, which as of this writing has been in place for about four years, currently has some 40 male and female students enrolled. A few other institutions such as the Islamic Society of North America and the International Institute of Islamic Thought in Virginia have held special training sessions for imams to help provide information on the American context. The Graduate School of Islamic and Social Sciences in northern Virginia recently received state accreditation for its chaplaincy training program. However, in the post-9/11 environment, it has ceased to offer on-campus training and has begun providing education through the Internet.

Islamic Education and the Challenge for Women

Young Muslim women often face specific concerns as they deal with practicing their faith in the American educational system, as several essays in this collection note. Shabana Mir provides a critical look at how Muslim women construct their identities on contemporary college and university campuses, where they often encounter an atmosphere hostile to religion in general and Islam in particular. She focuses on Muslim women's experiences with alcohol, their choices to drink or not drink and whether to participate in social occasions during which alcohol is served. Mir finds that the act of not drinking makes these women "not ordinary" in the eyes of their peers, placing them at the margins of college social life, which revolves to a great extent around drinking. Alcohol is a serious issue in whether or not Muslim women are seen as ordinary or acceptable by their classmates. Many of the women in her study said that they were eager to dispel stereotypes about Muslim women, especially after 9/11, yet their decision not to drink made that task more difficult. They wanted both to participate in college social life and to maintain their distinct Muslim identity and responded in different ways: some abstained from drinking and avoided social situations involving alcohol; others drank with their friends; and still others attempted to construct a third space in which they refrained from drinking but still socialized with friends at bars and clubs.

There is no question that since 9/11 more young women have chosen to identify themselves as Muslims by wearing some form of hijab or Islamic dress. The Muslim students of whom Mir speaks often find their identity on college campuses by associating with other Muslim women through local chapters of the MSA. It is increasingly rare in such groups to find young women who are not wearing one kind of head scarf or another. Head covering varies as cultures represented and individual inclinations vary, with some students dressed from head to toe in Islamically identifiable garb and others wearing jeans and shirts with scarves on their heads. For the moment, it is the unusual young observant Muslim woman who does not wear some kind of Islamic cover, although some who consider themselves practicing Muslims do not choose to dress identifiably and many others are not observant.

Educating the American Public about Islam

As was suggested above, providing Islamic education in the American context means more than simply teaching Muslim children and adults about their religion. It also must include education of those who are not Muslim, the general American public, who—despite the concentrated efforts of Muslims to decry terrorism in the name of Islam and to explain what the religion of Islam really is about—generally know little and attest to rising suspicions and concerns about Muslims.

Islamic educators are all too aware of the reality that Islamophobia is increasing in the United States, that growing numbers of Americans are expressing a sense of unease about Islam, and that such apprehensions generally are founded not on their personal interaction with Muslims but on what they read in the press. In reality most Americans do not know much about Islam and have had little if any contact with Muslims. Researchers Barbara Sahli, Christina Safiya Tobias-Nahi, and Mona Abo-Zena decided to find out whether actual contact between Muslim and non-Muslim students serves to help change attitudes and perceptions. They worked with the full-time Islamic Academy of New England (IANE), building on a project of yearly educational encounters between IANE students and those from several private schools. Sahli, Tobias-Nahi, and Abo-Zena began their investigations with the premise that authentic interactions between Muslim and other students would bring both more knowledge and better personal understanding. Their findings confirmed this result, as students attested that face-to-face meetings helped dismantle stereotypes, emphasize commonalities, and make differences seem less threatening. The researchers, recognizing that both public and private school teachers themselves can benefit from such personal interaction, hope that their experiment might serve as a model for other educators.

As is evident in the essays contained in this volume, the scope of themes under the main rubric of Islamic education is wide. Contributors here introduce the reader to the different kinds of education Muslims are attempting to give both to members of their own community and to the American public at large. They have looked at Muslim schools and at the teaching of Islam in public school curricula, at new forms of education for young Muslims, at concerns of dress and social choice for students at various educational levels, at the issues involved in homeschooling and the different venues for teaching the faith and practice of Islam, and at rising levels of anti-Muslim feeling in the American public and efforts to counter prejudice and misunderstanding in various educational settings. Much more research needs to be done on all of these topics, but the editors hope that the essays contained here will provide direction for future studies and will help highlight for the American public in general and for the Muslim community in particular the importance of Islamic education in all of its many dimensions.

NOTES

1. Daniel Pipes, "What Are Islamic Schools Teaching?" *New York Sun*, March 29, 2005, www.danielpipes.org/article 2489, accessed May 19, 2006.

2. See Associated Press, "Plans for New York Arabic School Draw Protests, 'Jihad' Labels," *International Herald Tribune*, April 15, 2007. The curriculum of the school is intended to be in line with basics required from public schools while integrating elements of its Arab culture theme.

3. Barbara J. Stock, "American Saudi Schools: Home Grown Sleeper-Cells," March 2, 2005, www.renewamerica.us/columns/stock/050302, accessed April 6, 2007; Kenneth Adelman, "U.S. Islamic Schools Teaching Homegrown Hate," FOX News, March 15, 2007, www.foxnews.com/story, accessed April 6, 2007.

4. "International Declaration, Islamic Schools Should Be Banned, Children Have No Religion," www.petitiononline.com/nofaith/petition.html. See also Freedom House, *Saudi Publications on Hate Ideology Fill American Mosques* (New York: Center for Religious Freedom, January 2006).

5. See, for example, Yvonne Yazbeck Haddad and Adair Lummis, *Islamic Values in the United States: A Comparative Study* (New York: Oxford University Press, 1987);

Yvonne Yazbeck Haddad and Jane I. Smith, eds., *Muslim Communities in North America* (Albany: State University of New York Press, 1994); Yvonne Yazbeck Haddad, Jane I. Smith, and Kathleen Moore, *Muslim Women in America: The Challenge of Islamic Identity Today* (New York: Oxford University Press, 2006).

6. For a thorough study of the Clara Muhammad schools, see Hakim M. Rashid and Zakiyyah Muhammad, "The Sister Clara Muhammad Schools: Pioneers in the Development of Islamic Education in America," *Journal of Negro Education* 61, no. 2 (1992): pp. 178–185.

7. Ibid., p. 179.

8. For more information on the NOI detailing its beliefs and practices, see, e.g., Sonsyrea Tate, *Little X: Growing Up in the Nation of Islam* (Knoxville: University of Tennessee Press, 2005); Vilbert White, *Inside the Nation of Islam: A Historical and Personal Testimony of a Black Muslim* (Gainesville: University Press of Florida, 2001).

9. Rashid and Muhammad, "The Sister Clara Muhammad Schools," p. 183.

10. Zakiyyah Muhammad, "What Makes an Islamic School Islamic? Theoretical Considerations. The Education and Status of Muslim Teachers" (paper presented at the conference on Islamic education at the Georgetown University Prince Alwaleed Bin Talal Center for Muslim-Christian Understanding, Washington, DC, April 6, 2006), typescript, p. 1.

11. Ibid., p. 4.

12. This reference to the Muslim American Society is to the Arab organization by the same name, not to be confused with an earlier name for the community of Warith Deen Mohammed.

13. Vincent F. Biondo III, "Integration versus Isolation: The Challenge of Islamic Education in Southern California" (paper presented at the American Academy of Religion, Toronto, November 25, 2002).

14. Both the Council on Islamic Education and the Council on American-Islamic Relations are working to eliminate stereotypical depictions, as well as ethnic and religious prejudice against Islam and Muslims, in public school texts, curricula, and classroom teaching.

15. Fakhruddin Ahmed, "How to Train Muslim Students to Interact with the Media" (paper presented at the Islamic Society of North America Education Forum, April 14–16, 2001), p. 1.

16. See its Web site, www.mynaraps.com/intro.htm, accessed November 17, 2005.

17. "Muslim School, Public School or Home School?" SoundVision, March 27, 2007, news@soundvision.net, accessed May 10, 2007.

18. Susan Sachs, "Demand for Muslim Schools on the Rise," *New York Times*, November 10, 1998, p. 1.

19. See www.masnet.org/school.asp.

1

Islamic Schools of America: Data-Based Profiles

Karen Keyworth

The very essence of Islamic schools is the teaching of Islam. It is what defines us. We have many Islamic curricula that fulfill the cultural and traditional needs and expectations of parents and communities; however, we continue to desire more spiritual content and real-life applications. We realize that if we want a curriculum for our children, we must look at Islamic curricula through the lens of our *children's* needs. What we teach and how we teach are of deep concern to Islamic schools, and the need to take up this challenge is now a top priority.

Though talk about such curricular needs has been bubbling up for years, it is only now that the community of educators has the capacity to act in a meaningful and connected way. The Islamic Schools League of America (ISLA) is facilitating this national dialogue on school leadership as it relates to spiritual curricula in K–12 Islamic schools and the curricula's impact on the future of American Muslim children through research, conferences, and online discussions.

Questions persist: What are the Islamic schools of America? How many are there? How are they structured? What stage of development are they experiencing: growth, plateau, reduction? How "connected" are the schools to the larger society and to each other? This essay will provide the major findings of primary research related to full-time K–12 Islamic schools in the United States, helping to create a more accurate profile of Islamic schools based on those data.

Data on Islamic schools are very difficult to obtain. A previous, and the only other known, primary research survey was published in

1989 by the Islamic Society of North America (ISNA) in an obscure booklet titled *In-Depth Study of Full-Time Islamic Schools in North America: Results and Data Analysis*.[1] In that booklet, the number of full-time Islamic schools was established at approximately 50. Today, there are approximately 235 such schools, and no other national studies such as the ISNA study and this study are known to have been carried out. This research is critical to the schools for establishing and identifying community, professionalism, standards, and shared educational philosophies as well as to the American Muslim community and the larger American society for a crucial understanding of full-time Islamic education that is based on fact rather than conjecture.

Establishing an Accurate List of Schools: Creating a Protocol

Before any research could occur, an accurate and current list of the schools needed to be created. As late as 1998, no such list of the full-time Islamic schools in the United States existed. The lists that existed were primarily voluntary lists where a school could self-register. No mechanism existed to ascertain the accuracy of any entry or follow up on that information over time. Consequently, the initial step in the research was to accurately identify the schools and obtain their contact information. This part of the research began in 1998 and continued until 2004. Current systems in place with the ISLA now accurately maintain up-to-date information.

Step 1: Consolidate Online Lists

The online lists used were available free on the Internet from various regional and national Muslim groups, and any list available was mined for contacts, with the majority of listings obtained in the years 1998–2000 from the "Islamic School Addresses in North America" section of the Muslim Students Association (MSA) Web site:

- The online lists were consolidated into one major list of over 600 school listings.
- Duplicates were eliminated:
  - Duplicate entries of the exact same name and street address were eliminated.
  - Variations of spelling were considered a "match" when determining duplicates if other information such as street name closely matched. For example, "Al-Huda" and "Alhuda" would be considered duplicates if they also carried the same street name.

- However, no variations of actual *names* were considered duplicates or eliminated even if the street name was similar or identical. For example, if one list presented "Alhuda School, 123 Main Street, New York, NY 12345" and another list presented "Universal School, 124 Main Street, New York, NY 12345," both entries were retained, listed separately, and evaluated as possible schools.
- Entries were eliminated in which any information indicated the school was a part-time school unless the information also indicated that the school was planning to become a full-time school.

Step 2: Verification

Initial verification was a lengthy process that followed a protocol: Telephone contact was attempted first. If that failed, then an attempt was made to obtain more information about the school telephone number via the Internet. Next, a query about the school would be sent to the Islamic Educators Communication Network (IECN).[2] In 2004, a land mailing was made to each school; any mail returned as undeliverable was set aside for further investigation. In a final step to verify schools, the online registration was established on the ISLA Web site for self-registration:

- *Telephone:* All schools with listed telephone numbers were called during normal school hours of operation. Many of the schools were reached quickly, but overall, this was not as fruitful as expected because of several different issues:
  - No one to answer the phone; no answering machine; messages left were not responded to.
  - Educators were sometimes surprised by the call, not commonly receiving calls other than from parents or local community members, and were initially suspicious and hesitant to provide information, particularly post-9/11.
  - School had moved physical location.
  - School had closed.
  - School had new telephone number or new area code.
- *Online:* After exhausting the phone search, an extensive search was conducted on the Internet. The two main search Web sites used were Google (www.google.com) and Langenberg Reverse Directory (http://reversedirectory.langenberg.com/).
  - The first step was to Google the name of the school. Results were cross-checked with name of school, street address, city, and local mosque.

- The second step was to conduct a reverse directory search on the old phone number, which would often yield a portion of the school's name or a city.
- The third step was an attempt to contact or identify a mosque in the area to inquire about the school, thus narrowing the search by helping to identify the current area code.

One of the greatest barriers to contacting the schools was the area code changes. This was severely problematic because new area codes were being added very quickly, and most of these schools are in urban areas where area codes were most likely to be added. Simply identifying *which* area codes had experienced a change was problematic. Furthermore, some school phone numbers experienced more than one area code change during the years 1998–2003, making initial contact difficult. For example, in Michigan, the three main area codes increased to 12 area codes by 2006. To complicate matters further, there is an area code assignment method called the *overlay* method that "places a new area code 'on top of' an existing one. Both area codes serve the same location."[3]

- *IECN:* The third part of the verification protocol was to query the IECN listserv about the school in question. Some of the more stubborn cases were solved that way because oftentimes a school would be in touch with at least one other Muslim educator outside its local area. Schools on the IECN would share contact information about schools in their state that were not yet connected via the IECN or other virtual means.
- *Mail:* A forth measure we took in verifying schools was to send mail via the U.S. Postal Service, that is, snail mail. In 2004, an initial mailing to all the schools for which there was contact information was conducted. When an envelope was returned as undeliverable, all previously mentioned measures in this protocol would be repeated in one last effort to contact the school. If this proved unsuccessful, the school was removed from the list. All schools are contacted on a yearly basis.
- *Online registration:* In 2002, an online database for school registration was created on the ISLA Web site. This registration not only requests basic contact information but also asks schools to answer a questionnaire.

Step 3: Keeping the List Current

The final step in the protocol to develop an accurate and current list of the schools is to keep the list current by periodically verifying and culling. ISLA continues to employ its verification protocol, keeping in mind that there are several factors that lead to inflated and inaccurate counts of schools in established lists:

- Double listings as a result of:
  - Similar name but different address because the school grew and moved—for example, Al-Huda at 1234 No Name Street in East Lansing, Michigan, builds a new and expanded school 1 1/2 miles away. When it moves, the new location is reported as "Al-huda" at "4567 Yes Name Street" in "Lansing, MI." Because both the name and the address are different, it wrongly appears as two schools.
  - Spellings of the school names—many are transliterated from Arabic, so the spelling often varies: for example, "Dar Ul Uloom," "Darul Uloom," "Dar ul-Uloom," and so on.
  - Schools with more than one name—for example, the School of Knowledge is also listed as Madrasa-Tul-Ilm.
- Charter schools—independent public schools. They are not parochial schools, but they have the flavor of a religious school because their student body is oftentimes as much as 99 percent Muslim.
- Schools that have closed or merged with another Islamic school but are not removed from the list.
- Schools that have closed (and are not removed from the list) and then reopen a year or two later under a different name but in the same location.

Unless the list is constantly verified and culled, it can build to some of the highly inaccurate numbers quoted in the media by both Muslim and non-Muslim organizations.

After eight years of following these protocols, a verified list of 235 schools in the United States and the U.S. Virgin Islands has now been built. This number is not absolute or concrete because there are some schools so young that they are not yet known. Additionally, there are some schools that might have closed, but that is also not yet clear. Nevertheless, the likelihood of there being 100 such unknown schools is extremely small. The number of missed schools in either direction of 235 is likely to be no more than 10–15. Overall, it is reasonable to rule out the larger numbers of 300, 400, 500, and 600 that have been erroneously but routinely quoted in the media. Furthermore, as a verified list of schools now exists, claims of other numbers need to meet or exceed the previously articulated level of assurance.

Data-Based Profile of Islamic Schools in the United States

Using the number 235 as the definitive total number of Islamic schools in the United States, the ISLA has gathered information on and analyzed two of its own data sources, collected since 2004. The first is the league *online registration survey* (106 schools = 45 percent of all schools and does not include league member schools), and the second is the league *membership application survey* (32 schools = 13.6 percent of all schools; see table 1.1). The online survey and the membership application survey are essentially the same, but some minor changes were made when preparing the survey to distribute as part of the membership application process. For example, in an effort to elicit more accurate information about accreditation, that question was expanded in the membership version of the survey. In the few areas where the survey was changed, the data are *not* presented in this report. In addition, there is an information source called Edustarz that is used with the permission of its publisher (97 schools = 41 percent of all schools). Input from this third source is not being presented as research data, but it will appear in the discussion as valuable anecdotal information. A summary of the data collection and its limitations is as follows:

GOALS OF DATA COLLECTION
- Provide a definitive profile of full-time schools based on data
- Determine trends
- Identify areas of concern

LIMITATIONS OF ALL DATA
- Self-selected—only schools that are interested and willing to offer the information are represented.
- Connectedness—if a school is not actively online and interacting with the Muslim educator community, it will not know of the league, the Web site, or membership or be able to share its information.
- Self-reported—the data are not observations; they are self-reported information.
- Limited scope—the survey tools are limited in length, and questions are focused on obtaining basic information such as growth, size, governance, budget, educator certification, and so on.

LEAGUE MEMBERSHIP DATA (SEPARATE FROM ONLINE LEAGUE DATA)
- Only schools applying for membership are represented in these data. Because membership fees are tied to the number of students in a school,

TABLE I.I. Source data.

	League Members	Online	Edustarz
Number of schools answering question	32	106	97
Actual number of students indicated	3,567	14,163	14,663
Average per school based on actual number	111	134	151
Extrapolated/estimated total students based on 235 schools	26,085	31,490	35,485

Note: Online and league members source data are exclusive of each other. Edustarz numbers include some schools from both groups.

larger schools are less likely to join. This could result in the member schools data being more representative of a profile for smaller schools.

The third source, information from Edustarz, is not being presented as research data because it was created as a for-profit publication—a booklet intended for school fund-raising entitled "Schools4Us." Despite the inability to use this data for research, when weighed against the dearth of information available anywhere on Islamic schools, it is too valuable to be discarded. Therefore, that information is included in parts of the discussion so that it might provide additional insight. It is *not* included in the data, only in the discussion of the data.

The Private/Parochial School Milieu

According to the National Center for the Study of Privatization in Education, Teachers College, Columbia University, "Approximately 5,953,000 students attend 27,223 non-profit schools. This comprises 11% of all students and 23% of all schools in the United States (National Center for Education Statistics, 2000). Most non-profit schools are small, located in urban centers, and possess a religious affiliation. About 80% of non-profit schools enroll less than 300 students (National Center for Education Statistics, 2000)."[4] Approximately 93 percent of private Islamic full-time schools enroll 300 or fewer students (fig. 1.1). Although this is higher than the figure for nonprofit schools in the United States, given the relatively young age of most Islamic schools, this is not surprising. Furthermore, one would expect that over time this percentage will decrease and come closer to the average of other parochial schools as the age and quality of the Islamic schools increase and the population of Muslims increases. The Edustarz schools indicate a very similar percentage—91 percent.

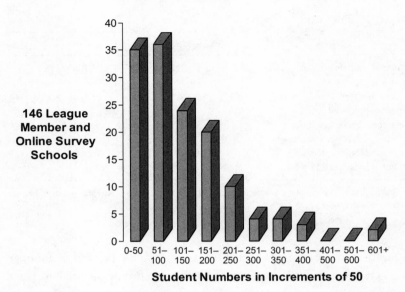

FIGURE I.I. Distribution of student enrollment. Chart represents 62% of all schools.

An estimated number of students—between 26,000 and 35,500 students—in Islamic schools can be extrapolated from the actual number of students reported in the data. After taking into consideration other factors, the most *probable* number of children in Islamic schools is approximately 32,000 students. Although this information indicates fairly clearly the actual number of children attending full-time Islamic schools, it does not, however, indicate the *percentage* of the Muslim school-aged population attending Islamic schools because the numbers for the Muslim population in general are still not well determined. Nonetheless, it is important for the Muslim community to know how it behaves regarding private schooling. Based on a conservative estimate of 850,000 Muslim children under the age of 18, one can estimate that the percentage of Muslim children attending full-time Islamic schools is, at the very most, 3.8 percent.[5] This is well below the national figure of approximately 10 percent of U.S. children attending private schools.[6] There is no evidence to indicate whether there is a large percentage of Muslim children attending private secular or non-Islamic schools.

Most Islamic schools are very young. Fully 85 percent are ten years old or younger (28 percent, 65 of 235), and 55 percent are six years old or younger (fig. 1.2). Even Edustarz information shows that almost half of those schools are ten years old or younger. This would indicate that many, if not most, of the schools will require a few more years before they reach that ten-year mark

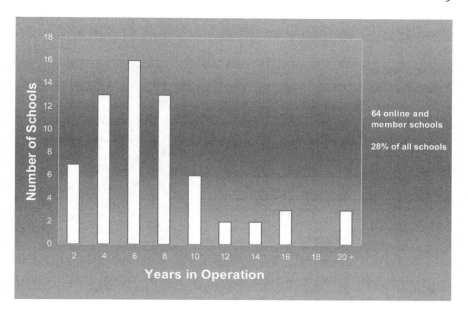

FIGURE I.2. Number of years school in operation.

that is so indicative of quality and stability and offers students a proficiency advantage. According to Caroline Hoxby in a Harvard study of charter schools, "[C]harter schools may do better as they become more experienced. . . . For instance, in reading, the advantage is 2.5 percent for a charter school that has been operating 1 to 4 years, 5.2 percent for a school operating 5 to 8 years, and 10.1 percent for a school operating 9 to 11 years."[7] Clearly, new schools need time to organize themselves before they can produce the quality education that is so important to building a solid reputation in their community.

When people in a community decide to start an Islamic school, they have no idea that the most important issue they will have to face is the physical space. Lack of sufficient and attractive physical space will present a larger barrier to a school's growth than even the school's actual academic performance. No matter how many students a school is able to attract, if it does not eventually acquire sufficient space for the children to run, play, conduct science experiments, and so on, the school cannot grow.

The data indicate that slightly under half of schools are in fairly young buildings of ten years or younger (fig. 1.3). However, slightly more than half of schools are located in buildings ten years or older, with approximately 25 percent of all schools in buildings of 30 years or older. The most telling

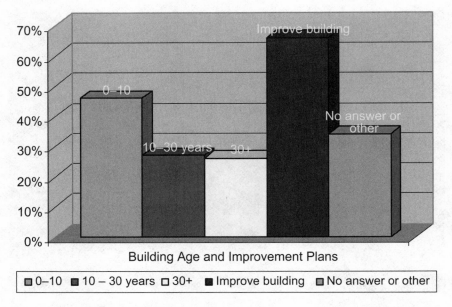

FIGURE 1.3. Buildings and growth.

statistic regarding the future of the schools is that fully 66 percent of schools either are currently involved in building improvement or have *written* plans to do so. This indicates a willingness and ability to invest in the future of the school. If these schools were not growing, there would not be such a large percentage making capital investments.

Next is the issue of teacher certification. Schools were to select the most appropriate response to the stem: *Our teachers are all state certified (to teach) in the United States.* In addition to indicating overall certification percentages, the response choices also allowed the schools to indicate a distinction of having all academic teachers certified and Arabic/Islamic studies teachers not certified—a very common occurrence in the schools. According to the data, in 10 percent of schools *all* teachers are certified, and in 36 percent of schools all *academic* teachers are certified (fig. 1.4). Thus, in 46 percent of Islamic schools, all academic teachers are certified. On the one hand, this is very positive, in that academic teachers constitute the vast majority of teaching staff in the schools, and the data show that these teachers are certified. On the other hand, a troubling figure for Islamic schools is that 36 percent indicated that the Arabic/Islamic studies teachers are not certified. When that figure is added to the 13 percent of schools indicating that *no* teachers are certified, the number of schools with uncertified Islamic studies and Arabic language teachers increases to 49 percent. As these teachers help define the very essence of an

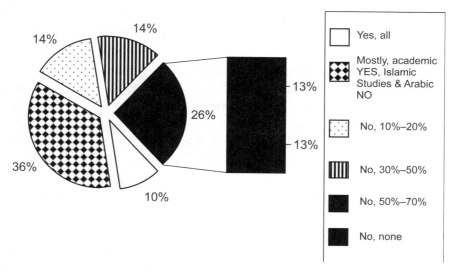

FIGURE 1.4. Teacher certification.

Islamic school, their lack of certification or their being perceived as less professional than their colleagues becomes more significant.

The issue of uncertified Arabic/Islamic studies teachers notwithstanding,
when looking at overall certification figures for Islamic schools, 60 percent
have a teaching staff where 80 percent of teachers are certified. Interestingly,
this demonstrates a higher level of professionalism in the schools than is
popularly believed by the Muslim community. Thus, given that enrollment relative to population is low, one might deduce from this information that schools
would benefit from conducting public relations programs to inform their communities about the level of professionalism in their schools. Contrarily and
interestingly, in 25 percent of schools, most to all of the teachers are not certified. There is likely a variety of situational reasons for this, for it is not often that
a school chooses to hire only uncertified teachers.

It is important to note that uncertified does not mean *uneducated*. Anecdotal information indicates that uncertified teachers have B.A., M.A., and even
Ph.D. degrees, but they lack teacher certification for K–12. Furthermore, to
paint a more accurate picture of Islamic schools, it is useful to place them into
the national context, where hiring uncertified teachers occurs more often than
most people think: "Private schools routinely hire unlicensed teachers. . . . The
rate [of uncertified teachers] for the public sector is 89.8 percent, whereas the
rate for private schools is much lower, particularly in non-religious schools,
where just 48.8 percent of teachers are certified."[8]

Further study is necessary to determine these figures more precisely and to determine what impact—negative, positive, or none—this might have on students. The question about certification is being hotly debated across the United States (regarding public schools), and attitudes are beginning to shift. Studies suggest that other factors are more predictive of student learning than teacher certification: "Simply put, a teacher's certification status matters little for student learning. We find no difference between teaching fellows and traditionally certified teachers or between uncertified and traditionally certified teachers in their impact on math achievement. . . . To put this in perspective, the advantage of being the student of a teacher in the top quarter of effectiveness rather than the bottom quarter is roughly three times the advantage of being taught by an experienced teacher rather than by a novice, and more than ten times any advantage created by teacher certification!"[9] Given the uncertain impact of uncertified teachers on schooling, the desire by Islamic schools to hire Muslim educators, and the sometimes serious shortage of certified Muslim teachers that Islamic schools often face, we can predict that Islamic schools are likely to continue hiring uncertified teachers when they feel it is necessary.

Despite how one might feel about the issue of certification, the fact remains that if schools are growing and seeking accreditation, these percentages will quickly change in the direction of greater certification. While the accreditation portion of the survey revealed problems too complex to provide reliable data on that subject, other factors and indicators outside the survey show clearly that accreditation is a swiftly developing trend. Given the other indications of growth, this is an important area in which to assist the schools as they grow and develop.

When asked to respond to the statement "Our school hires non-Muslim teachers," almost 50 percent of schools answered yes, with another 23 percent indicating that they were considering hiring non-Muslim teachers (fig. 1.5). The breakdown of the yes answers indicates an overwhelming percent of schools saying that approximately 10–30 percent of their teachers are non-Muslim. Curiously, one school indicated that 100 percent of the teachers were non-Muslim. Less than one-third of schools indicated that they do not hire or even consider hiring non-Muslim teachers. That notwithstanding, it is clear that the presence of non-Muslim educators is common in Islamic schools, and as schools move toward accreditation, the need to hire certified teachers combined with the short supply of certified Muslim teachers will likely push this figure higher.

Finally, the data regarding governance address a misconception about Islamic schools—the assumption being that full-time Islamic schools are controlled by their local mosques. The data show that fully 45 percent of Islamic

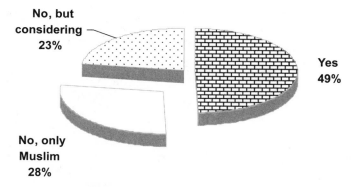

FIGURE 1.5. Schools hiring non-Muslim teachers.

schools are completely independent entities (fig. 1.6). Another 29 percent are connected to a mosque but make decisions very autonomously. Only 21 percent of Islamic schools are actually governed by a mosque. Overall, almost 75 percent of schools indicate that they are operating either independently or autonomously. This makes sense if, as has been supposed, schools oftentimes will begin life as an outgrowth of a mosque or "Sunday school"–related effort. They need the support of the larger and more established mosque to get them off the ground. Then, as other factors influence them and their needs become more complex and separate from those of the mosque, they move to become independent. Regardless of how or why a school arrives at independent governance, the majority of schools must view it as an advantage, or else they would not leave the financial security of a mosque. One advantage to independence is the ability to respond to parents, the conventional "clients" of private schools and the ones to whom the schools are most accountable. If a school is held accountable to the mosque rather than the parents, the governance dynamics and resulting system behaviors are changed and become more reminiscent of traditional public schools than private schools.

The Typical Full-Time Islamic School

Based on the data, we can now articulate a profile of the "typical" full-time Islamic school:

- Average size for a parochial school—100 students or fewer
- Young—six years or younger
- Growing
- Professionally oriented
- Independently governed

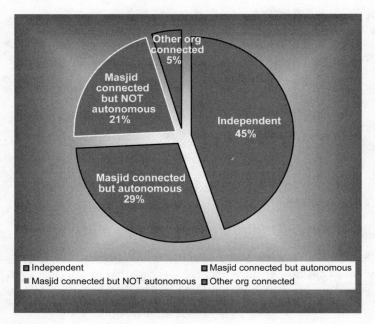

FIGURE 1.6. Governance.

Statistics for such a school are as follows:

Most common size	Under 100 students, 55 percent; under 150 students, 85 percent
Average number of students	121
Age of schools	Six years or younger, 55 percent; ten years or younger, 85 percent
Growth	Buildings—currently undergoing expansion or with written plans to do so, 66 percent
Professionalism	Widespread movement toward professionalism—in 60 percent of schools 80 percent of teaching staff are certified teachers

Recommendations

Full-time Islamic schools are in an extremely dynamic as well as precarious position. They are poised to grow if they are willing and able to take the necessary steps.

First, data indicate that schools are moving quickly toward the standards that parents expect, but their public relations efforts have not kept pace with this improvement. Schools will bring their public reputation into closer alignment with their actual quality if they spend more time communicating the good news of their development to the Muslim community, as this community remains unaware of the positive and recent changes.

Second, the fact that the percentage of Muslim children in private Islamic schools is roughly two to three times less than in the general public indicates that there are widespread negative beliefs and attitudes about private Islamic schooling in the Muslim community that Islamic schools and mosques might wish to address jointly. Whether and to what extent this is affected by immigrant-held attitudes toward Islam informed by the social and societal milieu of a history of colonialism in their countries of origin have yet to be studied. Nonetheless, the Muslim community in America is well situated to advocate its own blend of intellect, modernity, and Islam as reflective of the reality in which Muslims live in the United States; moreover, Islamic schools are the ideal place to promote that model and eliminate negative, self-nullifying stereotypes.

Third, the disproportionate number of uncertified Arabic language and Islamic studies teachers in conjunction with the trend toward Islamic schools requiring teacher certification indicate that the community of Muslim educators needs to address this issue. Alternative routes to certification are more available today than ever before, and Islamic schools and Muslim communities must facilitate this need. Islamic studies and Arabic language, it can be argued, are the very definition of an Islamic school. That these teachers are the *most likely* to be uncertified creates an atmosphere in which negative attitudes and stereotypes often held by Muslims about Muslims (i.e., religious people and entities are "backward" or "unprofessional") can be reinforced and perpetuated. As there are no legal barriers or requirements related to how private schools handle Arabic language and Islamic studies, the only barrier to equalizing and ensuring the desired level of professionalism in these areas is the Muslim community's willingness to do so.

Fourth, Most Islamic schools have an independent governance structure. To better facilitate this, when schools are conceived within the structure of an Islamic center or mosque, the founders (school and mosque) should plan from the very beginning for the school to grow toward independence. Embracing this wholeheartedly and incorporating it into the expectations of the community would help define it as a positive change. At times, a school's move toward independence can be misunderstood or mistakenly viewed by the mosque as negative and result in bitter discord. Planning ahead for this natural growth can diminish such problems.

Fifth, given the large number of non-Muslim teachers teaching in Islamic schools, an introductory course that offers these teachers basic information about Islam from the perspective of a teacher and containing classroom-related content seems useful. Furthermore, these teachers might serve as important interfaith bridges.

Sixth, Islamic schools and their communities need to deal with the fact that well over half of the schools are either currently in the process of building/ remodeling or about to begin such an effort. However, planning for such growth is difficult, in that it requires the community to cooperate along lines that can be very divisive, such as school location, classroom size, playground space, prayer space, parking, and more. These efforts can turn into bitter battles without the help of experienced professionals (such as architects, project designers, etc.) who are equally familiar with the dynamics of Muslim communities and how they use physical space.

Seventh, scholarships and trusts need to be established to support and encourage Muslim students to enter the field of academia on all levels— elementary, secondary, college, and university. In particular, Islamic schools need Muslim teachers.

And eighth, further research on *every* aspect of Islamic education is needed. Funding for that research will be equally critical. Small amounts of $2,000 to $5,000 can be extremely effective when directed at graduate students, schools, and organizations. Larger amounts can help fund longitudinal studies that are critical yet absent.

NOTES

The Islamic Schools League of America wishes to thank the Foundation for the Advancement and Development of Education and Learning organization for its steadfast support, without which this important work could not be conducted.

1. Islamic Society of North America, *In-Depth Study of Full-Time Islamic Schools in North America: Results and Data Analysis,* ed. Sha'ban M. Ismail (Plainfield, IN: Islamic Society of North America, 1989), p. 79.

2. The IECN is an interactive e-mail forum (a.k.a. listserv) with approximately 450 educators connected to full-time Islamic schools in North America and hosted by the Islamic Schools League of America.

3. "Types of Area Code Changes," Verizon, 2006, http://multimedia.verizon. com/customersupport/areacodes/change_types.html, accessed November 1, 2006.

4. "Private Schools," National Center for the Study of Privatization in Education, 2003, www.ncspe.org/publications_files/Private%20Schools-FAQ.pdf, accessed March 10, 2006, p. 2.

5. On the number of Muslim children under 18, see *Muslim Americans: Middle Class and Mostly Mainstream*, Pew Research Center, May 22, 2007, http://pewresearch.org/assets/pdf/muslim-americans.pdf, accessed May 22, 2007, p. 10.

6. S. P. Broughman and N. L. Swaim, "Characteristics of Private Schools in the United States: Results from the 2003–2004 Private School Universe Survey," NCES 2006-319 (Washington, DC: National Center for Education Statistics, 2006), http://nces.ed.gov/pubs2006/2006319.pdf, accessed March 27, 2006, p. 2.

7. Caroline M. Hoxby, "Achievement in Charter Schools and Regular Public Schools in the United States: Understanding the Differences," Harvard University and National Bureau of Economic Research faculty homepage, 2004, www.economics.harvard.edu/faculty/hoxby/papers/hoxbycharter_dec.pdf, accessed March 27, 2006.

8. Michael Podgursky, "Teacher Licensing in U.S. Public Schools: The Case for Simplicity and Flexibility," University of Missouri, Columbia, Department of Economics faculty homepage, 2004, http://web.missouri.edu/~podgurskym/papers_presentations/wp/Podgursky_pje_paper_2.pdf, accessed December 5, 2006. An earlier version of this paper was presented at the "Teacher Preparation and Quality: New Directions in Policy and Research" conference, American Enterprise Institute, Washington, DC, October 18–20, 2003. A later version was published in the *Peabody Journal of Education* 80, no. 3 (2005): pp. 15–43, DOI: 10.1207/s15327930pje8003_3.

9. Thomas J. Kane, Jonah E. Rockoff, and Douglas O. Staiger, "Photo Finish: Teacher Certification Doesn't Guarantee a Winner," *Education Next*, winter 2007: pp. 60–67, www.hoover.org/publications/ednext/4612527.html, accessed June 5, 2007, pp. 64, 66.

2

Safe Havens or Religious "Ghettos"? Narratives of Islamic Schooling in Canada

Jasmin Zine

Operating as a socially and spiritually based alternative to the secular public education system, independent Islamic schools take on multiple sociological roles in the Canadian context. For example, these schools attempt to create a "safe" environment that protects students from the "de-Islamizing" forces in public schools and society at large. Transnationalism and the experience of migrancy have led to cultural dissonance for newcomers from Muslim countries, unaccustomed to culturally permissive social norms such as consuming alcohol and partying, dating and premarital relations. Residing within culturally incongruent spaces, migrant Muslim communities seek to shelter their children and youth from negative outside influences. Immersion in a culturally incongruent environment has made parents more fearful for their children and the potential loss of their culture and religious way of life.

According to Nyang, self-definition and identity maintenance pose one of the primary challenges facing Muslim communities in North America.[1] He argues that while Muslims are beginning to conscientiously assert their identity within the public square, in the past newcomers were reticent to express their Muslimness openly and engaged in "survival strategies" such as the Anglicization of names to facilitate integration. Nyang refers to people in this category as "grasshopper Muslims": This type of Muslim is usually very eager to receive acceptance from the host society. For this and other related reasons, he or she may change his or her name to something else that is more familiar to the members of the majority community. This is why in the grasshopper category you find a Muhammed Jum 'ah going by the name Michael Friday and Musa Abdulla changing his name to Moses Abdullah.[2] Nyang notes that this survival mechanism helped many a Muslim immigrant to "weather the icy waters of racial or cultural prejudices."[3] Many Muslim parents fear that the assimilative forces within public schools threaten to "de-Islamize" their children.[4] For example, negative peer pressure, drugs, alcohol use, dating, and violence in schools pose many challenges for Muslim students attempting to maintain an Islamic lifestyle and identity while at school.[5] It is within the nexus of resisting cultural assimilation and engaging cultural survival that the need for Islamic schools emerges. These schools provide a culturally congruent space and a more seamless transition between the values, beliefs, and practices of the home and school environments. They also provide a space free from the racism and religious discrimination that many students encounter within public schools.[6]

Yet Islamic schools, like other independent religious schools, are also accused of "ghettoizing" students and not providing socialization within society at large and are considered inadequate arenas for civic engagement in a racially and religiously plural society due to their "particularist" orientation.[7] In the discussion that follows, these claims will be explored within the context of the narratives of Islamic school stakeholders. This chapter is drawn from broader ethnographic study of Islamic schooling that focused on four Islamic schools in the Greater Toronto Area. The study was based on interviews of 49 participants including students, teachers, school administrators, and parents as well as 18 months of fieldwork from September 1999 to August 2001 including classroom observations and action research–based teaching. The narratives of 14 high school students, seven teachers, and five parents are presented in this chapter and provide critical perspectives regarding the challenges and possibilities of Islamic schooling in Canada. As I am a Muslim scholar and parent of children who attend both Islamic schools and public schools, the outcomes and implications of this research are of personal as well as academic interest. Few studies have explored the social and cultural dimensions of Islamic schooling and their implication for diasporic Muslim communities. This research fills a void in the ethnographic literature by critically examining these processes and situating them within the political debates and contestations regarding separate religious schooling.

Background of Religious Schooling in Ontario

Figures from the Ontario Ministry of Education reported 2,240 children attending Islamic schools in 1999, but estimates from the Muslim community suggest that there were as many as 4,000 students enrolled.[8] Students are often added to waiting lists from birth, and some Islamic schools have waiting lists of 650 students and more. In Toronto and the surrounding areas there were 18 full-time Islamic schools and a total of 35 across the province of Ontario in 1999. With the exception of one school, all of these schools are part of the Sunni tradition in Islam, with the one exception being a Shia school, these two groups composing the predominant sects within Islam. An updated view of the growth of Islamic schools based on the most recent 2005 statistics of both the Ministry of Education and Statistics Canada reveals that approximately 3,500 Muslim students now attend Islamic schools, which is an estimated 7 percent of the total population of Muslim students at the elementary and secondary school levels.[9] In Ontario, full-time Islamic day schools are private and receive no government funding. Only Catholic schools are eligible for public funding under the Canadian Charter, despite the legal human rights claims of other minoritized religious groups in Ontario who are excluded from accessing such public support for their schools.[10] The Muslim community, consequently, has been involved within the multifaith coalition Ontario Parents for Equality in Education Funding in order to advocate for funding for religious schools. In 1999 their case was taken to the United Nations, which ruled that the Ontario government was in violation of human rights for funding only Catholic schools to the exclusion of other religious schools. The ruling has largely been ignored by educational officials in Ontario, and a controversial tax credit offered to private school students was recently repealed by the new liberal government.

The issue of religiously segregated schooling has often been contested on the grounds that it leads to a form of "religious apartheid." Defenders of the common school argue that claims for religious or culturally segregated schools are a rejection of liberal democratic values and discourage the positive possibilities of cultural pluralism.[11] In her book *God in the Classroom*, Lois Sweet also resists the balkanization of public schools into separate religious enclaves that, she argues, discourages the kind of dialogue and debate that can lead to effective citizenship in a plural society. Nevertheless, she argues that government inflexibility in dealing with religion in public schools has forced many religious families to opt out of the public school system. She argues that the success of liberal multiculturalism lies in the development of more inclusive practices, including a funding formula to keep religious schools inside rather than outside of public education.[12]

Beyond the politics of funding for independent schools, supporters of Islamic schools are put on the defensive with respect to how these schools are often seen as ghettoizing Muslim children and denying them opportunities to engage within the broader plural society. The term *ghettoizing* is used for its negative and racialized connotation to describe independent Islamic schools. Yet interestingly, the same negative terminology is not leveled against support- ers of the publicly funded Catholic separate school system, despite the fact that many critics also disapprove of the funding of these schools. Rather, the term is used strategically to undermine the claims of other more marginalized reli- gious groups. For example, Gutmann argues that religious or culturally based schools are part of a "separatist multicultural perspective" and are "designed primarily to sustain the separatist cultural identities of minorities and to bol- ster the self-esteem of students on the basis of their membership in a separatist culture."[13] Yet, as Halstead notes in his analysis of Muslim schooling in Britain, rather than committing themselves to self-imposed exile, Muslims in public schools face social isolation when white British parents refuse to send their children to Muslim-populated schools: "A pattern now emerging in some cities is for White parents to stop sending their daughters to a girls' secondary school when there is a substantial proportion of Muslim girls at the school, so that the school then quickly takes on the nature of a 'ghetto' school."[14]

This process of racial exclusion and social distance therefore leads to these schools becoming de facto separate institutions for Muslims, despite being part of the public education system.[15] Liberal educational thinkers like Gutmann view multiculturalism as a corrective to cultural bias by focusing on cultural diversity rather than cultural separatism. However, multicultural education has failed to move beyond a "tourist curriculum" that features "saris, samosas, and steel bands" as entry points into cultural knowledge. Yet this events-oriented focus in dealing with issues of cultural diversity has done little to decenter secu- lar Eurocentric knowledge as the privileged way of knowing in multiethnic/ multifaith public schools. I would argue that secular Eurocentric knowledge represents the hegemonic way of knowing in public schools that masquerades as universal and neutral space, when it is in fact a biased and culturally situated base of knowledge, which by virtue of its exclusivity imparts superiority and invalidates other ways of knowing, particularly those that are religiously cen- tered. Independent schools that are based on cultural or religious grounds, on the other hand, seek to move the realities and experiences of their students from the margins to the center of the educational focus. Gutmann argues, how- ever, that separate schools that bolster cultural self-esteem do so at the risk of undercutting mutual respect among citizens, because it is assumed that they are teaching the superior contributions of their ancestors and thereby contra- vening liberal conventions by imposing a particular view of the good life.[16] Yet, in providing a response to this critique from an antiracist standpoint, it can be argued that the contributions of marginalized communities have long been absent from the curriculum in many mainstream Eurocentric schools.

Reclaiming these historical contributions rather than undercutting mutual respect, this reinforces respect and neutralizes the superiority of the dominant culture. Theissen argues further that religiously and culturally based schools will enhance rather than hinder social harmony in a plural society: Allowing for schools that are an expression of cultural/religious traditions, while at the same time ensuring that these schools teach liberal democratic values, will do much more to create harmony within a pluralistic society than the imposition of liberal values and multicultural programs within an environment that is alien to students from minority cultural or religious traditions.[17] While opposed to independent schools, Gutmann does, however, support an inclusive curriculum in public education that represents cultural diversity and where all individuals have equal civic standing. Yet, while we can assert the notion of "equal civic standing," we have to do so in the context of unequal social conditions that mediate access to civic engagement. Not considering issues such as those raised leads to a bland, uncritical multiculturalism that does not address issues of power and privilege in society. Also from a liberal educational perspective, Callon examines the argument that the common school operates as a vehicle of civic education to perpetuate the ideal of "deliberative democracy," which encourages "open discussion in which diverse views are voiced and collectively evaluated, make, apply, and revise the norms by which their community lives."[18] Callon argues that religious schools, despite inculcating positive values, are not able to provide the required approach to a good civic education and therefore cannot produce a good liberal citizenry. Callon goes on to say: "Religious schooling may encourage much else that is laudable from a civic standpoint, but they *cannot* be arenas for inclusive deliberation by virtue of their exclusive religious identity."[19]

Yet it can be argued that mainstream public schools also impose a singular moral hegemonic viewpoint based on secularism and Eurocentrism. As argued earlier, these masquerade as universal ways of knowing but are culturally situated viewpoints that are in opposition to faith-centered worldviews and also engage fidelity to a particular partisan worldview or view of "the good life." McLaughlin argues that for various reasons the common school may not meet the needs of all students (whether on religious, cultural, or special needs grounds) and that, from a social justice perspective, there can be a view that supports separate schools from within a liberal framework, providing they are able to satisfy the conditions of developing critical rationality and independence. He argues that there can be a plurality of legitimate forms of liberal education and schooling that can be starting points for a child's journey toward autonomy and liberal citizenship and that these may start from a particular worldview or cultural identity.[20] Spinner-Halev calls this "moderate separatism," where early childhood and elementary education in religiously based schools can actually encourage greater knowledge of self without compromising the knowledge of others, and this knowledge of others may occur in sites other than schools or through transition to common schooling in higher grades.[21]

It should be noted that debates on religious education within the Muslim community also produce similar arguments against independent schooling. For example, posing an argument against separate religious schooling, Jafri and Fatah argue: "Most Muslim parents wish their children to grow and become educated in a climate of diversity, where they can learn to respect and understand the faiths of others, while being exemplary ambassadors of Islam and peace. Muslims do not believe in the segregation and ghettoization of their communities."[22] They further argue that the provision of tax credits to families attending private schools is a mechanism to further isolate religious minorities from the mainstream by encouraging separate social and educational enclaves.

Engaging the Narrative of Islamic School Stakeholders

In Canada, the challenges and debates surrounding religious education continue to center on whether religious schools lead to isolationism through the ghettoization of children and youth into separatist religious enclaves. The narratives of many of the students, parents, and teachers responded to these concerns through counternarratives of Islamic schools as "safe" spaces that provided protection from negative outside influences such as drugs, gangs, violence, and sexual harassment, and yet they rejected the notion that this constituted a form of "religious apartheid" or "ghettoization" as a result. Others did feel that the schools were not adequately preparing students to integrate into mainstream public schools or postsecondary institutions and were concerned about social isolation. Teachers, in particular, felt that systems of integration between independent and public schools needed to be set up so that information and resources could be better shared between these systems. The following discussion explores these issues and concerns relating to "protection" versus "isolation" as the by-products of independent religious schooling.

Racism and Opting Out of Public Schools

Many themes emerged from the student narratives in comparing their experiences in public schools and Islamic school. Students spoke of their experiences of disenfranchisement in the public school system and how their transition to

Islamic schools allowed them to feel a greater sense of belonging. For example, trying to "fit in" and accommodate to the social and cultural mores of the public school environment involved various aspects of cultural identification and practice, such as what kind of food it was "safe" to bring to school that would not lead to ostracism from other students. Nusaybah, a 16-year-old grade 11 student of Pakistani descent attending the Al-Rajab school, talked about how she finally felt comfortable bringing the kind of food she ate at home to school without the judgment and negative reactions from other students: "See here it's like Islam, so if you're Pakistani you can bring samosa, you can bring leftover food from the night before and it's like no one's going to care. It's like, 'Oh whatever.' But in public school, if you bring a sandwich and if it's like even slightly the weirdest thing they'll be like, 'Ooo why are you doing?! Why are you eating that?' So you pretty much have to stick to peanut butter in public school."[23] Having to "stick to peanut butter in public school" is a powerful metaphor for the dominance of Eurocentric practices within the culture of mainstream public schools, where any deviance from these socially enforced norms results in being labeled "weird" and, in Nusaybah's case, being forced to conceal any evidence of "ethnicness." Mundane experiences such as these lunchroom encounters actually have a profound effect on the identity and cultural self-esteem of ethnically minoritized students.

Parents also reported negative encounters when they approached public schools to register their children. Qassim and Sobia were Canadian-born parents of a four-year-old son at the Al-Shawwal Islamic school. They were both of Trinidadian origin and in their mid-20s. Whereas Sobia grew up attending Canadian schools, Qassim had returned to Trinidad for much of his schooling and had converted to Islam from Hinduism during his teens. During our interview, Sobia reported experiencing negative receptions from public schools when trying to enroll their son for kindergarten. They discussed how this affected their decision to send their son to an Islamic school instead:

JASMIN: What made you decide to choose an Islamic school out of all the choices that you have?

SOBIA: Well, we just moved to the area, and I went to the public school and I was rudely insulted there, and I was like, forget it!

JASMIN: What do you mean insulted?

SOBIA: They acted as if I had no knowledge of being in Canada in terms of filling out an application form or anything. And I was just like, if this is what the administrations are like for this school, I can't imagine how the whole school would be run.

QASSIM: I think more and more I find that public schools are not
meeting the needs of a diverse population. I think it pretends to be
inclusive, and it is in fact quite discriminatory. And I don't want my
child to be placed in an environment where he is being discriminated
against.

Sobia's experience of being treated as an immigrant who was not perceived by
school officials as having the cultural capital required to even fill out an application for her son was particularly insulting for Sobia, who was Canadian-born
and yet had the label of "foreigner" inscribed on her body because she was
racially minoritized and wore hijab. Based on their experiences with public
education, Sobia and Qassim felt that placing their son in an Islamic school
would allow him to build a strong sense of identity and self-esteem, free from
racial and religious bias and discrimination.

School as Family

As a result of the racialized pressures and exclusions encountered by many
Muslim youth in public schools, being able to fit in and be accepted in Islamic
schools was a significant theme in the narratives of students. Students reported
feeling less social differentiation on the basis of race, class, or culture in the
Islamic school environment in comparison with public schools. A particularly
salient theme in the student narratives was the way in which students characterized being in an Islamic school as being in a familial setting. Many students
talked about the school and the relationships that existed among students and
teachers as being "like a family" and said that they felt that Islamic schools had
more of a safe and comfortable environment for Muslim students than did
the public schools. Amal, an 18-year-old Arab student from Kuwait, described
the welcoming environment she encountered in the Al-Rajab school and how
"kind" other students were when she first came to the school. Amal had only
been in Canada for three years and spent the first two years attending a public
school. At the time of our interview she had been in Islamic school for one year.
For Amal, the relationships with friends and teachers that she developed in the
Al-Rajab school became like a surrogate family:

Uh, what I like is—or the most important thing for me is—friends.
Like my friends, we have the same beliefs. We can get together, we all
like the same things. And the thing is like the teachers they are more
like sisters and brothers to us than teachers. We're like . . . we're

free here. We can talk and express our opinions because—of course we have the same beliefs and the same religion—and the thing is they understand. They are more understanding, and we are like a community—like a small family. Not like public school. It's like I was really scared there. I had nobody there, and the teachers were like strangers to me. Here it's more like a sense of community. I remember from back when I first came to this school it was like: OK, this is so familiar to me.

Saira, a 14-year-old student of Pakistani descent who had recently transferred from the public school system to the Al-Safar Islamic school, had similar sentiments, referring to her school as being like "a big family and a community, everyone can rely on each other, we can help each other." Other participants also stressed the role of Islamic schools in creating spaces of solidarity and community among Muslims. Ibrahim, a parent and community activist originally from Sierra Leone, cofounded a grassroots organization that provides educational support and advocacy for Muslim families dealing with the public school system and Islamic schools. He spoke of Islamic schools as sites where community solidarity could be fostered in a way that would counteract "tribalism" or the fragmentation of Muslims into ethnic-based enclaves, by providing a mechanism for fostering greater cohesion on the basis of a common Islamic identity:

Also, another goal of Islamic education, or Islamic school, is the reinforcement of the whole question of solidarity among Muslims—children as well as parents—because we're united in faith. And we're united in building the bond of brotherhood and sisterhood within Islam. I think most times, as it is in the mainstream, this is where these relationships are reinforced so that kids, teachers, identify more as Muslim—much more so than where we come from. Because we always say that, you know, Islam is one body and we are brothers and sisters. But I think we have not acted this out in our daily interaction, and I think schooling allows that possibility to happen. You know, as kids grow up in these schools, the color line is erased. They begin to see more and more of each other as children who are the same—not thinking about where they come from.

Deqa, a 16-year-old grade 12 Somali student who had attended the Al-Rajab school for three years, also saw Islam as a force of social cohesion among the culturally diverse student body in her school: "We're all from so many different countries and different backgrounds and we all have different cultures, but the only aspect that brings us together is Islam. So this makes Islam more pure to us." Ali, an 18-year-old student of Bangladeshi descent who had attended the Al-Rajab school for three years, also associated his relationship with teachers and fellow students to that of a "family" situation. He referred to teachers as "brothers" in a familial sense, which, although a common reference in the Muslim community where people customarily refer to one another as "brothers" or "sisters" within Islam, held a higher significance of being more as a "true" family. He remarked that he felt he received more attention from teachers in the Islamic school and felt that this was qualitatively different from and more positive than his treatment in the public schools. In the same vein, Deqa felt that the school provided her with a more "comfortable environment." When I asked her if she felt that she faced any challenges in the Islamic school, she replied that there were greater challenges outside the school than inside: "Challenges? Maybe you better ask somebody else because I can't think of any challenges. It's not too difficult, because it's actually more challenging to be outside because then you have to deal with more stuff. Around here all you have to deal with is being around fellow Muslims and just discussing faith, it's basically like a much more comfortable environment." Being in a faith-centered environment, therefore, provided a source of comfort, familiarity, safety, and cultural congruence. Yet critics of separate schools argue that this sense of "safety" and comfort breeds an unhealthy insularity by secluding these children and youth from other non-Muslim peer groups.

Non-Muslim Friends

Many students spoke of their relationship with friends from outside the community. Saira, who was a recent migrant into the Islamic school system, noted that although the majority of her friends were from public school and were not Muslim, the friends that she had made at the Al-Safar school in only the past year were actually closer to her. She felt that this was because they had more in common from an Islamic point of view and they had a better understanding of her feelings and experiences as a young adolescent Muslim girl, since their experiences were similar. Noora, a classmate of Saira's who was also 14 years old and of Guyanese descent, had been one of the first students to enroll at Al-Safar when it began in 1993. She also found it easier to socialize with Muslim friends, arguing that non-Muslim friends are a more likely source of negative peer pressure and often do not understand and question the religious lifestyle that they have chosen: "With your non-Muslim friends, they don't understand you, and they'll keep questioning you about your religion, and they might not only ask just to know, they might ask to try to shake you or to bend you."

Many students noted changes in their relationship with their non-Muslim friends due to the shift in values and perspectives many of them had when they became part of the Islamic school environment. This reflected more of a sense of "growing apart" from these friends, rather than a deliberate attempt to distance themselves. Iman, a 17-year-old grade 12 Somali student who had attended the Al-Rajab school for three years, spoke of the changes in social practices that students underwent as they acclimatized to the new values and mores of the Islamic school, leaving behind often un-Islamic practices from their public school days: "When you come into an Islamic environment, people tend to change a lot of the time. So it's like calling up an old friend and that person might have been the same or might have even changed worse, but you're like more on the positive side." Deqa also agreed, noting that since "Islam was an everyday thing," she found it more comfortable to share friendships with fellow Muslims.

Among the male students, there were similar sentiments about needing to be with Muslim friends or resist the negative peer pressure that many of their friends outside of school encouraged. Yet they felt that the moral grounding that they received from Islamic school did enable them to build resistances to negative peer pressure. Sabbir, 19, and Saadi, 17 years old, are brothers, and both had been attending the Al-Rajab school for 18 months. They were both born in Canada but are of Pakistani descent. They reflected upon their new interactions with friends they left behind in public school:

> Yeah, I still have non-Muslim friends who I used to hang around
> even before I was in the public schools. I still hang around them now,
> but you don't get influenced by their ideas. We don't get influenced
> by non-Islamic culture. But they are still my friends. They respect the
> fact that I'm Muslim. They always have. There are some people who
> don't accept you because you are Muslim, especially in the area that
> I live now. (Sabbir)

> I have a lot of Jewish friends too. We don't discriminate at all. Just
> because we go to a Muslim school, when we come out, it's not like we
> can only talk to Muslim people. It's not like that at all. (Saadi)

It is significant that both Saadi and Sabbir maintained ties with non-Muslim friends who came from different cultural backgrounds and faith communities.

They demonstrated that religious schooling need not be a form of "religious apartheid" and that it is possible to maintain cross-cultural and interfaith ties outside of school.

Ghettoization

The fact that Islamic school students were, by and large, open to maintaining ties with non-Muslim friends from outside of school, despite their noted concerns about negative peer pressure, goes a long way to dispel attitudes against religious schooling on the grounds that it breeds the insularity of already marginalized groups. Students, parents, and teachers addressed the criticisms leveled against independent parochial schools as being "religious ghettos." Farida and Shazad, Guyanese parents in their mid-30s from the Al-Safar Islamic school, pointed out, for example, that a certain amount of isolation was necessary in order to "minimize the risks" of children falling into unacceptable kinds of behavior that exist within mainstream culture. Farida went on to note how the inculcation of values in a separate and culturally congruent environment was necessary to first build a sense of identity within Muslim children that would then help them integrate into mainstream society without losing their Islamic values and identity: "I guess that some of the things they're being taught in the public school, and you have to, like, you know, just wonder what, because they teach them things that are non-Islamic too, and you want to isolate them from some of that when they're young so that, not that you don't want them to be exposed, but if you give them too much of that, they will eventually be, so you try to isolate them and gear them into Islam as early as possible. Eventually they'll be going into the public system. You're preparing them for that too, but they'll be stronger as their identity builds."

There were some concerns, however, that without more engagement with the mainstream society, some schools did run the risk of socially and intellectually isolating their students. Even among Muslims, there were negative stereotypes attached to the idea of Islamic schools. Shahnaz noted that many of her family and friends from back home in India were opposed to her decision to send her daughter to Islamic school: "My in-laws, everyone, they said, you know, 'Why are you putting her in an Islamic school?' My friends—they're calling from India, 'Why are you putting her in an Islamic school? You're in Canada! You should put her in the public school system.' You know, 'Why are you making her backward like that? And why are you doing this to her?' They weren't against the hijab or the Islamic dress code or anything, but they were just, you know, 'She's going to go out in the real world. Why do you want her to be just sheltered like that in the school system?'" Shahnaz's family and friends back home saw social and cultural integration as the goal of school-ing for their diasporic relatives in Canada. The fact that they felt that keeping Shahnaz's daughter in an Islamic school would not only be sheltering her from mainstream society but also be making her more "backward" in the process is indicative of the way that, due to the colonial legacies and growing West-ern cultural imperialism and hegemony, Muslims equate Westernization with progress and view tradition and faith as an anachronistic hold on less socially desirable traits.

Rukhsana, a mother of three children attending the Al-Safar school who was of Pakistani descent, felt that having an Islamic education should not stand in the way of being active participants and contributors in society and was critical of those who allowed themselves to become too insular: "OK, they obviously should have the Islamic teaching, but they should have to integrate in society. They can't be just Muslim. You have to be Muslim, obviously, but you can show that you can contribute to society. You can get involved in the community, you know, do something volunteer. There's food banks. There's a lot of things that they can get involved in. They're an integral part of the soci-ety. We can contribute to the society. We can contribute with our academics. There are hundreds of ways to contribute, but they're not contributing. They want to stay within themselves. They don't want to spread out. I don't know why." Sister Mehrun, the principal of the Al-Safar school, also disagreed with the perspective that Islamic schooling disallowed Muslim children to have healthy interactions with children from different religious and cultural back-grounds. She argued that children from her school were engaged in activities outside of school that put them in contact with people from the broader com-munity and that the self-esteem and confidence they were developing in their own identities as Muslims were just as important as cross-cultural interaction: "We are living in the society—we are not that completely isolated—the chil-dren go shopping, the children are watching television, they go for picnics and all that, and you know they are aware. But at the same time, I think having a good self-concept and being comfortable with who they are is just as impor-tant. And after all, basically I came from another country, and I don't think I had any trouble adjusting to the society. So those children that are grow-ing up here, they are not completely isolated. Inshallah, once they are older, they will have a good understanding, maybe a better understanding than what we have." Therefore, in Mehrun's view, the children from her school were being equipped to deal with their identities as Muslims, and being rooted in their own sense of identity was the basis for developing an understanding and knowledge of others.

Leila, a grade 12 student of Somali descent who attended the Al-Rajab school, had similar sentiments, arguing that being prepared to live out their identities as Muslims provided them with the life skills that they needed to maintain their identity within the plurality of society and to develop a basis from which they could interact with others: "Well, you know being prepared in the sense of not being out there, it's not such a big deal, 'cuz like you take the bus with everybody. It's like our lives interact with different people, but it's just that the school prepares us Islamically—giving us an Islamic perspective on how to deal with everybody—and in that sense they are preparing us, like for the world." Other students were offended by the suggestion that they were isolated or that they were not aware of the world outside of them. In my interview with Zarqa, Aliyah, and Nusaybah, grade 11 students of South Asian and Afghani descent, they were defensive of their choice to be in an Islamic school and did not feel that it impinged on their ability to know about other cultures and ways of life. They also defended the choice of those who wanted to focus on their own faith as a central aspect of their education:

But like you have a right to your own religion, and if you want to put yourself into a box and only do your religion and only know about your religion, it's your choice. It shouldn't matter. I know it's like a good thing to know about other religions and respect other religions and understand other religions, but how to explain it? (Zarqa)

You should also know about your own. (Aliyah)

Countering the argument made by liberal theorists that being among a diverse community of students in public schools allows for greater opportunities to gain cross-cultural knowledge, the students argued that the Eurocentric hegemony of the public school meant that their learning centered on Anglo-Canadian traditions and history and prohibited learning about other cultures, as they discussed in the following exchange:

JASMIN: What about the opportunity to, say, learn about different cultures?

ZARQA: That's good. I think that's a really good idea.

ALIYAH: But we've learned that. We've been learning all our lives before we came here. We've been learning about other people's religions, other people's holidays, other people's things. The teachers, they'll be talking about what the Inuits did in the olden days or what the Christians did.

They talk about all that stuff, but you don't really hear them talk in a positive way about Muslims.

NUSAYBAH: But like Islam was never really talked about in public school. And only like the French holidays, or the English holidays, not like Chinese holidays or Buddhist holidays. None of those are really respected or taught in public school anyways, so how are you supposed to know about other cultures? I only know about Christianity and Hinduism from Indian movies, right? But those are the only three religions that I know; they don't really teach you in public school, or you don't learn from other people.

Therefore, as they argued, they learned more about other religious ways of life from "Bollywood movies" than they did from their public schooling. Opportunities to learn about other cultures and faiths from their peers were also limited, they noted, since most minoritized youth were more concerned with conforming to the traditions of the dominant culture or going to malls than discussing the finer points of theology:

I don't know that they really show you their culture. They all act that one culture, they all act that one Canadian, typical Christmas, Halloween, whatever. (Zarqa)

You won't have the Hindus talking about their temple or whatever, they all talk about malls, clothes, they don't talk about their religion anyways, so what's the point? (Aliyah)

Students noted that the cultural demographics of Islamic schools, where Muslims from South Asia, Africa, and the Caribbean as well as North American converts could be found, were very diverse. Therefore they did not feel "cheated" out of having access to cultural diversity by being in an Islamic school. Deqa, for example, did not feel that being in an Islamic school was an impediment to understanding and engaging in Canadian multiculturalism since Islamic schools already had a culturally diverse student body: "I think that's especially not true for Islamic schools because we're so like, multicultural, and in that sense we are very open-minded and we accept each other's different cultures. And even though we have Islam as what brings us together, we also have many things that are different. And that's why we accept each other in that way; and we do deal with people—outside people basically, and it's not like a big deal. And it's not like we get a shock outside later on."

Religious diversity was taken up at the high school level through world religion courses that were offered as electives, as they are in public schools. I was very impressed by some of the projects that the grade 10 world religion students presented at an exhibition of the school's work at a local civic center. One group of students had prepared a PowerPoint presentation on Buddhism, and another group had constructed a model of a concentration camp in their presentation of Jewish history. This demonstrated to me that these students not only had access to knowledge of other faith communities but also had an interest in learning about other religions and developed their presentations with both pride and respect. In elementary schools there were fewer curricular opportunities to integrate knowledge of other cultures, since Islamic schools followed the same Eurocentric curriculum mandated by the provincial government as did public schools. Teachers in these schools individually tried to make their curriculum more inclusive, since, as Ruqayyah, a teacher at the Al-Safar school, noted, she did not want the children to grow up as if they were "living in a bubble":

> That's something [ghettoization] that I know myself—and I know
> some of the other teachers—we are scared of sometimes that it
> might happen. But, inshallah, I won't because I want them to realize
> that they have to learn about everything. They have to interact with
> everybody. So that's my main take. I personally have received criti-
> cism about teaching things like the Olympics. Some parents think
> it's an un-Islamic thing. Not all of the parents, just a couple. But I
> said—without getting defensive—that I understood where they were
> coming from, but that to me is almost like living in a bubble. There
> are so many non-Muslims that know more about us than we do about
> them. I just think it's important for them to learn about everyone
> and everything. We're back to the Prophet of Islam. He knew about
> everyone. He knew about all the lifestyles and everything. And there's
> no harm in learning just for the sake of knowing and thinking, OK,
> this is what this group does, and this is what that group does.

Ruqayyah, therefore, was attentive to the need for students to have a broad education that includes knowledge of other ways of life aside from their own, and she situated this as integral to the practice of the Prophet Muhammad as an example for all Muslims to follow. Nevertheless, she also had to contend with the narrow viewpoints of some parents who expected only Islamic knowledge to be represented—a position very much in contrast to the historical Islamic traditions of pedagogy and knowledge production that built upon the earlier knowledge of the Greeks. Ruqayyah feared that such attitudes and the absence of a multicultural curriculum would lead to divisive social attitudes that would lead students into reproducing the "us" versus "them" dichotomy as a means of relating to the world outside the school: "I hope, inshallah, we're not ghettoizing them because I know it's not just me, myself, I know a lot of the teachers are teaching them about different things, different projects. Last year

I was teaching about Native cultures. So, inshallah, I hope we're not doing that [ghettoizing]. It is scary because I don't want any child coming out of the school having an 'us' versus 'them' approach."

Being attentive to the way that Islamic schooling could potentially lead to an "us versus them" way of thinking about the world is a significant concern. This is largely due to two reasons. The first is due to the current geopolitical context and the impact of the post-9/11 world: the backlash against Muslims in North America, the bombing of Afghanistan, the war against Iraq, and the oppression of the Palestinians. As a result of these events, many Muslims feel victimized on a global scale, and children are not immune to internalizing these feelings of oppression and resentment toward those complicit in the causes. The binary notions of "us" and "them" framed within "the clash of civilizations" paradigm popularized by Huntington have some saliency on a psychosocial level, where marginalized groups who are "otherized" within dominant discourses and geopolitical narratives also return the gaze in equally distancing and pejorative terms.[24]

The second factor in this dynamic is the relational narrative espoused by many religious leaders who refer to nonbelievers in their *khutbas,* or sermons, through the derogatory reference of *kafirs.* While Christians and Jews are referred to in the Qur'an as *Ahl al-kitab,* or "people of the Book," referring to the common theological heritage shared by Christians, Jews, and Muslims, the term *kafir* is reserved for apostates or nonbelievers. The term *kafir,* however, is a label often generically applied to non-Muslims and one that frames a particular reference point for Muslim children as they view others outside their community. In this way, some religious authorities use religious discourse in destructive ways to reinforce separatist boundaries between Muslims and non-Muslims.

This was evident to Bilquees, a teacher in her late 60s of Indian descent, from the Al-Shawwal school, who saw such attitudes trickling down from the religious leaders who were also administrators of the school. She discussed the inappropriateness of these attitudes and her resistance in seeing these reproduced within the school: "I think, they do get the feeling, oh, we are Muslims, they do get that identity eventually, but in a way, they are kind of discriminating other kids, by saying that they are kafir and we are Muslim. That kind of attitude develops into them, between Muslims and non-Muslims a lot. Oh, those are kafir and we are Muslim, more like arrogance and you know pride. Of course, we are supposed to be proud of our religion, but not in the way that they are doing it. Like, oh yeah those are kafir schools or kafir this. And I said, 'Don't say that,' you know. It's not appropriate for us to say that. It's good to be a good Muslim, but you cannot put down somebody else." Bilquees resisted the construction of an Islamic identity through "arrogance" or self-righteous pride, in a way that was constituted through the construction of the abject social difference of non-Muslims. She rightly argued that these attitudes, espoused by some community leaders, were themselves un-Islamic, and she felt that it was important that the schools did not reproduce this cultural ignorance among students.

Other teachers also spoke of the need to make sure that children grew up with an open mind and were tolerant of other social differences. Rima, a teacher in her mid-30s of Egyptian background, expressed fears that children were too sheltered in their Islamic school environment: "We should equip them and have them open-minded to know what's going on out there . . . not to live in that cocoon. That's another problem of having Islamic school environment is having to live in this cocoon—in our school anyway." Both Ruqayyah and Rima—teachers from two different schools—used similar metaphors of "enclosure" to express some of their fears and concerns regarding the possibilities of "ghettoizing" students. They described their concerns over students living in a "bubble" or "cocoon" as potential and sometimes actual by-products of socially isolated Islamic school environments. In the case of the Al-Shawwal school where Rima worked, many families were newcomers, having come to Canada as immigrants and refugees, which contributed to their social isolation. Their social ties were primarily through the mosque community and the school. Children, therefore, had less exposure to other environments. Many newcomer families from Muslim countries find it difficult to come to terms with what they see as an overly permissive society that legitimizes many practices that they see as contrary to Islam such as drinking alcohol and premarital dating and sex.[25] Islamic schools are more attractive, by contrast, since they provide a culturally congruent environment where family-centered values are reinforced.

At a forum on community education and activism, a Somali activist with a women's settlement organization described how Somali Muslim families saw children as their "RRSPs"—in other words, as an investment that would provide a "return" to them in their old age when their children would be expected to provide for and look after them.[26] She explained that many families feared losing their children to the dominant social mores of Western culture, which is based more on individualism at the expense of communal and familial responsibilities. Islamic schools, in this sense, were viewed more as a means of protecting their children and, therefore, protecting their investment in the future of their family and community.

Desegregation and Integration into Public Schools

Other participants did acknowledge the "ghettoizing" effects of segregated schooling that may make transitions to public secondary or postsecondary institutions more difficult. Bilquees acknowledged the problems of integration without adequate preparation: "If we are isolating our children from the rest of the world, and eventually when they go into high school or say even after high school, we have a university that will not be an Islamic university or anything, so they eventually have to merge into some system that is not going to be Islamic. So if the child is not prepared from the beginning to go into these institutions, how is he going to progress? You know, I don't understand how we can do that." Sakhina, a teacher in her late 20s at the Al-Rajab girls' high school who was of Pakistani descent, had similar concerns about making sure students would be prepared to integrate and succeed in postsecondary schooling. She noted that ghettoization was a dual process, one that occurred as the result of how those looking at the school from the outside regard the students as being culturally apart from dominant norms and then how the students themselves would relate to the outside world: "The people who were outside looking in would see these girls in their [Islamic-style] uniforms. And it's like, 'What goes on in there?' That sort of thing. The people who were inside looking out—like the students themselves—sometimes they don't know how to interact with our society, and they have to learn. So I'm for the Islamic schools, but I'm also afraid of that whole ghettoizing aspect. Are we going to be able to function in society?" Students, therefore, seemed to exist within a fishbowl, where they were being scrutinized by those on the outside and yet were so contained in their own environment that the fear was that they might literally feel like fish out of water once they had to integrate into mainstream schools and institutions.

Amira, a teacher of Pakistani descent in her mid-30s from the Al-Safar Islamic school, also agreed that students had a certain distance from the dominant culture but argued that they were not completely cut off from their social or cultural surroundings. She echoed the views of some students who felt that being in public school was more isolating in many ways for Muslim students who are living a faith-centered lifestyle: "Well, in terms of knowing what's out there, all of them, like, they live in a society where they see the kind of things that go on. They know, they are sort of aware of the things non-Muslims do. But it's sort of at a distance. Its not, like, when they're at high school they're put in an environment where they will feel like the oddballs and there will be pressure to be like the others." Peer pressure was also a concern regarding students who would be migrating out of the safety of the Islamic school environment and be facing many social and cultural challenges in the public school system. The process of desegregation and the student's preparedness for resisting the negative peer pressure that they would likely confront, such as the pressure to date or use recreational drugs and alcohol, were issues of concern to parents and teachers.

For Amani, an Ethiopian teacher in her early 30s from the Al-Safar school, some fears were allayed by the recent graduates from her school who went on to high school and were successful both academically and in maintaining their Islamic identity in the face of social challenges and pressures to conform to mainstream norms: "I'm glad you brought that up because this is one of the concerns that all parents have. They constantly worry: Are they going to be able to handle [public] high school? Like last year we had our first graduates, so in fact we want them to come back and tell us how they survived their first year, to talk to the grade 8s that are about to graduate and to tell them, you know, I mean they were hearing lots of myths about how bad the high schools, public schools are. . . . I always tell my students: If you know who you are and you feel confident about yourself and your identity and your place in this society, you can go anywhere and survive, you can go to the moon, you can go to Mars."

Receiving a faith-centered learning that rooted these students in their sense of identity, self, and purpose in life was, for teachers like Amani, the key to preparing students to negotiate their identities and experiences in mainstream society and still retain their Islamic way of life. She felt that students needed guidance and support to make the right choices in their lives: "Even right now, as grade 8s we keep telling them they're the role models and the ambassadors. So we're preparing them, psychologically we're preparing them that you know, you guys are now mature adults, you can make your own choice, you can be responsible. And the other thing also that we tell them is that you always know where to come when you need help. Like we try, we give them a support system." Amira also pointed out that, from an Islamic point of view, as many of these students reach puberty they cross the threshold from childhood into adulthood and, therefore, are now considered accountable to Allah for their religious obligations. With a limited number of Islamic high schools, many Muslim adolescents migrate into public schools during this period, when the onus is on them to be spiritually responsible and accountable for maintaining their five daily prayers, fasting during Ramadan, and other religious requirements. Therefore, she argued that the need for developing life skills starts early in their schooling through inculcating a form of values education to help guide students toward making correct moral choices in their behavior and actions when they leave the more regulated environment of the Islamic school:

> What we do, starting from grade 6, we start teaching them, we start
> telling them, like you know, it's high school, this is what you're going
> to encounter . . . and then also we start telling that they're going to
> be their own decision makers and that being in an Islamic school,
> there are teachers everywhere so there will always be someone there

to pull you back and say, "You know, you shouldn't be doing this," so that will no longer exist in high school. So we tell them . . . no one is going to tell you, your parents will probably never find out what you do in high school, so . . . the onus is on them, they have to make their own choices. And that we have tried our best to show them the choices and what the consequences are for the choices. A lot of that starts in grade 6 . . . you know, relationships, drugs, everything that is encountered. And we talk, openly and frankly, about all these things, especially the relationship with boys and girls and dating. We talk about the consequences and what can happen . . . [sexually trans-mitted] diseases and things like that. So, we sort of tell them that it's between you and Allah, and you have to seriously start saying to yourself, Oh, what choice do I want to make? Do I want to make one that goes towards the straight path? Or do I want to make one that's going to lead me to the wrong path?

Teachers described several strategies that they had already implemented to help students make the transition into public schools. For example, Amira explained the steps taken at the Al-Safar school to create dialogues and discus-sions around peer pressure. The majority of the teachers in Al-Safar had grown up in Canada attending public schools, unlike most teachers in other local Islamic schools, who were more recent immigrants. These teachers had a greater understanding of the challenges that their students would be facing and were conscious of the need to develop proactive strategies to help them cope:

Like we have to, we just have to be very open about it. Um, because I don't think they're that open about it with their parents. We talk about gangs, being involved in certain cliques or groups in high school, or doing things because a group is doing it, we even had some seminars on gang violence, and things like that. We had the police come in, and they were talking about consequences and the Young Offenders Act and what constitutes arrest and so and so, so they have a better idea. . . . And, that's all we can do, and just pray that they will make their life choice, 'cause there's no longer someone watching you or someone telling you or someone even enforcing . . . like if someone just goes and starts using foul language in every sentence, like who's going to enforce it? Whereas if they're with us, OK yeah, they're going to be in trouble, it's a big deal.

Students migrating out of Islamic schools, therefore, become more morally re-sponsible for their behavior, where un-Islamic practices like swearing, as Amira pointed out, that are highly sanctioned in Islamic schools, become more common and less regulated by public school authorities.

Sakhina felt that the key to integration was through community engagement through individual and school-based interactions: "I think the key is through community work. Not necessarily with Muslim organizations but non-Muslim organizations too. Like community service where the school, as a community, goes to a senior citizens' home . . . you know, because I think, like, work within the community that way. If you're working with senior citizens, you're working with the elderly. You're helping them. Go to the library and be part of a reading club for young kids who come there." Sakhina felt that opportunities like these needed to be sought out by Islamic schools since they provided the type of interaction that would be consistent with their religious values rather than being a compromise. Some of the Islamic schools were involved with public schools through track meets and science fair competitions, which allowed opportunities for collegial interaction through sports and academic events. Teachers spoke of the need to develop more opportunities like these, such as through spelling bees or speech competitions that would create further linkages and networks between the local public and independent schools.

Independent schools were not seen as being completely separate from the public system since students often migrated back and forth between these systems and Islamic school students eventually graduated and moved on to public high schools or universities. Therefore, it was felt that the public schools should have a vested interest in the students in the Islamic schools since many would, at some time, have to reintegrate into public education. Rima had some concrete recommendations and requests for support from public schools that would help fill some of the resource gaps in the Islamic school and help students make their transitions into the public education system smoother, such as the assistance of guidance counselors or English as a second language support. However, she added that because of pervasive racism and Islamophobia, there was still a lack of trust with the mainstream system and how guidance counselors, for example, might respond to issues in the community by calling in Children's Aid authorities and having children removed to non-Muslim homes:

> Bringing in some of the helpers that could help the kids could be
> from outside in the public school system if we could get them, like
> guidance counselors or remedial help would be good. Maybe guid-
> ance helpers are limited though because if somebody gets hit or
> something, you know, they get abused at home or somebody's going
> to complain, then it's going to be more of a problem for our com-
> munity. We're being alienated in dealing with organizations like

Children's Aid because of the way they're treating us. And so that alienates us. You know, this is very important, but at the same time I don't want to make more problems for our community. I know the Children's Aid is very prejudiced, so we feel that even though some kids might need their help, we don't tend to go to them because of what they might do.

Rima's fears of turning to guidance counselors or Children's Aid come from a history of experiences where these authorities have been quick to remove children from their homes before abuse could be corroborated. For example, at Rima's school a child of one of the teachers had been removed from the family on allegations of abuse laid by doctors when the mother brought the child in to seek medical assistance. Police came to the school and interviewed this teacher's grade 1 students to see whether she had been abusive toward them, and her other children were removed from her care. Two weeks later, medical tests determined that the child had not been abused but suffered from a chemical imbalance in his brain. Members of the community charged this as a case of Islamophobia that caused authorities to act against the parent and level suspicion against the school before other medical possibilities were ruled out. Community fears of differential negative treatment by authorities are, therefore, often a barrier to seeking out professional help and services, and many prefer to deal with situations of conflict or distress internally with the help of religious leaders, rather than being potentially exposed to mistreatment.

In other ways local public schools have stepped in to provide logistical support to Islamic schools. For example, sister Mehrun, the principal of the Al-Safar school, described the connections she fostered with a local public school to provide various kinds of support to the school, particularly in a crisis situation: "We invited the principal [from the public school], and we took them to dinner as well and showed the whole building, the office. Two years ago we went and borrowed some equipment for our play day, like ropes or whatever. And also we made an arrangement with them, in case of an emergency, you know, because they're on a main road and being a Muslim school and place of worship, in case of threats, or some kind of problem like that bomb threat, we made an arrangement with them to go to their school." Evacuation planning became imperative after the Oklahoma City bombing, when Islamic centers across North America, including Al-Safar, received bomb threats as Muslims and Arabs were mistakenly accused of the terrorism. The alert was high again right from the day of the September 11 attacks. By the afternoon of September 11, Muslim men from the community left work early and formed a security perimeter around Al-Safar, which is both a mosque and a school, for fear of attacks—despite the fact that it was not yet known who was responsible for the acts. The burden of collective guilt and punishment for the tragedy of September 11 has left an imprint on the way Islamic schools and centers now regard their own safety in the community.

Interestingly, students pointed to the lack of government funding for Islamic schools and society's lack of knowledge of Muslims as the main factors contributing to their "ghettoization," as the following students from the Al-Rajab school explained:

> Some of the challenges will be like, the school, its not government-funded so there's a lot more, you know, involvement amongst the community and yourself, so in public school everything is basically given to you in your lap basically. You just come to school, write the stuff, and then just go home, right. Here it's a lot more harder than that, because like I said the school is not properly equipped sometimes. (Daood)

> See, we're not subsidized. Being segregated from different communities doesn't mean that we're not aware of the things that are going on, the social conflict going on around the world. But like, we pretty much know a lot of these things. We hear things, but we're just not like in tune with them all the time. (Iman)

> And just because this is Islamic school, they might not think that we're well educated, right? And that's a problem. (Summaya)

> The Ministry of Education come in, and they check out our school, the work that we're doing, you know look at the binders and stuff. We're pretty much like normal people. There's no difference, just the religion, being tight with your religion, that's the number one key. (Iman)

Therefore, in their view, the issue of being separated out was an effect of the discriminatory funding policies of the government and the way in which they felt positioned by the dominant society and culture, rather than a conscious attempt by Muslims to self-exile from society. Students clearly respond to the peer support, religious freedom, and camaraderie that Islamic schools engender but do not see themselves as essentially living separatist lifestyles or not being conscious of the world around them. In other words, they do not see centering their Islamic identity as a negation of their Canadian identity or their role as active citizens.

The challenge for both public and Islamic educational systems is to develop ways to have a complementary coexistence as parallel systems that implicate one another. More inclusive funding formulas may provide a means to keep independent religious schools within the public purview while at the same time offering alternative faith-based education for families who choose a more spiritually centered education. Such an arrangement can avoid the segmentation of schools into separate cultural and religious enclaves that have no connection with one another. A system that engenders more cooperation and interaction between the various religious and secular public schools would provide a mutual opportunity for growth and learning. Secular Eurocentric schooling in Canada can no longer masquerade as an ideologically neutral space when it affirms particular identities and discourses and marginalizes others. By recognizing religious pluralism as a positive and intrinsic aspect of society, a truly inclusive school system centering the knowledge and experience of communities on the margins would weather well the challenge of social fragmentation along racial and religious lines.

NOTES

An earlier version of this essay appeared as "Safe Havens or Religious 'Ghettos'? Narratives of Islamic Schooling in Canada," *Race Ethnicity and Education* 10, no. 1 (March 2007): pp. 71–92, DOI: 10.1080/13613320601100385. It has been reproduced here with the permission of the publisher, Taylor and Francis.

1. S. Nyang, "Islam, American Society and the Challenges," *The Message,* 2000, www.icna.org/icna/publications/the-message-magazine.html, accessed August 15, 2001.

2. Ibid., p. 2.

3. Ibid.

4. K. Murad, *Muslim Youth in the West* (London: Islamic Foundation, 1986); A. Yousif, *Muslims in Canada: A Question of Identity* (Ottawa: Legas Press, 1993); M. Parker-Jenkins, *Children of Islam: A Teacher's Guide to Meeting the Needs of Muslim Pupils* (London: Trentham Books, 1995); M. A. Khan-Cheema, "British Muslims in State Schools: A Positive Way Forward," in Muslim Educational Trust, ed., *Issues in Islamic Education* (London: Muslim Educational Trust, 1996), pp. 83–90; G. Sarwar, "Islamic Education: Its Meanings, Problems and Prospects," in Muslim Educational Trust, *Issues in Islamic Education,* pp. 7–23.

5. J. Jacobson, *Islam in Transition: Religion and Identity among British-Pakistani Youth* (London: Routledge, 1998); R. Shamma, "Muslim Youth in North America: Issues and Concerns," in A. Haque, ed., *Muslims and Islamization in North America: Problems and Prospects* (Beltsville, MD: Amana Publishers, 1999), pp. 323–330; J. Zine, "Redefining Resistance: Toward an Islamic Sub-culture in Schools," *Race, Ethnicity and Education* 31, no. 2 (2000): pp. 293–316; J. Zine, "Muslim Youth in Canadian Schools: Education and the Politics of Religious Identity," *Anthropology and Education Quarterly* 32, no. 4 (2001): pp. 399–423.

6. Murad, *Muslim Youth in the West;* G. Rezai-Rashti, "Islamic Identity and Racism," *Orbit* (Ontario Institute for Studies in Education, Toronto) 25, no. 2 (1994): pp. 37–38; Zine, "Redefining Resistance"; Zine, "Muslim Youth in Canadian Schools."

7. A. Gutmann, "Challenges of Multiculturalism in Democratic Education," in R. K. Fullwider, ed., *Public Education in a Multicultural Society: Policy, Theory, Critique* (Cambridge: Cambridge University Press, 1996), pp. 156–179; L. Sweet, *God in the Classroom* (Toronto: McClelland and Stewart, 1997); E. Callon, "Discrimination and Religious Schooling" (paper presented at the Canadian Centre for Philosophy and Public Policy Conference, University of Toronto, Toronto, October 1997); E. J. Theissen, *In Defence of Religious Schools and Colleges* (Montreal: McGill University Press, 2001).

8. L. Scrivenor, "Islamic Schools a 'Safe Space,'" *Toronto Star*, February 25, 2001, p. D-8.

9. N. Memon, "Colonizing Muslim Schools from Within: An Analysis of Neo-liberal Practices in Toronto's Islamic Schools" (paper presented at the Rage and Hope Conference, Ontario Institute for Studies in Education/University of Toronto, Toronto, February 24, 2006).

10. I use the term *minoritized* to refer to the social, political, economic, and cultural forces that conspire to relegate world majority groups of people to a subordinated status. See also Sweet, *God in the Classroom*.

11. Gutmann, "Challenges of Multiculturalism in Democratic Education."

12. Sweet, *God in the Classroom*.

13. Gutmann, "Challenges of Multiculturalism in Democratic Education," p. 158.

14. M. Halstead, "Radical Feminism, Islam and the Single Sex School Debate," *Gender and Education* 3, no. 3 (1991): pp. 263–278. See p. 275.

15. In a recent study of schools, religion, and public funding, M. Parker-Jenkins, D. Hartas, and B. A. Irving (*In Good Faith: Schools, Religion, and Public Funding* (Aldershot, UK: Ashgate, 2005) outline a distinction among Muslim schools, schools for Muslims, and Islamic schools in the European context. "Muslim schools" are qualified as those where "the intention is to develop an entire ethos consistent with religious values," whereas the "schools for Muslims" have similar aspirations but in actuality tend to be schools characterized by a shared religious identity where the integration of religious ethos and curriculum is not feasible due to staffing or financial constraints. The authors note that greater access to state funding can help offset these concerns. What is qualified as an "Islamic" school is a school where Islamic epistemology and praxis are embedded into the formal and hidden curricula and where all subjects are taught from an Islamic perspective (Parker-Jenkins et al., p. 40). In the Canadian context, schools overall aspire to this same ideal, and therefore the term *"Islamic" schools* is applied universally.

16. Gutmann, "Challenges of Multiculturalism in Democratic Education."

17. Theissen, *In Defence of Religious Schools and Colleges*, p. 244.

18. Callon, "Discrimination and Religious Schooling," p. 24.

19. Ibid., pp. 24–25; emphasis in the original.

20. T. McLaughlin, "The Ethics of Separate Schools," in M. Leicester and M. Taylor, eds., *Ethics, Ethnicity and Education* (London: Kogan Page, 1992), pp. 100–113.

21. J. Spinner-Halev, "Extending Diversity: Religion in Public and Private Education" (paper presented at the Canadian Centre for Philosophy and Public Policy

Conference "Citizenship in Diverse Societies," University of Toronto, Toronto, October 1997).

22. R. Jafri and T. Fatah, "Muslims Oppose Funding," *Toronto Star,* July 14, 2003, p. A-17.

23. The participants and schools in this study are identified through the use of pseudonyms to protect their privacy and anonymity.

24. S. Huntington, "The Clash of Civilizations," *Foreign Affairs* 72, no. 3 (1993): pp. 22–28.

25. R. Berns-McGown, *Muslims in the Diaspora* (Toronto: University of Toronto Press, 1999); Shamma, "Muslim Youth in North America"; Zine, "Muslim Youth in Canadian Schools."

26. *RRSP* refers to Canada's "Registered Retirement Savings Plan," which is a retirement fund that individuals can contribute a portion of their income to, tax free. The saliency of this reference is as a metaphor for children being an investment for one's future.

3

The Case for the Muslim School as a Civil Society Actor

Louis Cristillo

Although the vast majority of American Muslims do not live
in economically depressed physical ghettos, many live in a
psychological ghetto caused by the lack of acceptance they feel
from their neighbors and colleagues, especially in the post–
Sept. 11 era. This psychological ghetto may prove the largest
challenge in the war on terrorism.
> —Salam Al-Marayati, "America's Muslim Ghettos,"
> *Washington Post*, August 15, 2005

Whenever I speak in public about the full-time Muslim school
in New York City where I conducted ethnographic research for
my dissertation from 1999 to 2000, someone inevitably asks me,
"Wouldn't these kids be better off in public school where they could
learn civic values to help them assimilate into American society?" The
assumption is that the Muslim school is a cultural and institutional
ghetto where, at best, the kids will grow up pious Muslims living
quietly in the margins of mainstream American society. Or at worst,
and this is the thrust of Al-Marayati's op-ed piece penned after the July
7, 2005, London subway bombings, American-born Muslims, like the
misguided "homegrown British Muslim lads," might easily fall prey to
"political and religious radicalization."[1]

Despite his appeal for American Muslims to embrace the
populist ideal that "Islam is American-based, not Arab- or South
Asian–based," Al-Marayati's faith in American pluralism is unlikely

to mitigate the pervasive fear of the immigrant "Muslim Other." A conservative blogger, for example, recently inveighed against a Democratic congressman's visit to a Muslim school in Queens, New York. What was most stunning, however, was the cavalier stream of comments that followed, including this one: "Nationalist groups thrive where there is a common ethnic identify. They also thrive where there is a common religious theme. First-generation Muslim adults are isolating American born children and indoctrinating them with pro-Arab fascist Muslim ideology."[2] Ignoring the fact that public schools fail to prevent some children from slipping into bigotry and intolerance—*Brown v. Board of Education* notwithstanding—this blogger would sleep better knowing that American-born Muslims were getting a wholesome public school education. The irony in this is that 97 percent of all Muslim schoolchildren are already in public schools.

Even so, it is the other 3 percent whom, if pushed to the fringes of society, right-wing bloggers and some apprehensive American Muslims worry may turn out like the "homegrown British Muslim lads." Evidence from the classroom suggests that such worries are overblown. In the case of the Muslim school I studied in New York City, more than 85 percent of the teacher-student contact time is devoted to secular instruction; the curriculum is adopted in its entirety, and in total accordance with, the content, standards, and educational laws set forth by the State of New York; the school's fourth and eighth graders endure the same citywide standardized tests of math and language arts and bury their noses in the same textbooks as do their public school peers.[3]

Intolerance toward minority religious groups in public discourse on American education is, of course, nothing new. For over a century and a half, the Catholic parochial school system educated virtually millions of immigrants and their offspring—Polish, German, Lithuanian, Irish, and Italian to name a few—belying the bigotry of 19th-century nativists who reviled the "heathen papists" as unpatriotic corruptors of an imagined Anglo-Protestant mainstream.[4] Jewish immigrants, whose numbers swelled to over one million between 1830 and 1905, fared little better. For even though most Jewish immigrants at the time preferred the American *public school*—not the segregated schooling they left behind in European ghettos—the promise of assimilation, portrayed romantically in Israel Zangwill's 1908 play *The Melting Pot*, gave way to the harsh reality of anti-Semitism ingrained in the cultural hegemony of the Anglo-Protestant mainstream.[5]

In this chapter, then, I take an alternative approach by examining the Muslim school outside the conventional frame of curriculum and classroom. I explore how the Muslim school becomes a major actor in a nexus of institutions—the mosque, the local professional and business sector, the family, and the state—and in so doing I provide evidence to correct the misconception that the Muslim school marginalizes youth inside a real or imagined ethno-religious ghetto. The analysis reveals, in fact, that participation in the founding and life of a Muslim school produces overlapping social networks to bring individuals and groups into greater involvement in American civic life and participatory democracy.[6]

Background to the Muslim School Movement

In the short span of the past two decades, Muslim schools founded by diaspora communities have joined the long-standing institution of faith-based alternative schools in the United States.[7] Counting the several dozen Sister Clara Muhammad schools established originally by the Nation of Islam but now part of the African American Sunni community, there are about 235 Muslim schools across the country, catering to the educational and religious needs of an estimated 26,000–35,000 children.[8]

For many Muslim Americans today, the Muslim school represents an institutional firewall against the loss of religious identity by the wholesale assimilation of future generations of American Muslims. Just as born-again Christians heap criticism on America's public schools for failing the moral education of their children, observant Muslims likewise view the public school as an unhealthy microcosm of a larger society increasingly plagued by random violence, drug abuse, and widespread sexual promiscuity. Whereas many American Muslims speak proudly of their private schools, there are non-Muslim Americans, as I noted earlier, who see them as a worrisome presence in post-9/11 America. The Muslim school conjures up images of a Taliban-style madrassa, where children are robbed of the opportunity to acquire core moral and civic values of American democracy best learned through a public school education.

Both of these perceptions, Muslim and non-Muslim alike, rest on the faulty assumption that Muslim schools in America live an insular existence impervious to penetration by American culture, mores, and civic values. Ignorance, fear, and misconceptions abound in both camps, for in post-9/11 America, draconian national security measures, coupled with a readiness to accept the simplistic allure of the "Clash of Civilizations" thesis, have ushered in a new round of American nativism. Islamophobia is worse now than it was in the first few months after 9/11 when Muslims were facing a national backlash. A recent Washington Post–ABC poll, coinciding with the start of the fourth year of the War in Iraq, revealed that 46 percent of those surveyed—up 7 percent from just after the 9/11 attacks—expressed unfavorable views toward Islam and regard Muslims to be disproportionately prone to violence.[9]

Reframing the Analysis of Muslim Schools

My central argument is that the establishment and operation of a full-time Muslim school produce a network of social relations and structures that fosters, rather than fetters, the civic integration of Muslim diaspora communities into American civil society. Looking at the existing albeit scanty literature on Muslim schools in the United States, I believe it is time to reframe our analysis. To date, two theoretical frameworks—reflecting both journalistic and academic impulses—have tended to define the research: (1) the Muslim school is conceptualized as a transnational space where Islamic identity is negotiated and contested in a pluralistic, multicultural society or (2) the school is viewed as a (counter-)cultural alternative to the perceived hegemony of white Anglo-Protestant culture prevalent in public schools.[10] My own dissertation research straddled both frameworks.[11] I now feel, however, that these approaches have run their course and offer little in the way of new insights. What is needed, I believe, is a broader structural analysis of the overlapping social, cultural, economic, and political contexts in which the school and its many actors are situated and interconnected.

The concepts of structure, civil society, and religiosity provide the theoretical scaffolding for this broader analysis. My use of the term *structure* draws from Anthony Giddens's understanding of the concept. Structure refers to the rules and resources that human beings use in the daily practices that constitute social life, and these include language and the communication of meaning, material and symbolic resources of power, and norms and sanctions that underpin an implicit moral order.[12] It is these rules and resources that both structure and give meaning to social interaction in whatever institutional form it takes: for example, a family, school, neighborhood association, religious organization, business enterprise, government agency, and the like. A structural analysis thus implicates the Muslim school in a web of social relations and cultural meanings that, among other things, overlaps the boundaries of other institutions constituting American civil society.

The modern concept of civil society is understood as the space "between individuals and government that assures that social justice and democracy are features of the social order and not a 'gift' of government."[13] It is that social arena where citizens may associate, voluntarily and uncoerced, with other citizens in organizations "formed for the sake of family, faith, interest, and ideology."[14]

It is where a person can join a church, temple, or mosque; volunteer in a neighborhood association or join a labor union; become a member in a fan club, art club, or fraternity; enroll in a professional society or register in a political party; or start up a nonprofit. Civil society is thus vital to the democratic ideal of a pluralistic society, where diversity—racial or ethnic, cultural or religious, political or ideological—is recognized and protected.

The importance of religiosity to civil society in America is undeniable, for by some accounts almost half of the American population is affiliated with faith-based organizations.[15] Analytically speaking, religiosity can be understood as human agency informed by beliefs, values, and attitudes that are legitimized by faith-based principles and teachings. Analogous to the way that speech is related to language, religiosity describes the ways that people intentionally actualize their religious identity in any instance of social interaction.[16] It is thus more than what a religious person does in "religious" situations, such as attending prayers; participating in ritual ceremonies related to birth, marriage, and death; or celebrating annual holidays and so on. Conceived this way, one avoids the analytically meaningless dichotomy of "religious" versus "secular." How, for example, would religiosity be measured for a so-called secular Muslim who rarely if ever prays but sends her children to weekend school at the local mosque? Or what about the Muslim owner of a convenience store who piously fasts during Ramadan and donates to charity yet deals in the sale of liquor, adult magazines, and lottery tickets, behavior that is excoriated in the Friday sermon at the local mosque? In this chapter, therefore, I emphasize religiosity and not "religion" per se in examining the emergent role of the Muslim school in American civil society.

The Mosque and the Business Community: Religiosity and Civic Engagement

The genesis of a full-time Muslim school is often the result of a partnership between a community mosque and the professional/business sector that supports it. The following excerpt, taken from field notes documenting my participant-observation at a Brooklyn mosque in 1997, illustrates this important relationship:

> "We've got to start at the top," Marwan said resolutely as he handed
> the letter back to Najeem, a Moroccan immigrant who taught
> math and science at a local high school in Brooklyn. The letter,
> drafted by Najeem, was a petition to New York City's department of

education to make Arabic an official foreign language offering in Brooklyn high schools. "We start with the superintendent," Marwan advised, "because that way the principals won't have the first option to refuse." Najeem nodded. At that, Marwan, a Lebanese American businessman who volunteers as the public relations officer for the mosque, hurried downstairs to join the throng of worshippers assembling for Friday prayer.

At the conclusion of the prayer, Hajj Amr, a respected elder and spiritual leader of the local Palestinian community, rose and stood at the microphone. "$100,000," he called out. "Al Noor School needs $100,000. Who will be the first to pledge for the sake of the children?" Looking every bit the respected patriarch, Hajj Amr declared that the school, where many of the community's children attended, desperately needed to build more classrooms for the hundreds of children on the waiting list. "Listen," he pleaded, "all it takes is twenty people, just $5000 each. Come on, brothers, do it for the sake of the children!" No one was willing to pledge that high. With the enthusiasm of a champion auctioneer, Hajj Amr gradually reduced the pledge amount till finally at the $1000 level, hands began to rise. With each pledge, Hajj Amr excitedly cheered, "takbir!" ("praise Allah") to which the congregation shouted back, "Allahu akbar!" ("Allah is most great!"). Hajj Amr didn't rest until he made his target—$100,000.

This vignette shows the dynamic intersection of actors, structures, and practices working together in the faith-based sector of American civil society. Marwan is a prosperous and respected business entrepreneur, born in Lebanon, from where he emigrated to the United States in the 1970s to flee the civil war. He is a founding board member of the mosque, volunteers on many of its committees, and played a leading role in the founding of the community's full-time school, Al Noor. Najeem emigrated from Morocco in the early 1980s. He holds a teaching credential in secondary school and teaches biology at one of Brooklyn's most prestigious high schools. He volunteers at the mosque and also volunteers at Al Noor, where he tutors students preparing for the state Regents Exams. Two of his children attend Al Noor's elementary school, and he is an active member of the school's parent-teacher organization. Hajj Ali is a religious scholar who has served as imam at several Brooklyn mosques and was a leading figure in mobilizing the fund-raising efforts of five New York City mosques to purchase the building that now houses Al Noor School.

By appealing to the religiosity of the members of the local business establishment at this Friday service, Hajj Ali was not only generating donations but also engendering social connections between the business sector and the school. The many Muslim-owned businesses in the neighborhood represent a substantial financial base for charitable donations, called *sadaqāt* (sing. *sadaqa*), which help to support both the mosque and the school. This fact, in combination with the mandatory religious practice of almsgiving (*zakat*) in Islam, means that the faith-based philanthropy of the local Muslim business community creates multiple social linkages that overlap and reinforce connections among home, mosque, and school. There is thus a constant intersection of religious and secular practices, with businesspeople increasingly supporting the neighborhood mosque and school.

Facing a growing sense of disconnectedness because of widespread racialized prejudices in the post-9/11 era, the neighborhood mosque, like other faith-based community associations, helps people find ways to pool resources, receive and distribute aid, hold meetings, learn about public issues, and recruit members for committees and projects. In the case of the Brooklyn mosque described above, the leadership regularly recruits volunteers from its congregation to participate in civic projects cosponsored by coalitions of secular and faith-based organizations. These activities include working with local hospitals and clinics to raise the cultural sensitivity of medical personnel toward Muslim patients in their care, combating stereotypes of Arab Muslims through outreach to local news media, engaging in interfaith dialogue, and cultivating relationships with elected officials and local political committees of both the Republican and Democratic parties. Muslim diaspora communities are thus reinventing the mosque, creating space to cultivate experiences, civic values, and personal networks easily transferable to other forms of local civic and political engagement. The establishment of a full-time Muslim school is a prime example of this transference.

The Full-Time Muslim School: Genesis of a Civil Society Actor

Not every mosque in America opens a full-time day school, though the desire is one that most mosques share. Large mosques with a strong community base, often called "Islamic centers," are able to provide after-school or weekend religious instruction. Findings from several studies suggest that only one in five mosques in the United States ever establishes a full-time school.[17] Most immigrant communities simply do not have the capacity to sustain the enormous investment of financial and human resources to establish and maintain a full-time school. In New York City, for example, only 4,000 of the city's estimated 90,000 school-aged Muslim children attend the city's 14 Muslim schools. All of these schools, of which only three go up to grade 12, have long waiting lists almost as large as their total enrollments.

A popular misconception about the founding of a Muslim school and its relationship to a mosque must be corrected. It is widely assumed that American mosques, under the supposed domination of foreign-born imams, hold sway over the affairs of a day school. Findings from six years of research on Muslim communities in New York City, corroborated by informal interviews with religious and lay community leaders in other cities, paint a different picture.[18] Muslim schools tend to function as autonomous institutions, both administratively and financially, even when they are located on the same premises as their founding mosques. Autonomy does not mean the absence of structural connections, however.

The sharing of common sources of social capital guarantees that mosque and school are structurally entwined. The membership of a mosque's board of trustees and a school's board of directors often overlap considerably. This is because the founders of American mosques are typically not religious elites; rather, they are middle-class professionals and businesspersons, almost always men and of the same ethnic group, whose wealth, property, occupational prestige, and personal piety generate social capital and power. These resources of power provide them political leverage to mobilize their local communities to establish mosques, cultural associations, and schools. Not surprisingly, these same movers and shakers often end up as key players on the governing boards of the mosques and the schools they help to establish.

With the founding of a full-time school, the state and its education laws and regulations now enter into the mix. As will be discussed below, the addition of the state as a partner in the operation of the Muslim school propels its chief stakeholders—the mosque, the professional and business sector, and local families—into the arena of American civil society.

Locating the State in the Muslim School

Nonpublic schools in New York State, whether religious or secular, must comply with state-mandated education laws and policies that dictate everything from curriculum content and instruction to discipline and labor relations. As mentioned above, most of the schoolwide curriculum is composed of secular subjects and content over which the school has little or no control. At Al Noor School in Brooklyn, for example, "Islamic studies" constitutes only four out of 35 class periods (11 percent) per week.[19] Al Noor thus represents a hybrid form of schooling in which the religious elements of a weekend "catechism" school merge with the secular content and structures of an American public school.

This hybridity is illustrated in the myriad ways that state-mandated (secular) laws, policies, and practices influence Al Noor's schooling environment.[20] As in public schools, students at Al Noor must attend school for a minimum of 180 days; by law, the principal is required to keep students' attendance and health/immunization records on file and to produce them if requested to do so by city authorities; English must be used as the primary language of instruction; and the curricular content and instructional methods must be "substantially equivalent" to what is offered in the public schools. According to the New York State Educational Code, the course of study for the first eight years "must include arithmetic, reading, spelling, writing, the English language, geography, United States history, civics, hygiene, physical training, the history of New York state and science." And beyond the first eight years, "instruction must include the English language and its use, civics, hygiene, physical training, American history including the Declaration of Independence and the Constitution of the United States, and may include a course in communism and its methods and its destructive effects."[21]

Textbook adoption further aligns Muslim students with the public school curriculum. New York State law stipulates that all nonpublic schools be offered the free loan of the same textbooks supplied to public schools. Al Noor, like other Muslim schools in New York City, saves thousands of dollars annually in textbook costs by taking advantage of this provision; but there is a catch. As a condition for receiving indirect state aid, which includes textbooks, Al Noor is required to administer statewide standardized tests in English language arts and mathematics to the fourth and eighth grades, as well as the Regents Exams in core subject areas for high school students.[22] This testing regime all but guarantees the adoption of state-approved textbooks since the tests are produced by the same publishing companies that market the textbooks. For this reason, teachers dare not deviate from the state-mandated curriculum content for fear that their students may score poorly on standardized tests. This alignment of textbooks and subject matter means that the academic, civic, and even cultural education of Al Noor's students is indeed "substantially equivalent" to that in the secular public school system.

Another significant outcome of the "public/private" hybridity of the Muslim school is that it creates structures to foster the civic integration of teachers and administrators. At all three of the Muslim secondary schools in New York City, full-time teachers and administrators participate in professional development workshops organized by the city's Department of Education and funded by Title II of the U.S. Department of Education. Many teachers and staff also take advantage of Title II resources to enroll in education courses for college credit at local colleges. Two of the high schools require their full-time faculty to take at least one college course per year and the principals of several schools in the city, including the female head of an elementary school, have taken college courses in educational leadership. Participation in these professional activities by Muslim teachers and administrators not only fosters conformity to the state's curricular and management standards but also fashions social networks linking the Muslim school with the educational and civic goals of the public school system.

A significant consequence of professional development bears mentioning. Immigrant Muslim women are major beneficiaries since their numbers likely constitute at least 80 percent of the teaching staff at most schools.[23] Muslim women immigrants often have fewer opportunities than men to acquire institutional experience outside the domestic sphere. Even in mosques, key leadership and committee positions are dominated by males. Employment at a day school is thus a valuable mechanism by which women may gain workplace knowledge and skills, network with others outside the circle of family and kin, and develop social capital in ways that promote greater public and civic engagement. A good example of this is a female principal of a Muslim elementary school in Queens who rallied her school to join a coalition of a local neighborhood associations and a public elementary school. At issue was the flow of two-way traffic on a narrow street that was putting schoolchildren at risk. With this formidable community partnership behind her, this Pakistani-born principal successfully lobbied the local community board to change the road to a safer one-way traffic pattern. This capacity to transform social capital into civic engagement is also evidenced in the agency of American-born Muslim youth in Muslim schools.

The Day School as Civil Society Actor

The claim that Muslim schools imprison students in a "mental ghetto" might be plausible if the schools made no provision for the development of social capital beyond the social and cultural boundaries of their religious and ethnic communities. This allegation, however, has little to support it. First, the idea of social capital is understood to be a set of social and cultural resources that lead to increased cooperation between individuals, without which the achievement of personal and collective goals would be tough or impossible.[24] This is why "church life" in the United States continues to be one of the most important dimensions of American civil society. It fosters social networking and forges associational ties. The denser these networks, for example, by coalition building with other groups or associations, the more powerful social capital becomes as a resource for civic and political engagement.[25]

There is growing evidence—mostly from the news media but also supported by some research—that Muslim schools are promoting the development of social capital for students, staff, and parents in their communities. A few illustrations will make the point. One of the most significant changes in the curriculum of Muslim schools since the events of September 11, 2001, has been the introduction of courses in comparative religion and the addition of workshops, guest speakers, and field trips to foster interfaith dialogue and tolerance. All three of New York City's Muslim high schools now have such programs. At Razi School in Woodside, Queens, for example, students and teachers participate in an interfaith sensitivity project called "Religion in Dialogue." Twice a month, all students in grades 7–12 participate in an interactive assembly with Jewish and Christian religious leaders and educators and sometimes with classes from local public and private sectarian schools. Muslim spiritual leaders and students reciprocate by visiting Christian and Jewish schools. Another school in Queens, Al-Iman, participates in a program called Abraham's Vision, a New York–based nonprofit dedicated to peace education and interfaith dialogue among Jewish, Palestinian, and Muslim high school and college students.[26]

This inclusion of interfaith awareness and dialogue into the curriculum requires interaction with non-Muslim voluntary associations, obliging the Muslim school to reimagine itself as an actor in a religiously diverse civil society. The principal of Razi School in Queens sees interfaith partnerships as a vital policy in counteracting the post-9/11 marginalization that he feared might victimize his students: "It was necessary for the school to open up. We had to find a way to help students see that they are not isolated or separated from the diversity of the community; so this program has a kind of therapeutic value as well as educational." In other words, it is via the renewal of social trust and faith in American pluralism, so weakened by the rise of Islamophobia in the aftermath of 9/11, that a "ghetto mentality" can best be averted.

Social trust—a belief in the value of associating with other people based on perceived mutual trust and respect—is a fundamental building block of civil society.[27] It is a key factor, I believe, behind important education reforms in Muslim schools across the United States. Nowhere is this more evident than in extracurricular programs and activities—framed in the language of Islamic religiosity—to foster citizenship and civic responsibility. Each of the three largest Muslim schools in New York City has a student government, with class representatives and officers who campaign and debate to win office. A variety of student academic and service organizations provide structures in which youth and their faculty sponsors become engaged in discourse and debate on major social and public issues of the day. These include debate clubs, academic interest groups, and student organizations focusing on activist causes such as environmental protection, human and civil rights, and social justice. Students and adults in the environment club at one school participate in neighborhood cleanup campaigns organized by city and nonprofit community organizations. The debate club at Razi School is extremely popular. Each morning at the school assembly, selected students present and defend positions on controversial issues such as cloning or euthanasia, and recently they took up the matter of free speech and religious tolerance in the wake of the Danish cartoon controversy. At Al Noor School, a 12th grade girl offered this perspective: "We participate in the political system. We went to rallies and to protests. We went to the rally in front of the consulate of Denmark in Manhattan against the cartoons. In this school, we are all the time being discriminated against [after 9/11], and we have spoken and made our voices heard. We go into the media. There are newspapers and televisions that come here, and we speak to them. So we're pretty much more out there, because we're in Al Noor, than [students] in the public schools, like being on TV like we are."

In one of the biggest moves to foster civic consciousness among students since 9/11, New York City Muslim high schools now require a minimum of 100 hours of community service as a graduation requirement, the same policy for students in the city's public schools. Al Noor School, for example, has arranged for students to intern at local hospitals; volunteer during elections to show people to polling stations; organize blood drives for the New York Blood Center; and even intern at Brooklyn's criminal justice court. In addition, several schools and mosques in New York City sponsor Boy Scout and Girl Scout troops as a way to encourage community building and civic responsibility among students. The Boy Scouts of America reports that there are some 112 troops chartered to Muslim schools or mosques.[28]

In many cases, students exercise civic leadership by taking their own initiative to mobilize their schools in responding to civic and humanitarian issues. In one example, a senior girl at Al Noor did volunteer work with one of Brooklyn's oldest Latino community-based organizations and persuaded the school to partner in its project to revitalize Brooklyn's rundown waterfront area. Another group of students at Al Noor, with the sponsorship of the high school principal, started a chapter of Key Club, one of the oldest and largest service programs for high school students in the United States. The student leader of the group, a 12th grade girl, explained proudly: "Last year we started this club, the Key Club, where we focused on countries suffering from natural disasters. And we began saving up from bake sales and other events to raise money. They featured us on ABC News, talking about our fund-raising. I think we raised around $2,000."

In another example, the mostly South Asian students at a K–6 Muslim school in Flushing, Queens, worked with teachers and parents to raise money in their communities for victims of the earthquake in Pakistan in 2005 and for survivors of Hurricane Katrina in Louisiana that same year. Most of the relief money was generated at a charity bazaar in which local merchants donated food items and merchandise, with the profits going to charity. The principal proudly told me that her students raised $9,900 in relief aid for the victims of Hurricane Katrina, almost $2,000 more than what they were able to raise for the Pakistan effort.

From the above discussion, it is clear that the Muslim school is serving as a pathway for students as well as adults to cultivate social trust, leadership skills, and community values commonly associated with citizenship and civic engagement.[29] By partnering with local grassroots organizations, the local business sector, and national service organizations, the Muslim school is playing a key role in the development of an emerging American Muslim civic identity.

From the Family Sphere into the Public Square

While participation in voluntary associations is a hallmark of civil society, new immigrants, particularly those who are either self-employed, in low-wage labor, or undocumented, find it difficult to get involved in local community or professional organizations. They often have less free time than most other families for activities beyond family and workplace, a fact that impedes their ability to develop the social, cultural, and linguistic skills to engage in the wider arenas of American associational life. Muslim community leaders in New York City, for example, point out that very few Muslim parents with children in public schools attend PTA meetings. Not from indifference, they point out, but, rather, to avoid public embarrassment due to limited English or unfamiliarity with cultural expectations and behavior.

It is my observation, however, that the Muslim school creates a transitional space for immigrant Muslims to test the waters of associational life outside the private domain of the family or the limited sphere of the workplace. At Al Noor School, for example, where most of the students are American-born children of Arab immigrants and there is a sense of shared identity, values, and culture, activities such as parent-teacher conferences, "family days" and community picnics, and end-of-the-year ceremonies draw students' families into the communal life of the school. Moreover, parents can be found volunteering to support cocurricular activities like chaperoning on field trips; working as teachers' assistants; cooking and baking for school functions; donating money or merchandise for fund-raising events; and volunteering technical expertise like networking a computer lab, or talking at a school assembly about issues of mental health and hygiene.

Informal activities like these, in addition to the formal structure of the PTA, also provide frequent opportunities for parents to meet face to face with schoolteachers and administrators and voice their views and concerns about school policies and procedures. By thus creating a nonthreatening environment constituted of structures and practices common to American voluntary associations, the Muslim school is helping immigrant families to acquire knowledge and skills, norms and values—social capital—that are potentially transferable to other domains of life in the American public square.

Conclusion

In this chapter, I have argued that the Muslim school is a civil society actor, functioning in many ways like other voluntary associations that constitute the faith-based sector of American civil society. By framing the analysis more broadly than the tendency to narrowly focus on classroom behavior and curriculum content, I have illustrated how the founding and operation of full-time Muslim schools produce networks of social relations and structures that, among other things, provide ways for people to give money, receive an education, hold meetings, recruit members for other associations or community projects, learn about public issues, and take part in civic and political engagement. And by locating the Muslim school in a nexus of people and institutions—the mosque, the professional and business sector, the family, and the state—I have also endeavored to challenge the Islamophobic assumptions in public discourse that have fueled the widespread misconception that attendance at a Muslim school isolates American-born youth in a real or imagined ethno-religious ghetto.

NOTES

1. Salam Al-Marayati, "America's Muslim Ghettos," *Washington Post*, August 15, 2005, p. A.15. Salam Al-Marayati is the director and cofounder of the Muslim Public Affairs Council, a nonprofit advocacy organization "working for the civil rights of American Muslims, for the integration of Islam into American pluralism, and for a positive, constructive relationship between American Muslims and their

representatives" (Muslim Public Affairs Council, "About MPAC," www.mpac.org/home_about.aspx, accessed March 18, 2006).

2. Tim Blair, "Future President Promises Prohibition," December 31, 2005, http://timblair.net/ee/index.php/weblog/2005/12/, accessed March 18, 2006.

3. Louis Cristillo, "God Has Willed It: Religiosity and Social Reproduction at a Private Muslim School in New York City" (Ph.D. dissertation, Teachers College Columbia University, New York, 2004), p. 121.

4. JoEllen McNergney Vinyard, *For Faith and Fortune: The Education of Catholic Immigrants in Detroit, 1805–1925* (Urbana: University of Illinois Press, 1998); Timothy Walch, *Catholicism in America: A Social History* (Melbourne, FL: R. E. Krieger, 1989).

5. Nathan H. Winter, *Jewish Education in a Pluralist Society: Samson Benderly and Jewish Education in the United States* (New York: University of London Press Limited, 1966).

6. Michael Walzer describes this as the pluralist, multiculturalist model of civil society, wherein the state is understood as a "union of social unions" (or a "nation of nationalities" in the case of the immigrant-based United States) and where ordinary citizens, taking up the slack of the professional civil service, engage in voluntarism to "serve each other, committing themselves to the everyday work of welfare, schooling, communal upkeep, and celebration" ("Rescuing Civil Society," *Dissent* 46, no. 1 [1999]: pp. 62–67).

7. By "Muslim school," I mean a full-time nonpublic school offering a conventional public school curriculum in self-contained classrooms in addition to religious studies courses. Homeschooling is not included in this definition.

8. See Ihsan Bagby, Paul M. Perl, and Bryan T. Froehle, *The Mosque in America: A National Portrait* (Washington, DC: Council on American-Islamic Relations, 2001); see also chapter 1 in this volume by Karen Keyworth.

9. Washington Post–ABC News Poll, March 6, 2006, www.washingtonpost.com/wpsrv/politics/includes/postpoll_iraqwar_030606.htm, accessed March 12, 2006.

10. Mollok Roghanizad, "Full-Time Muslim Schools in the United States, 1970–1990" (Ph.D. dissertation, University of Maryland, College Park, 1990); Patricia Kelly, "Integrating Islam: A Muslim School in Montreal" (M.A. thesis, Institute of Islamic Studies, Montreal, 1997). Although Kelly's study examines a Canadian Muslim school, her analysis is relevant to this discussion. See also Susan Sachs, "Muslim Schools in U.S.: A Voice for Identity," *New York Times*, Late Edition, November 10, 1998; Tara Bahrampour, "Between Two Worlds; For Young Muslim Women, Coming of Age in New York Is a Complex Journey," *New York Times*, Late Edition, December 12, 1999. See also Frederick Erickson, "Transformation and School Success: The Politics and Culture of Educational Achievement," *Anthropology and Education Quarterly* 18, no. 4 (1987): pp. 335–356; Kamal H. Ali, "Muslim School Planning in the United States: An Analysis of Issues, Problems and Possible Approaches" (Ph.D. dissertation, University of Maryland, College Park, 1981); Qadir Abdus-Sabur, "A Muslim School's Response to the Dilemma of Ghetto Life" (Ph.D. dissertation, University of Virginia, Charlottesville, 1998); Robert Dannin, *Black Pilgrimage to Islam* (New York: Oxford University Press, 2002); and Hoda Badawi, "Parental Reasons for School Choice: A

Case Study of an Islamic School in the United States of America" (Ed.D. dissertation, University of Minnesota, 2005).

11. Cristillo, "God Has Willed It."

12. Anthony Giddens, *The Constitution of Society: Outline of a Theory of Structuration* (Berkeley: University of California Press, 1984).

13. Richard M. Lerner, *Liberty: Thriving and Civic Engagement among America's Youth* (Thousand Oaks, CA: SAGE Publications, 2004), pp. 19–20.

14. Michael Walzer, in E. J. Dionne, ed., *Community Works: The Revival of Civil Society in America* (Washington, DC: Brookings Institution Press, 2000), pp. 123–124.

15. The American Religious Identification Survey of 2001 reports that more than half (54 percent) of the adult population in the United States live in households where either they themselves or someone else is a member of a church, temple, synagogue or mosque, or some other place of worship. See Barry A. Kosmin, Egon Mayer, and Ariela Keysar, "American Religious Identification Survey 2001," www.gc.cuny.edu/faculty/research_studies/aris.pdf, accessed February 16, 2006.

16. See Clifford Geertz, "Religion as a Cultural System," in Michael Banton, ed., *Anthropological Approaches to the Study of Religion* (London: Tavistock Publications, 1966), pp. 1–46.

17. Bagby, Perl, and Froehle, *The Mosque in America*; Louis Abdellatif Cristillo and Lorraine Minnite, "The Changing Arab New York Community," in Kathleen Benson and Philip Kayal, ed., *A Community of Many Worlds: Arab Americans in New York City* (New York: Syracuse University Press, 2002), pp. 124–139.

18. Bagby, Perl, and Froehle, *The Mosque in America*; Cristillo and Minnite, "The Changing Arab New York Community."

19. Cristillo, "God Has Willed It."

20. New York State Education Law stipulates that all nonpublic high schools—religious or independent—that issue a high school diploma must be registered with the Board of Regents. See the U.S. Department of Education, "State Regulation of Private Schools—June 2000: New York," www.ed.gov/pubs/RegPrivSchl/newyork.html, accessed July 10, 2007.

21. Ibid., §§ 3204.2–3.

22. Any nonpublic school that participates in these examinations, and complies with the system for pupil attendance and reporting, is eligible to receive state monies to cover its actual costs for participating in these exams; in addition, nonpublic schools may qualify for other forms of federal support for special needs students and professional development opportunities for teachers and administrators. Al Noor is a recipient of such funding.

23. During the 1999–2000 school year, women accounted for over two-thirds (68 percent) of Al Noor's entire teaching staff and virtually all of the elementary school homeroom teachers. Given that in the United States women fill 80 percent of the elementary school positions, Al Noor is thus no more gender biased in this regard than public schools. See Francine D. Blau and Marianne A. Ferber, *The Economics of Women, Men, and Work* (Englewood Cliffs, NJ: Prentice-Hall, 1992).

24. Corwin Smidt, "Religion and Civic Engagement: A Comparative Analysis," *Annals of the American Academy of Political and Social Science* 565, no. 1 (1999): pp. 176–192.

25. Ibid., p. 178.

26. See Abraham's Vision, www.abrahamsvision.org/, accessed July 10, 2007.

27. Jan Delhey and Kenneth Newton, "Who Trusts? The Origins of Social Trust in Seven Nations," *European Societies* 5 (2003): pp. 1–45.

28. Jessica Ravitz, "Our Little Adventure: Utah's First Muslim Girl Scout Troop Gives Members a Place to Gain Confidence, Make Friends with Similar Values and Rack Up the Badges; Muslim Scouting Is Part of a National Trend," *Salt Lake Tribune,* December 10, 2005, p. C1.

29. Daniel Hart and Robert Atkins, "Civic Competence in Urban Youth," *Applied Developmental Science* 6, no. 4 (2002): pp. 227–236. See also James Youniss and Miranda Yates, *Community Service and Social Responsibility in Youth* (Chicago: University of Chicago Press, 1997).

4

Teaching about Religion, Islam, and the World in Public and Private School Curricula

Susan L. Douglass

This chapter describes four interlocking areas of work in education, both in public or mainstream schools and in Muslim private or community-based schools in the United States. The first of these four areas involves teaching about world religions, specifically the effort to improve content about Islam, as both religion and historical civilization. The second area involves teaching world history and world geography, which is the major arena in which teaching about religions appears in the curricula of both public and private schools, but it is a highly significant arena of work beyond anything to do with teaching about religions. The third area involves the movement to develop, adopt, and implement academic standards in all subject areas during the 1990s. The fourth area concerns the process of developing an integrated curriculum based on the use of national and state content and skills standards and the effort to disseminate these ideas in the U.S. educational arena, both public and private, with emphasis on the integration of social studies and science curricula. A significant focus of the chapter is to detail the ways in which efforts to improve curriculum in these areas flow seamlessly among the arenas of work involving mainstream public schools and Muslim community-based schools. It is significant that this work also involves the academic arena of university-based scholarship in world history, religious studies, and education.

This chapter also describes the work of the Council on Islamic Education (CIE), which has recently been absorbed into a new and broader organization, the Institute on Religion and Civic Values.

Recognizing the problems with teaching about Islam in the schools, CIE was founded to engage policy-makers as a nonadvocacy research institute, with the awareness that teaching about Islam was not to be dealt with as a single issue but as one situated in a much broader educational and political context. Accordingly, the work of the organization has expanded organically to embrace the relationship between teaching about Islam and teaching about religions in general and, in turn, to explore the context in which teaching about religions and the cultures and civilizations that are associated with them—in short, world history and geography education—takes place in the schools. These areas have been affected by tremendous changes and restructuring in recent years, as part of ongoing curriculum reform and in the scholarship of teaching and learning. As a result, the work that has taken place during the past two decades must be seen within a very broad framework.

Teaching about World Religions

Since teaching about Islam and Muslim civilization formed the entry point for CIE's work, it makes sense to begin the story there. It is absolutely essential to note that by the time the organization was founded in 1990, there was no need to exert any pressure to find a place for teaching about Islam in the public school curriculum. State and district social studies curriculum required content on Islam as it did other world religions, and it had therefore acquired a firm place in commercially produced textbooks. The reasons for this will be examined below in some detail, but the scope and placement of such instruction can be quickly summarized.

Content about world religions is found almost entirely in world history and world geography courses taught in middle grades 5–7 and in high school, though elective courses on world religions are becoming more common in some high schools. There is some content at the elementary level, which is related to community studies and teaching about ethnic, religious, and cultural diversity in the United States and the local region. Coverage of Islamic celebrations is the typical material studied at the primary level, with some background on Islam, for which a number of trade books are used in many schools.[1] Apart from other brief mentions, systematic coverage comes in connection with teaching about the world. Coverage of *all* world religions has been gradually increasing in scope and prominence during the past two decades, as a comparison of world history or geography textbooks published between the 1980s and today would demonstrate clearly. Textbooks from the mid-1980s covered each major world religion in a paragraph or a brief subtopic. By the early

1990s, most textbooks for middle and high school contained a full lesson and sometimes an entire chapter on each world religion. By the end of the 1990s, Judaism, Christianity, and Islam were covered in an entire unit in textbooks produced for adoption in certain states. In response to state standards for world history and geography written during the late 1990s, between one and three chapters would cover origins and basic beliefs, the rise and spread of the faiths as organized religions, including their political and territorial expansion, and finally, their spread and the description of the world civilization and cultures associated with it. For example, Buddhism is associated in the textbooks with the civilizations of India and China, and coverage includes its spread into Japan, Korea, and Southeast Asia.[2]

Improving the coverage of any world religion obviously was related to improvement of all of them, since their rise in prominence as topics of study proceeded as part of a larger process that had been ongoing for several decades. This process of building public and professional consensus that religion is a significant, valuable, and teachable topic in American public schools is described and historically documented in a publication by the First Amendment Center (FAC), which is the organization largely responsible for the success of that process over the past 20 years.[3] A key factor in the acceptance of teaching about religion in public schools is the existence and dissemination of the FAC guidelines for teaching about religion, which have become a matter of broad consensus in the United States for at least the past decade. These guidelines are discussed below in detail.

There is no doubt among those who have studied content in social studies books from the 1970s and 1980s on the topic of the Middle East, Islam, or Muslims that the coverage of these topics could not be characterized as fair, accurate, or balanced. The texts were rife with errors of several types, including significant errors of omission. One could compose an extensive rogues' gallery of errors in the description of Islam, its origins, beliefs, and practices, to which entries might be added with each textbook cycle. For example, misconstrued names of the founding individuals and even the name "Islam" itself could then still be found occasionally represented as "Mohammedanism." Upside-down images from artistic Qur'an pages, inverted images of Arabic script, and miscaptioned images of angels, prophets, and other figures, usually taken from artworks produced centuries after the period covered in the text, were inserted as if they were journalistic snapshots of the protagonists. Orientalist canards discredited for decades could be found in the textbooks presented at face value, without any attribution of source or indication of differing views among scholars or advances in scholarship over the past century. Examples include flat statements about Muhammad, the teachings of Islam, and the Qur'an as a scripture that, if true, would mean that the religion of Islam is false, or Muhammad was a deceiver, or both. Among the errors of omission, early textbook coverage of Islam seldom mentioned the similarities and continuities among Islam, Christianity, and Judaism. The geography of Muslim regions was often presented within a Middle Eastern or merely Arabian context. Along with this, the impression was conveyed that desert characterizes most of the lands where Islam is the majority faith. One draft chapter of a middle school textbook had the subtitle "Sand, Sand, Sand" to introduce the geography of the region. Even the Arabian Peninsula itself was implicitly or explicitly defined as covering only a part of the land bridge between Africa and Asia called today Southwest Asia, cutting off the Fertile Crescent or the Holy Land in the eastern Mediterranean coast without providing any specific geographic designation of the remaining region. In terms of chronological scope, the history of the region was often confined to the period from Muhammad to the Abbasids, effectively covering the period from about the sixth to the tenth century, omitting much of the past millennium of Islamic history. The Ottoman, Safavid, and Mughal periods were usually presented as a sort of last gasp of Islamic history before the upheavals of modern times and even then, scantily.

The description of Islam's rise is a case study in itself. Regularly, textbooks have conflated the two distinct historical processes that constituted the rise and spread of Islam—the rapid expansion of territory under Muslim rule and the gradual process by which Islam spread in the lands under Muslim rule and beyond, until it reached majority status. Many textbooks have simply described the "expansion" of Islam in the first hundred years, as though it had achieved instant majority status upon conquest. As an exercise in teaching history, this confusion is egregious, and its effect in the text is to create a lot of ambiguity around the issue of Islam being spread by the sword, in effect reproducing the old polemics about Islam by default. Many other historical issues of importance were often glossed over, with the effect of reinforcing conventional-wisdom stereotypes about the role of women and the role of men, for that matter, and about the vital matter of Islamic law, or Shari'ah. Very few textbooks until recently did any more than toss these terms carelessly about in the text, with neither conceptual nor historical explanations of any value.

Another case study of textbook language could start with the popularized rather than accurate transliteration of Arabic terms and place-names. *Moslem* versus *Muslim, Mohammed* versus *Muhammad, Mecca* versus *Makkah*, and *Koran* versus *Qur'an* are just a few. Shorthand terms such as *strict* were paired regularly with *Islamic* to characterize Islamic law, secular historical phenomena, and sometimes even regional customs associated rightly or wrongly with Islamic norms. In discussion of contemporary phenomena, the word *Islamic* formed many oxymorons with words like *radical, extremist,* and *terrorist.* Use of undefined or ill-defined terms such as *fundamentalist* and *Islamist* and the dropping of simplistic statements combining these terms made for difficult going for the reviewer and the reader, whether student or teacher. Improvement of these terms through textbook review has been a seesaw affair, and the net effect has sometimes been the intrusion of conventional wisdom where scholarship should be.

Other historical issues often neglected in textbook coverage of Islam are related to the interactions among cultures, civilizations, and regions during the formative periods of Muslim history and the recognized contribution or role of Islam and Muslim civilizations in world history. Textbooks whose reference point is European civilization have often maintained the pretense that cities were something that disappeared with Rome and only appeared in Europe in the late Middle Ages; in other words, one of the major periods of urbanization in human history was simply ignored, with the exception of "showcase" cities like Abbasid Baghdad or Andalusian Cordoba. The role of urban growth in the spread of Islam among the population was virtually never found in earlier generations of textbooks.

An earlier battle waged with some success by multicultural advocates involved the attribution of major human achievements to various civilizations, Western and non-Western, in the parlance of some standards documents. Generations of world history books from the 1950s to the 1970s were well known for virtually ignoring the achievements of classical Indian, Chinese, African, indigenous American, and Muslim civilizations, and the period from Rome's dying glory to the Renaissance was often portrayed as though human intellect and creativity had taken an extended vacation until Europeans miraculously rediscovered the classical arts and sciences. The typical multicultural solution to all of these omissions has been the shaping of chapters on various world civilizations that conclude with a checklist of items that "we" modern Westerners "got" from "them [name of culture or civilization]" or of phenomena that "they" "also had created" aforetime. This has been a major area where improvement over multicultural contributions has been sought via improved scholarship and expanded global scope of inquiry. For example, Muslim contributions in areas like algebra, astronomy, medicine, and geometry are consistently listed in the chapter on Islam, but these items on the multicultural scorecard are detached from the historical context that brought them forth. Trade, transfers of technology, development, and publication in the sciences and mathematics have not been described with the dynamism that characterized interaction across linguistic, religious, and regional barriers or with the dynamism that characterized European cultural development itself. Most importantly for recent scholarship in world history, improvement would mean tracing the paths of transmission, agents and arenas of transmission, and entry points into the receiving culture or society, in context. Such structural change has been slow in coming at the K–12 level, but it would dramatically improve teaching about the world, as well as boosting the level of scholarship in the textbooks.

Another issue is geographic representation. Coverage of the modern Middle East was often made to stand for coverage of all Muslim regions of the world, ignoring the Muslim populations east of Islam's demographic center in South Asia. This Middle East–heavy portrayal was often quite reductionist and abnormal in comparison with coverage of other world regions, with topics limited to petroleum, the Israel/Palestine foreign policy issue, and Islam portrayed as a struggle between religious traditionalism and secular modernism. One benefit of the standards movement was precisely that frameworks for basic coverage in geography and history allowed for a more evenhanded approach to each region. Here, too, change in the textbooks has been glacial in pace, despite the mandates and call for improved scholarship in the letter and spirit of the standards. These examples show how the improvement of coverage of Islam entails general improvements in the way history and geography are taught. The same set of improvements, furthermore, would improve the coverage of all other faiths, and more integrated, global history would improve the incorporation of arts, economics, literature, and civics as well.

The basic issue illuminated by this brief characterization of the problems in the factual and conceptual coverage of one world religion is that these examples refer to errors that would not be admissible in any academically rigorous environment. This brief summary is not the place for detailed citations of these problems, which have been documented elsewhere.[4] Much of it would be laughed out of class among well-informed specialists. It involves material that was discredited as history decades ago or is oversummarized from other sources. For example, it has been known and widely documented in mainstream Western historical sources for at least 75 years that Muslim civilization influenced the Renaissance intellectually and technically. New knowledge on these interactions has recently emerged, but the basic idea has only crept into the high school textbooks over the past ten years or so and then, only piecemeal.

In short, a lot of work has been needed to improve teaching about Islam in the schools where many citizens receive all the world history education they will ever get. This process has been affected by publishers' own willingness to improve, met by efforts to undertake extensive research, review, and outreach with the publishers, the state standards commissions and development process, public school systems, civic education organizations, university outreach programs (mainly area studies departments but increasingly history departments), and especially centers for world history research. For the Council on Islamic Education, it would have been possible to work productively in the education arena doing nothing further than working diligently to improve the coverage of Islam and Muslim history by offering a scholarly basis for change in the textbook coverage—the words students read—on these topics. This does not, however, describe what has taken place in over 15 years of work, given the organization's efforts to work in a broader capacity regarding the coverage of religion and history in instructional materials.

Instead of remaining narrowly focused, the work came to embrace the whole enterprise of teaching about the world. It moved far beyond teaching about Islam, beyond public education or Muslim education, to involve working toward a model of teaching that improves education about the world for everyone. It is a vital civic enterprise that involves the application of rigorous but creative academic standards, constitutionally appropriate education about all world religions, and global world history education based on ongoing interdisciplinary, international scholarship. It is an enterprise that is also of great relevance to the growing phenomenon of Muslim education in the United States and other Western nations, as well as in nations where Muslims form a majority or significant portion of the population.

Constitutional Guidelines for Teaching about Religion

How did world religions get into the curriculum? Some post-9/11 press coverage has tried to show that Muslims have exerted lots of pressure to force Islam into the public school curriculum, and nearly as often the mirror opposite appears, repetition of journalistic conventional wisdom that God has been banished from mention in the schools. To the contrary, there has been no multicultural battle to include Islam, Muslims, or the geographic regions where Muslims live. Today, and for the past 15 years at least, Islam as a religion and Muslim regions as geographic and historical topics have been a firm part of the curriculum in public schools. The other major world religions—Christianity, Judaism, Hinduism, Buddhism, and in many states and textbooks, also Confucianism, Daoism, Zoroastrianism, classical religions of ancient Greece and Rome, ancient Egypt, Mesopotamia, and the pre-Colombian Americas—are covered as well. This inclusion or reinclusion of religion in the history and geography curriculum also incorporated the American religious experience as a component of standard U.S. history courses. American and world literature and fine arts curricula also include appropriate content on the topic. This inclusion in the curriculum became codified, so to speak, through the academic standards movement of the 1990s. This process continues with standards revision cycles, refinement of accountability testing at the state level, and detailed curriculum development at the district level. These documents demonstrate the clear consensus among educators, and by extension, the political leadership and departments of education that adopted the standards after a long process of development and public comment. The clear conclusion drawn through these efforts was that learning about the human religious experience is part of a basic education.

The Constitutional Guidelines

Achievement of this consensus was dependent upon a process that goes back almost five decades, wending its way from the studies of U.S. theologians to the Supreme Court, flowing out into the public square through civic organizations. The core achievement was to develop and test constitutional guidelines for teaching about religion with fairness, accuracy, and balance and then to disseminate them and take the necessary steps toward educational implementation; this has happened in large part through the work of the First Amendment Center at Vanderbilt University and Freedom Forum, Washington, D.C., and its earlier iterations. This work is traced in the document *Finding Common Ground*.[5]

During the mid-1990s, the promulgation of academic standards in the core subjects by commissioned national organizations and then by official state standards commissions provided the opportunity to assess the extent to which this dissemination and development process had taken hold across the United States. Conducted over six years and jointly published in 2000 by the FAC and the CIE, the study *Teaching about Religion in National and State Social Studies Standards* surveyed all of the national and state standards in social studies (and a sampling of language arts and fine arts standards) and concluded that all of the national documents—especially those in history and geography—demonstrate the consensus that students ought to learn about the role of religions in world and U.S. history.[6] Furthermore, the wording of standards on religion was shown to adhere, with few exceptions, to the FAC constitutional guidelines for teaching about religion in public schools.

The FAC guidelines for teaching about religion can be summarized as follows:

- The school's approach to religion is *academic*, not *devotional*.
- The school strives for student *awareness* of religions, but does not press for student *acceptance* of any religion.

BOX 4.I.   First Amendment Center guidelines for teaching about religion.

Educate but do not promote or denigrate any religion.

Natural inclusion: teach in humanities and social studies.

Fairness, accuracy, and balance:
- Portray beliefs and practices as adherents understand them
- Teaching is open-ended, seeks to understand
- Teacher states no religious or irreligious views

Respect for differences:
- Religious truth claims may not be made or denied
- Use words of attribution to avoid personal judgments ("Muslims believe that . . .")

- The school sponsors *study* about religion, not the *practice* of religion.
- The school may *expose* students to a diversity of religious views, but may not *impose* any particular view.
- The school *educates* about all religions; it does not *promote* or *denigrate* religion.
- The school *informs* students about various beliefs; it does not seek to *conform* students to any particular belief.[7]

The implications of these guidelines for instruction in the classroom require some elaboration, which has been culled from various consensus documents, teacher-education publications, conferences, and workshops conducted over the years, including my own. A slide used in many such presentations lays out these implications (see box 4.1).

Working with the FAC Guidelines

The First Amendment Center guidelines became part of the Council on Islamic Education's work in preparation of teaching resources, review of commercially produced and state-adopted textbooks, and teacher training. Reviewing text-books that covered all of the world religions and working with teachers who use them quickly made it clear that the problems in teaching about religion were not limited to content on Islam, nor did they end with the relatively brief thumbnail sketches provided in the chapters on Hinduism, Buddhism, Juda-ism, Christianity, and Islam. The key to improving teaching about religions in world history lay in raising the level of scholarship and skill acquisition in world history and geography courses generally.

Meeting the challenge of including teaching about religion in the curriculum has become a valuable asset to history teaching in general. Uncovering the rich historical experience across cultures and the role of religion not just as a perennial cause of conflict but as a source of preserving knowledge and a vehicle for the transfer of artistic, scientific, and technological advancements has opened up exciting ways of involving teachers and students in actively learning history.

The problems of creating a comfort zone for teachers who would discuss "our deepest differences," as Charles Haynes describes religious diversity, require research in current scholarship, the development of teaching materials that make it accessible to teachers, and work with curriculum developers, administrators, and textbook publishers to incorporate the various elements of good practice and good scholarship. Despite the widespread mandates to teach about religion, there is little or no training for this task, and indeed, courses on religion usually do not count toward certification, nor are there any requirements for teacher certification in social studies that would fill this need. In-service training is a very important way to bridge this gap. The problems and challenges of teaching about religions extend to private schools, and despite the lack of constraints on teaching religion in private schools, including Muslim schools, the guidelines should be disseminated in that milieu, because they provide a good civic framework for educating children and adults to discuss religion in a diverse community, nation, and world. Efforts toward such dissemination in Muslim private schools have included many workshops around the United States at individual or regional school professional in-service workshops and at conferences such as the Islamic Society of North America (ISNA) Education Forum held in Chicago each spring.[8]

Having provided examples from a rogues' gallery of common errors of fact, approach, and scholarship above, it is worthwhile to demonstrate how the FAC guidelines provide a framework for avoiding them. These examples will show how the principles and practices in the FAC guidelines function with regard to instructional content and methodology. The principle of "natural inclusion" is simply discussed. It means that wherever discussion of religion fits into the curriculum naturally, it may and should be the subject of lessons. An art appreciation lesson on Michelangelo's *Pietà* or the Sistine Chapel ceiling, for example, or a study of Byzantine icons makes little sense without an understanding of the faiths that underlie these works. Thanksgiving is not a religious holiday, but explanation of the religious nature of the community that held the first feast is indispensable. In fact, natural inclusion has often been upheld in the courts and forms the basis for the consensus on teaching about religions in world and U.S. history.

The principles listed above differentiate *teaching religion* from *teaching about religion*. What this means is that no *truth claims* may be made in the sense of *describing in direct terms* the nature of God or belief in prophets, miracles, and scriptures or holy books. The guidelines do not require academic secularism, or placing religious beliefs in the realm of sociological phenomena and thus explaining them away. This had been considered an editorially neutral position by some textbook writers and flowed naturally from the academic sources that were first used to write textbooks. The guidelines clearly state that religious truth claims can be neither made nor denied, under the principle that religions may not be promoted or denigrated. Conventional academic secularism was in fact a judgment on the veracity of religion. By the same token, the guidelines do not permit face-value statements that might imply truth claims. For example, a recent textbook manuscript contained the following summarizing statement: "Recall that Allah, the god of Islam, is the same god of the Jewish and Christian traditions." As CIE's reviewer, I suggested to the editors that this statement, while true for a Muslim, must be attributed, so as not to imply that the author (to students, the omniscient voice of the textbook) is telling the reader that something is true on its face. The text change that was suggested was as follows: "*The Qur'an teaches that Allah, the name of God in Arabic language, is the same as God in the Jewish and Christian traditions.*" The requested change illuminates several points in the effort to bring instructional materials into alignment with the letter and spirit of the FAC guidelines. First, the key to accurate but religiously neutral description is attribution. A phrase such as this one can be simply attributed to Islamic beliefs, Islamic teachings, or the teachings of its Prophet or spiritual founder. Better, however, from the point of view of teaching history, is to name the exact source from which the belief or practice was conveyed to the religion's followers. In this case, it is not legend, or hearsay, or a saying of Muhammad (though such statements on the topic exist) but the primary scripture of Islam, the Qur'an, that directly teaches, in many verses, that the God of Abraham is the God of Islam, whose name in Arabic is Allah. Convention in writing would, incidentally, capitalize *God* as a proper name, rather than as a noun meaning "deity." Attribution of beliefs to their source, then, is really the key to achieving accurate coverage of any religion that is forthright and honest.

Using this principle makes possible the achievement of direct, accurate, and authentic explanation of religious beliefs and teachings, without imposing ideas or engaging in doctrinal competition. Discussion of beliefs by careful and accurate attribution is in fact the instructional equivalent of the "wall of separation" because it provides a piece of safety glass between the student learning about a religion and the truth claims of the religion itself. Academic secularism puts a smoke screen between the student and the faith, in effect dismissing the beliefs as human or cultural in origin and denigrating or denying them in the process. Direct statements of beliefs without attribution, such as "God spoke to Moses and gave him the Ten Commandments," remove the safety glass and make it impossible to teach without promoting. Attribution creates a comfort zone that was created in earlier iterations of textbooks by simply omitting mention of those beliefs that the writers found uncomfortable or not in alignment with their own beliefs. For example, although the rites of the Islamic pilgrimage cannot be understood or accurately described without reference to Abraham and his family, many textbook accounts of the hajj omitted the patriarch altogether. Similarly, it took quite a while before textbook writers were willing to acknowledge Islamic teachings about Jesus and the other monotheistic prophets and scriptures. With attribution, the writer finds accuracy but escapes intimacy with the beliefs being described.

From this point of departure, accuracy becomes easier, and classroom practice is infused with a basic level of respect for beliefs, as well as respect for historical sources that supports the textbook voice and requirements to present historical evidence in instructional materials. This respect also points the way toward respectful and accurate interaction with the material by teachers. Classroom simulations of worship and role-playing activities that involve asking students to simulate belief in other religious teachings do *not* meet the guidelines for two reasons. One cannot and should not be asked to pretend to believe something one does not; in any case, simulating religious rituals without belief is disrespectful to the faith being imitated. A student cannot be asked to inhabit a faith, because it is too close to asking for conformity to that belief, however temporarily or artificially.[9]

Another very important aspect of the guidelines that Charles Haynes and the First Amendment Center have stressed from the beginning is the need to differentiate between the religions as ideals and teachings and the historical actions of their adherents. This requires accuracy in the use of terminology and explains why the term *Islamic* cannot be a catchall adjective to describe everything that any Muslim or Muslim society may have carried out in the 1,400 years since its inception. Achieving this standard has been an uphill battle, not least because so many academic sources use the term *Islamic* so haphazardly. Using the term *Islam* as shorthand for the sum total of Muslim history is problematic but all too common. Referring to the Islamic world is little better, especially when Muslim regions, throughout their history, exhibited tremendous religious diversity. The FAC guidelines lay out principles for dealing with the issue of judgment in historical studies. How do textbooks deal with the atrocities committed by adherents of Christianity during the Crusades or the conquest of the Incas, or the problem of the Holocaust in Europe and of terrorist acts committed in the name of Islam, or teaching students to differentiate between the policies of Israel and the tenets of Judaism? Instructional materials that fail to make these distinctions through accurate use of sourcing, labeling, and describing actors in conflicts and peaceful activities alike are *not* in alignment with the guidelines. Similarly, referring to Islamic achievements or Muslim contributions in science is inaccurate if it fails to note that some of its important contributors were in fact Jews, Christians, and adherents of other faiths, even if they were working within a Muslim cultural and an Arabic linguistic framework. The hallmark of good coverage here is historical accuracy and careful attention to fair and balanced discussion and differentiated terminology. For a reviewer or a writer, consistency is key. It may be tempting for a reviewer or writer who adheres to a particular faith to give a free pass to text that favors one's own position, but that must be avoided. Without careful adherence to these principles, the consensus on teaching about religions—any religion—is placed in jeopardy.

It did not take long for CIE scholars in their roles as a reviewers and workshop providers to discover that poor teaching and poor textbook coverage of Islam or any of the other world religions was at its worst when too little recourse to historical scholarship was apparent. Conflation of historical processes that should be discussed systematically, inaccurate or vague attribution of sources, failure to acknowledge historical debates in the field, and poorly constructed narratives, as well as inaccurate descriptions of beliefs and practices, all testify to the unfortunate fact that K–12 textbooks are seldom written by specialists, do not always reflect recent (or even standard) research, and seldom engage historical investigation instead of flat narrative recitals. Teachers, on the other hand, readily admit that they need information and access to reliable scholarship in order to teach effectively, and they are well aware that textbooks often do not supply that need. It is for this reason that the enterprise of improving teaching about religion very soon moved into the enterprise of improving the teaching of history overall. That journey struck out on very fertile ground.

World History Education and the New World History

For several decades, historians working in various disciplines and specializations were responsible as part of their teaching load for teaching undergraduate Western civilizations or "world history" survey courses. From a variety of vantage points that can be explored in the foundational literature on the emerging field of world history, these historians began to explore the possibilities of a larger scope of inquiry. Most importantly, in tandem with this scholarly research across disciplinary and specialization boundaries, they began to explore world history as a teachable survey course.[10] Parallel to this development, the past two decades have witnessed the reentry of professional historians into matters of K–12 education and curriculum in what has come to be called social studies. This effort, though tentative at first, has become increasingly prominent in professional historical journals of late.[11]

What came to be known as the standards movement intersected with this process. For history education, a watershed document was the Bradley Commission on History in Schools report issued in 1988 and sustained by the National Center for History Education as a force in curriculum development.[12] The most important impact of the Bradley Commission was its support for social studies programs that restored history to a position as the centerpiece of K–12 programs and advocated for chronologically sequential survey courses in U.S. and world history across multiple school years. Another organization, the National Center for History in the Schools (NCHS), surveyed school history education and was awarded a grant by the National Endowment for the Humanities to lead the development of the *National Standards for History*.[13] The work of the NCHS involved a collaborative effort that included professional historians and a broad spectrum of K–12 teachers and curriculum developers and resulted in a set of standards that reflect both interest in the scholarship of teaching history and ongoing research in world and U.S. history. The well-known negative reaction to its publication did not prevent the *National Standards for History* from having a significant impact on the development of state standards. Another important and related development was the development of an Advanced Placement (AP) World History course by the College Board with the aid of numerous prominent world history scholars and support for teacher training in the new course from the World History Association and the National Endowment for the Humanities.

The importance of these developments in history education for CIE's work was to open a field of inquiry that resulted in the development of teaching resources and in intensive research into standards across the United States. By the mid-1990s, the national standards published in the four core disciplines of social studies (geography, history, civics, and economics) in addition to *Expectations of Excellence*,[14] a standards document published by the National Council for the Social Studies that combined the four core disciplines and six areas of social sciences, began to demonstrate their influence in the development of state standards documents. From 1995 onward, a project to track the influence of national standards and other models on state standards documents began, which has continued to the present.

If it has become clear that teaching about religions is an integrated enterprise, improvement in the way world history is taught conforms to the economic metaphor of a rising tide lifting all boats. The national standards for geography and history both pointed the way toward more comprehensive surveys of the world's regions and cultures, religions, trade and technology, humanities, and social institutions, in addition to the usual political and military history. In particular, a new area of study—the interaction of cultures over time—was emerging from advances in world history scholarship. Recognizing that the spread of world religions and the interactions among them transcend the boundaries of civilizations and large states, coverage of the spread of trade, technological borrowing, law, arts, and letters was shown to deeply involve the human spiritual experience. A sound and global model for world history can enhance the coverage of all topics, and in addition, the attention paid by world historians to the scholarship of teaching added significantly to the potential for improvement in the teaching of world history.

The hallmark of the new world history as it came to be embodied in the *National Standards for History* was its organizing principle or course structure. Whereas survey courses and textbooks had long been built around describing a series of civilizations, the new structure for teaching world history was organized chronologically into a series of eras across the entire globe. Within each era, regional societies, civilizations, and the interactions among them found a place that was awkward at best in the older model. Recent scholarship and older research that had been left out of traditional courses were much easier to integrate into the global model. The four core disciplines and the humanities, whose integration into history was always touted as a desirable goal, could be incorporated in many new ways, particularly in terms of interactions and influences among societies. Paths of transmission of inventions, styles, and ideas and the spread of religions flowed easily into the new model.

It was frustrating to find that the debate swirling around the teaching of history ignored this important issue of how courses would be structured and instead focused almost entirely on facts, details, and a cultural contest over "who's in and who's out" of the content standards. Much of the discussion seemed disingenuous, and the contested content pointed not to a rising of all boats but toward a grim zero-sum game about which facts about the West versus the Rest students would be exposed to and tested on.

One interesting outcome of the research into standards was of course the consensus on teaching about religion. Another was the clear consensus among educators and the public that learning about the world is part of a basic education. To reiterate, the fact that state standards were officially commissioned, developed by educators statewide, and submitted to the public in a lengthy process that often included soliciting comments nationally meant that state standards provided a snapshot of what was considered desirable to teach. The fact that many states did in fact pay attention to the structure of history courses and the skill set needed to learn history was heartening, even while the public debate ignored that important area. During the past decade or so, a more comprehensive curriculum model has emerged through the collaboration of world history scholars and secondary world history teachers, AP World History has seen tremendous success among students and educators, and a wealth of teaching resources and in-service opportunities has become available.

Unfortunately, at this writing there has not yet been much movement in the way world history textbooks for middle and high school are structured, and the content seems mired in the past for the most part. Despite the embarrassment of riches in the collegiate world history textbook market, the politicization of the adoption market and other factors related to the production of K–12 textbooks have so far limited the incorporation of new scholarship and pedagogy into the status quo ante in terms of the standards movement's most positive and promising aspects. True, the books reflect a mechanical adherence to laundry lists of content but little else. The standards research continues in the attempt to illuminate what is of lasting value and to point out areas of consensus. As this chapter was being written, CIE's study of teaching about the world in the K–12 classroom was forthcoming in publication.

The Council on Islamic Education has been working in all three areas identified above. During the past 15 years, the organization and its staff have conducted in-service and preservice training for thousands of teachers. The organization has researched, designed, and published dozens of teaching resources, both print and online, as well as Web resources for publishers and journalists. In addition to providing information on Islam, the authors of these materials have tried to explore disciplinary connections across the curriculum and investigate historical scholarship. The "Emergence of Renaissance" teaching unit, for example, was an exercise in gathering historical evidence of interactions between Europeans and Muslims that contributed to the Renaissance and making it accessible to students, but it was also an effort to explore teaching about cultural interactions as a distinct topic of study, answering questions about the paths of transmission, the agents of interaction, and the places and circumstances that favored the transfer of knowledge, goods, and techniques. Institutional outreach and the publication of articles have encouraged a consolidation of advances in world history and geography scholarship and instruction at the secondary level where most citizens acquire their first, and often final, exposure to study of the world and its peoples.[15]

Integrated Curriculum and Standards in Public and Private Schools

While press coverage of education often harped on doomsday views of students who could not read and did not know who or where Washington is, something more important was happening. The collaborative effort between scholars in the disciplines and teachers of K–12 students approached the issue of how to best incorporate the mass of new knowledge generated in the past half century. Its best outcome in disciplines like geography, history, and the sciences was to restructure these bodies of knowledge to teach with greater meaning and skill enhancement.

If nothing else, standards flipped the teaching equation on its head to emphasize not what teachers send out but what students take in and demonstrate they can do as a result. In fact, study of the standards documents shows that clear patterns of consensus on many subjects can be identified, among them the idea of integrating disciplines within subject areas and across them. My research into standards was carried beyond social studies or history on an informal basis, in part because the publication of teaching supplements for use in Muslim education predated work with the Council on Islamic Education and because for a teacher of numerous fields in social studies, interdisciplinary work is very close to the surface because of the breadth of the subjects covered. The standards research conducted on behalf of CIE in mainstream social studies, combined with an awareness of the movement to restructure the other disciplines that was a part of the better, more optimistic side of standards, eventually led to imagining a standards-based, integrated curriculum project, which has independently been steadily developed and tested in the Muslim school context.

During the past five years at several Muslim schools in the Washington, D.C., metropolitan area, work with teachers on interdisciplinary curriculum development has resulted in the development of course modules in social studies, science, and language arts. Begun as an individual effort, the work on integrated curriculum has expanded beyond the region to involve collaboration and dissemination among other Muslim schools in the United States, and there are opportunities to share the results of this curriculum work with educators in the mainstream. For example, several workshops on integrated curriculum flowing out of this work involve demonstrating how Muslim schools can use the recently published National Geographic Society school division publications series *Windows on Literacy* and *Reading Expeditions* in yearlong or unit-length modules to implement round-the-curriculum integration of social studies, science, language arts, and math.

This work is a logical extension of the research in content and curriculum that originally grew out of the problem of effective teaching about Islam in social studies in Muslim schools. Taking an interdisciplinary, integrated approach rather than treating it as an add-on to an existing public school curriculum, the natural inclusiveness of social studies led to research and lesson development that involved the sciences, math, literature, the arts, and religious studies. A series of supplementary units that was published in the mid-1990s actually began its development in the classroom in the late 1980s.[16] After publication of the series, work with their dissemination led to invitations to conduct teacher workshops at Muslim schools around the country and to awareness of the severe dearth of original curriculum development taking place at those schools. This need stimulated the desire to find ways to share resources among Muslim educators in order to realize the potential of these schools for excellence in teaching and creative approaches.

Since their founding during the past decade or so, most Muslim schools have lacked the resources and know-how to develop curriculum on their own. Recently founded and even fairly well-established schools have ongoing challenges related to their physical plants, hiring qualified teachers at below-market salaries, and finding principals trained for the myriad tasks they are asked to perform, from fund-raising to discipline, teacher training to curriculum oversight. Those community members who found and support Muslim schools are not necessarily educators, nor are the parents who form the school. Both groups' expectations of curriculum may be based on their knowledge of local public schools, which are the major alternative to Muslim private schools. Many in both groups often incorrectly assume that accreditation and legal status depend on adherence to state or district curricula. Even without this assumption, it is a daunting task to produce a customized curriculum that covers both the academic and the religious needs of students. Few Muslim educators have the time to comb through the plethora of public curriculum documents that have become available with the expansion of Internet resources during the past decade. It has seemed much easier to adopt the standards, programs of study, and even textbooks that are used locally. Administrators know they are readily available, free, and aligned with the wishes of the parents to have their children partake of the two halves of the curriculum—the secular and the religious. Muslim educators are also aware of their students needs, and the school community's expectations to cultivate Islamic knowledge, practice, and values and spiritual awareness in their charges.

It is clear that exclusive reliance on the public school curriculum has drawbacks for Muslim schools. The most obvious problem is the uneven quality of district and state curricula, allowing the accident of location of a Muslim school to determine the quality of its curriculum. Second, programs of study designed for mass education do not make best use of the advantages of smaller, private schools, nor overcome their disadvantages, nor do they compensate for the constraints that go into developing a public school curriculum. Third, Muslim schools are trying to implement what amounts to a "double curriculum." With their school day and year equal in length to those of ordinary school schedules, Muslim schools teach between two and four additional subjects. These include recitation of the Qur'an in Arabic, religious studies (which sometimes includes the former), and Arabic language (or an additional one). Classroom time for these subjects affects subjects such as art, physical education, or even core subjects like social studies and science. Fourth, many Muslim schools have low student populations in some grades and use multiage classrooms. Multiage instruction has advantages of its own, but the practice makes a highly grade-specific public school curriculum very challenging to implement.

On the other hand, the tradition of American private schools offers a rich heritage of innovative, effective, and enriching curriculum, and it seems more natural to move Muslim schools in that direction, in part by raising awareness of the advantages of doing so and in particular by bringing to bear on the problem the cumulative experience with standards research and instructional design of the past 20 years. Innovative curriculum development that meets the demands of parents for academic excellence and meets the challenges of increased subject matter and the holistic task of Islamic education that lies at the heart of their missions seems to offer the best solution to the need for efficient learning and developing well-rounded, motivated Muslim learners. Islam is viewed by its adherents as a way of life, and the incorporation of Islamic values is most effectively taught if it is infused into the curriculum rather than isolated in one or two subjects. With *tawhid*, or unity of God and the creation at the center of Islamic beliefs, the notion of bifurcated knowledge and artificially separated disciplines seems inimical to achievement of the goals of Muslim schools.

Twenty years of work designing interdisciplinary instructional materials for social studies and a decade of reviewing textbooks have made it apparent to me that the best solution to the Muslim school curriculum is systematic integration of the subjects. A decade of work with standards at the national, state, and district levels, including membership on the Governor of Virginia's Standards of Learning Revision Task Force in 1999–2000, and consulting with local school districts on curriculum and teacher training led me to the realization that standards could serve as a platform and tool for curriculum integration.

Many educators in Muslim schools, private schools, and public schools have been striving for cross-curricular instruction to maximize the impact, depth, and interest value of topics being taught. Among the best known and most comprehensive integrated education projects is the Tarbiyah Project, which was developed by Dawud Tauhidi and is being implemented under the administrative guidance of Sommieh Uddin at Crescent Academy in Canton, Michigan.[17] A major obstacle to achieving this goal in a systematic manner has been the difficulty of knowing exactly what is taught at which grade levels in all of the subjects. The development of national standards models by academic and professional organizations—both those commissioned by the Goals 2000 legislation and others—resulted in the articulation of performance standards in all of the subjects in the K–12 curriculum. There was little or no coordination across subject-area boundaries in these efforts, however. Beyond the politics associated with their unveiling, standards represented a significant collaborative effort between scholars in the fields and teachers practicing in the classroom. A number of national documents represented innovative approaches utilizing cross-disciplinary investigations of major topics, intensive skill development, and increased incorporation of advances in scholarship within the subject areas. The skills identified as essential for acquiring and processing information showed much in common among core subjects—as a result of coincidence in the true sense of the word: they *are* very similar skills across the school subject spectrum, so we may as well teach them in tandem, with awareness of the congruence, rather than taking a decontextualized, additive approach to skill acquisition. Research into recent trends in curriculum strengthens the case for integrated curriculum, in addition to its other advantages for Muslim schools.

The problem, however, was to gain an overview of the standards across the nation, both national and state (and even including some innovative districts), and to knit these together into a framework that would enable them to be used by Muslim schools in a systematic manner. The curriculum development project that began five years ago compiles public documents consisting of (1) academic standards identified by the commissioned organizations that produced the history, geography, civics, economics, math, English, science, and other standards; (2) selected state documents that effectively distill essential content into teacher-friendly formats; and (3) auxiliary disciplines such as Arabic where educators utilized the methodology of standards to create improvement models. The fourth component is a set of essays defining an integrated approach to each subject and a correlation of skills to be acquired across each grade level or cluster in all of the disciplines. An additional section on lesson planning models helps schools train teachers to record and evaluate curriculum development that emerges from praxis. Materials for explaining the goals, process, and outcomes of integrated curriculum help to win over the school community to its advantages over local public school curriculum.

The second tier of work involves pilot projects consisting of multiage classroom modules that integrate language arts (in Arabic and English), social studies, science, Islamic studies, and math and the arts. These outlines and detailed lesson plans are the result of collaborative work with teams of class-room teachers, including the development of original instructional materials and adaptations of existing materials. These efforts dovetail with trends in the larger educational environment, such as the expansion of the National Geo-graphic Society's school publishing division, using research-based efforts to integrate science, social studies, and math content with cultivation of reading and writing skills. The National Geographic Society materials from the *Read-ing Expeditions* (for grades 4 through 7 or 8) and *Windows on Literacy* (for pre-K through grade 3 or 4) series are based on national standards in science, the four core disciplines of social studies, and extensive research on reading and writing in the content area as means of developing reading ability and critical thinking, in addition to the skills and content knowledge identified and elaborated in the national standards efforts.

The integration of common topics across the science and social studies divide takes this integration a step further. For example, one of the integrated modules developed for grades 3 and 4 combines earth science and human ge-ography, both of which subject areas are usually introduced separately in that middle elementary grade cluster, though the content overlaps and even dupli-cates the effort. Unfortunately, however, even self-contained elementary class-rooms have mainly taught this content separately, missing the opportunity to gain depth and instruction time. Topics such as the dynamic movement of the earth's crust in earthquakes and volcanoes, the reasons for seasonal fluc-tuations in the hemispheres and climate zones, weather patterns, and so on are taught in both social studies and science. Acquisition of map skills and knowledge is introduced in the remaining time. On the other hand, topics that would benefit from integration are the science topic of earth's biomes and the social studies topic of human culture regions. By combining science and social studies into the same year and working through topics with recourse to content best suited to a given discipline, time is gained for more thorough attention to hands-on activities and to build skills and concepts. By incorporating language arts instruction into both, attention is given to comprehension and processing abilities, and even more time is made available for reinforcement or extension. Literature and the arts are not left out either, with units on poetry describing the wonders of nature, folktales, songs, music, and stories from the various regions, often featuring plants and animals native to these biomes. Indigenous arts and crafts are a "natural" for the elementary classroom.

Teacher training on integrated instruction begins with opening up the pos-sibilities, finding methods for recording instructional development, and help-ing a school to connect such "nodes" in the curriculum content areas, using language skills as a tool for knowledge acquisition, adding connections to religious knowledge, math, and literature and the arts. Several such modules for grade clusters paired in multiage classrooms can be cycled through the grade cluster over a few years with or without focused repetition. A wide variety of textual, visual, and electronic resources have been marshaled to teach these units, including real-life experiences such as a garden project, construction of clothing, and visits to local sites. The schools have recently become better connected, so that a project to make this research available now has greater potential than even just a few years ago. Places where the project has been presented include the ISNA Education Forum mentioned above, the Islamic Schools League of America's Web site and listserv, the Islamic Educators Communication Network, teacher workshops across the country, and one-on-one work with teachers and administrators. The goal is to encourage integrated instruction and tap into the resources of many schools, ultimately creating units, modules, and courses and sharing them via conferences, online forums, and Web sites.

The project has already demonstrated that curriculum integration is neither a pie-in-the-sky idea nor an impossible dream, and parents as well as community members have come to support the idea. It has proven a boon for teachers striving to awaken the interest of their students and give them greater depth of exposure to content, to avoid overly compartmentalized instruction, to spend school year time more effectively, and to make learning more meaningful. In schools where it is being tried, it offers great relief in terms of the demands of the "double curriculum." Using standards as a platform for integrated instruction, the project nourishes the dream of bringing the academic, language, and religious instruction worlds a lot closer together.

Conclusion

The two-decade journey described above with respect to CIE's work and other experiences in education has hopefully illuminated both the extraordinary and the very ordinary aspects of this work that swings freely among various public school, academic, and private religious and secular educational arenas. Like the attempt to develop meaningful, integrated educational experiences for students and schools, the fields described above are interlocked and interlinked in many ways that have their own internal logic. The most important quality of this work, however, is that there are no sharp boundary lines that can or should be drawn around the Islamic educational dimension and the public (some would call it "mainstream") dimension. Both strive to educate students who would pursue knowledge willingly and with an open spirit of inquiry, engage and serve society as responsible and well-informed citizens, and make sound individual life choices.

NOTES

1. For a list of such books, see AMIDEAST at www.amideast.org/pubs_one/, the Council on Islamic Education Web site at www.cie.org, Arab World and Islamic Resources at www.awaironline.org/, and others.

2. Susan Douglass, *Teaching about Religion in National and State Social Studies Standards* (Council on Islamic Education and First Amendment Center, 2000); Susan L. Douglass and Ross E. Dunn, "Interpreting Islam in American Schools," in Hastings Donnan, ed., *Interpreting Islam* (London: Sage Publications, 2002), pp. 76–98; and Susan Douglass, "God Spoke: Guidelines and Coverage of Abrahamic Religions in World History Textbooks," *Religion and Education* 25, nos. 1–2 (winter 1998): pp. 45–58.

3. Charles Haynes and Oliver S. Thomas, *Finding Common Ground: A First Amendment Guide to Religion and Public Education* (Nashville, TN: Freedom Forum First Amendment Center, Vanderbilt University, 1998–2001).

4. Douglass and Dunn, "Interpreting Islam in American Schools"; Douglass, "God Spoke."

5. Haynes and Thomas, *Finding Common Ground.*

6. Douglass, *Teaching about Religion in National and State Social Studies Standards.*

7. Charles Haynes, "A Teacher's Guide to Religion in the Public Schools" (Nashville, TN: First Amendment Center, 1999), www.religionpublicschools.com/ teachers guide.pdf, accessed June 11, 2007, p. 3.

8. See "Modeling Methods for Integrated Curriculum—Three Teaching Units" and "Teaching Resources on Islam in World History/Cultures and Geography Courses for Elementary, Middle and High School" (papers presented at the 2005 Islamic Society of North America Education Forum conference, Chicago, 2005), www.isna. net/conferences/educationforum/2005downloads.html, accessed June 11, 2007. At the 2004 ISNA Education Forum, for which papers are not available online, two presentations were given to the Muslim educators who attended, one introducing the Freedom Forum First Amendment Schools Project (www.firstamendmentschools. org/about/aboutindex.aspx, accessed June 11, 2007) in order to encourage Muslim schools to apply to the project and the other on teaching about religion and world history curriculum.

9. For a more detailed discussion, see the CIE essay "Should Teachers Use Role-Playing Activities in Teaching about Religion?" December 26, 2003, www.cie. org/ItemDetail.aspx?id=N&m_id=29&item_id=227&cat_id=56, accessed June 11, 2007, and other essays posted under "Essays and Articles" on the "Educators" page.

10. The large number of important works in this field would be too long to mention here, but three that touch on education as well as research are Marshall G. S. Hodgson, *Rethinking World History,* ed. Edmund Burke III (New York: Cambridge University Press, 1993); Ross E. Dunn, *The New World History: A Teacher's Companion*

(New York: Bedford/St. Martin's, 2000); and Patrick Manning, *Navigating World History: Historians Create a Global Past* (New York: Palgrave/Macmillan, 2003). The *Journal of World History* published at the University of Hawaii and edited by Jerry H. Bentley offers a window on scholarship and teaching in the field. David Christian's *Maps of Time: An Introduction to Big History* (Berkeley: University of California Press, 2004) illustrates the interdisciplinary nature of the field of world history, which figures in this article as an entry into integrated curriculum for K–12 education.

11. For a historical and methodological overview, see Robert Orrill and Linn Shapiro, "From Bold Beginnings to an Uncertain Future: The Discipline of History and History Education," *American Historical Review* 110, no. 3 (June 2005): pp. 727–751; Gilbert Allardyce, "The Rise and Fall of the Western Civilization Course," *American Historical Review* 87, no. 3 (1982); Peter N. Stearns, Peter Seixas, and Sam Wineberg, *Knowing, Teaching and Learning History* (New York: New York University Press and the American Historical Association, 2000).

12. National Council for History Education, *Building a History Curriculum: Guidelines for Teaching History in Schools* (Westlake, OH: Bradley Commission on History in Schools, 1988).

13. National Center for History in the Schools, *National Standards for History* (Los Angeles: National Center for History in the Schools, 1996), http://nchs.ucla.edu/standards, accessed June 11, 2007.

14. National Council for the Social Studies, *Expectations of Excellence* (Silver Spring, MD: National Council for the Social Studies, 1994).

15. Susan Douglass and Karima Diane Alavi, *The Emergence of Renaissance: Cultural Interactions between Europeans and Muslims* (Fountain Valley, CA: Council on Islamic Education, 1999).

16. Susan Douglass, *Supplementary Social Studies Units on Islam and Muslim History, Grades K–6* (Herndon, VA: International Institute of Islamic Thought, 1993–1996).

17. Documents describing the Tarbiyah Project and its design, research base, and implementation can be downloaded at Islamic Schools League of America, "Welcome to the Tarbiyah Project," www.4islamicschools.org/tarbiyah.htm, accessed June 11, 2007, and further explored at www.tarbiyah.org/.

5

Muslim Homeschooling

Priscilla Martinez

Muslim families are considered to be the fastest-growing demographic of homeschoolers in the country, according to Shay Seaborne, president of the Organization of Virginia Homeschoolers (previously known as the Virginia Home Education Association).[1] Indeed, anyone who attends a local or national homeschooling conference, or even participates in online homeschooling discussion forums and support groups, will notice the marked increase in the presence of Muslims over the past ten years.

The timing of this increase coincides with the rise in tolerance teaching and diversity awareness in public schools. We live during a time in American Muslim history in which we see the gradual emergence of quality full-time Islamic schools. Yet the number of Muslim homeschooling families is growing by leaps and bounds. Why do Muslim parents choose to take on the responsibility of educating their children at home? As is the case for many Muslim parents, the initial reasons my husband and I have chosen to homeschool our children have been substantially added to throughout the years as we realize, through firsthand experience, the many benefits afforded by homeschooling.

Generally speaking, Muslim homeschooling families are a microcosm of the greater homeschooling community. Some choose to homeschool in order to allow more in-depth study and higher academic achievement than what is available in highly structured public and private Islamic full-time schools. Others may feel better able to customize their child's education—including those with special needs—based on the child's specific learning style. Some families may simply enjoy the lifestyle afforded by homeschooling, including spending more time together as a family, traveling more than otherwise allowed by a school calendar, consistently guiding children in their family's unique values, or simply keeping their children safe from gangs, drugs, and guns. Even though there are virtually as many reasons to homeschool as there are homeschooling families, the underlying motive common to both Muslim and non-Muslim families is the desire for freedom and flexibility to educate our children in a manner that we feel is best.

Islamic Imperatives

It is the Qur'an itself that influences and distinguishes the determination of some Muslim families to homeschool. The Qur'an prescribes religion as not only a part of life but indeed the whole of it. Islam, Muslims believe, is life itself and incorporates what they do, what they think, and what they feel. There is nothing secular—that is, nothing outside the realm that is governed by God alone. Public schools operate on the separation of secular and religion, state and church, as guaranteed by the First Amendment of the Constitution. Separating the secular and the religious in such a way that God is removed from all subjects is contrary to a Muslim's belief. Muslims are commanded to live their lives with God-consciousness. God instructs in the Qur'an: "So believe in God and His Messengers. If you believe and maintain awareness (of God) yours will be a fast reward" (*Imran* 3:179).

Muslim homeschoolers understand that it is their responsibility to teach their children how to achieve God-consciousness and strengthen their Islamic identity through their own example in every aspect of their lives. This can only be instilled in an environment that fosters God-consciousness, not through the social and educational environments of public school settings.

Muslim homeschoolers view their children as gifts from God, a trust bestowed on them by God Himself. They are entrusted with teaching children the knowledge and morals God revealed in the Qur'an. Homeschoolers believe that children must be raised and educated according to God's divine law and that not to do so violates the trust God has bestowed on them: "O you who believe! Betray not the trust of God and the Messenger, Nor misappropriate knowingly things entrusted to you. And know ye that your possessions and your progeny are but a trial; And that it is God with Whom lies your highest reward" (*Anfal* 8:27–28).

Thus, placing children in public schools is seen as a violation of that trust. Homeschooling gives Muslim families the freedom and flexibility to educate and instruct children in the principles of Qur'an and Sunnah, as they believe God requires. Learning those basic principles then facilitates the acquisition of all other types of knowledge.

Choosing a Curriculum

Once parents have decided to homeschool their children, the next logical concern is the legality of homeschooling. While it is technically legal in every state, individual state legislatures determine their respective homeschooling laws. As a result, legal requirements vary greatly. In some states families do not even need to notify the state that their school-aged child will not be attending school, whereas in others monthly visits/evaluations are required with continuous monitoring of students' attendance and materials covered in each subject. In order to homeschool in compliance with the laws of their respective state, families are obligated to fully research the laws governing their right to homeschool. A simple Internet search using the word *homeschool* and the name of the specific state yields virtually unlimited results, including links to specific statutes.

Included in the many kinds of homeschooling methods available to homeschoolers is the option to follow a state-approved curriculum. There is a wide range of choices—including "Islamic" curricula—easily within the reach of any parent with an Internet connection. Families seeking an "Islamic" curriculum that includes the "secular" subjects as well as Islamic, Qur'an, and Arabic studies have several choices, including the well-known Kinza Academy, which was founded by Imam Hamza Yusuf Hanson and on whose board John Taylor Gatto serves.[2] Families who wish to use a "secular" curriculum, supplemented by their own choices for imparting Islamic, Qur'an, and Arabic studies, can purchase a curriculum from companies such as Calvert School, Oak Meadow, and Clonlara School.[3] Generally, purchasing a prepackaged, off-the-shelf curriculum is called "school-at-home" because its approach to educational theory and methods and teaching techniques very much mirrors the approach taken by the school system.

On the other end of the spectrum is an approach called "unschooling," which is commonly defined as "child-led learning." The term *unschooling* was first coined by educator John Holt, a teacher, school reformer, and author of many books on education.[4] Widely ranging estimates place the number of homeschooled children nationwide at 1.5–2 million, with unschoolers making up approximately 10 percent of those. There are as many ways to define unschooling as there are unschoolers. Despite their diverse approaches to learning, unschoolers agree that an education is not found solely in curricula, that children are learning all the time, that children's learning strengths and weaknesses should be taken into consideration when teaching them, that the world around us provides a richer learning environment than a classroom, and that trusting children's innate abilities and interest in learning ultimately leads to the best education a child can receive. Unschooling parents often describe themselves as "facilitators" of their children's education rather than "teachers."

Between the school-at-home and unschooling ends of the spectrum lie other educational philosophies embraced by homeschooling families. The bulk of homeschoolers can be categorized as "eclectic" or "relaxed" homeschoolers. They may use the Saxon curriculum for mathematics but allow their children to learn to read simply by being read to.[5] Or they may use Hooked on Phonics to teach their children to read but allow them to learn math by baking cookies and shopping for groceries.[6] Play, games, puzzles, and electronic media usually round out the list of a typical relaxed homeschooling family's activities. Eclectic homeschoolers piece together a diversity of unschooling and school-at-home approaches.

Muslim homeschoolers may also subscribe to specific educational theories whose methods they then apply to their homeschooling. For example, the Charlotte Mason method, named for a British educator who died in 1923, includes narration, nature study, math manipulatives, fine arts appreciation, foreign languages, poetry, literature, and real-life applications.[7] This method is known for being very flexible and gentle in its approach, especially with respect toward younger children. Charlotte Mason believed that a child's home environment is superior to the artificiality of a school environment, that a child's natural curiosity is the driving force behind his or her education, and that child's play is as important as lessons.

The Waldorf approach, developed by Rudolf Steiner, conveys knowledge experientially as well as academically, working with the hands throughout every day.[8] With an emphasis on artistic handwork and craft activities, the Waldorf approach is particularly concerned with steering a child away from the dominant materialist culture. One of its appeals for Muslim homeschoolers is that its approach is based on the first seven years, then the second seven years, and finally the third seven years of a child's life. Waldorf education is strongly rooted in the anthroposophy movement, a spiritual view of humanity and the cosmos based on knowing rather than on faith.

Finally, dubbed the "classical model of education," the approach outlined in the book *The Well-Trained Mind,* by Jessie Wise and Susan Wise Bauer, is increasing in popularity among Muslim homeschoolers.[9] Generally, classical education bases its techniques on the ideas that in the early school years students should spend their time memorizing rules and facts, in the middle school years students begin to learn to think through arguments and ask "Why?" and in the high school years students begin to learn to express themselves through writing and speaking following the rules of logic. The overriding principle is that learning is best accomplished by focusing on language—written and spoken—rather than on images such as pictures and television.

Flexibility

Whether choosing from these approaches and methods or others, Muslim homeschoolers find it quite easy to merge their educational philosophies with their Islamic way of life. The key is to maintain flexibility. Muslim family homeschoolers believe that flexibility is used to the child's advantage as they pick and choose which portions they will use from various curricula, research the educational philosophy they agree with, and complete the package with field trips, various classes, and community service. But perhaps the biggest factor influencing a family's homeschooling path is awareness of a child's learning style.

Homeschoolers are persuaded that theirs is the only method in which a child's education can truly be customized. Parents are uniquely attuned to how their children enjoy discovering and exploring a subject. Families can observe the time frames in which their children grasp and embrace a concept to form their individualized education. Many homeschoolers subscribe to the idea that God created every child with "multiple intelligences," formulated by Howard Gardner, Hobbs Professor of Cognition and Education at the Harvard Graduate School of Education.[10] Gardner's list includes eight intelligences: linguistic intelligence, logical-mathematical intelligence, musical intelligence, body-kinesthetic intelligence, spatial intelligence, interpersonal intelligence, intrapersonal intelligence, and naturalist intelligence. Understanding children's specific learning styles within these intelligences enables parents to nourish their strengths and strengthen their weaknesses, entirely on their individualized time frames. Parents then continuously use their observations of their children to make adjustments to their methodologies as personal judgment directs. This allows children to work more efficiently and at a level that is best for their developmental stages, with skills and concepts introduced at the right time. This in turn encourages children to develop the ability to pace themselves and to take responsibility for their education, in contrast to classroom learning that is designed to keep every child busy all the time. Personal responsibility encourages a child to work for internal satisfaction, rather than for external rewards, and instills confidence.

One of the main advantages of the flexibility inherent in homeschooling is that even families with diverse learners within the same family can still homeschool. Even if their children have Down syndrome, autism, or attention deficit disorder or are highly gifted, parents can lead them through their studies at the pace that works for each individual child—an advantage unique to the homeschooling environment. The home environment also provides children with the ability to follow their body's physical needs—eating, drinking, and visiting the restroom on their own body's rhythm—which is especially crucial to children with physical challenges. Contrary to our first instinct to hand our special needs children over to "professional" educators trained to teach these children, homeschooling is becoming widely recognized as the preferred educational approach. Because parents are the individuals most in tune with their children's needs, learning styles, and diagnosis, they make the best advocates for their children. Support groups for families homeschooling their special needs children are in abundance, which is especially helpful during times of frustration or disappointment.

The flexibility that allows for a customized education is only one of many benefits of homeschooling. Parents also find numerous personal and social benefits that help both their children and themselves. Spending many hours with their parents on a daily basis enables children to develop essential life skills—balancing a checkbook, filing taxes, changing a car's oil, and cooking, for example—in a natural way by observing and assisting the adults around them. Islamic holidays and special family days can be commemorated. Homeschooled children are able to spend their days with family and friends who really love and care about them. Homeschooling families believe that working and playing together, as well as fasting and praying together, strengthen the bonds between family members.

Socialization

Socialization—while often mistakenly perceived as absent in homeschooling by those unfamiliar with the homeschooling movement—in fact can be achieved very successfully. Peer pressure is greatly reduced, if not eliminated, in a homeschooling environment, which results in less pressure to mature too quickly—especially with respect to interest in the opposite sex—and less pressure to have or buy the latest game, brand of shoes, or backpack. Interactions with other children can be based on common interests, rather than on factors as arbitrary as a child's age or the randomness of the school boundary in which he or she lives. Further, true multiculturalism can be incorporated into a child's life, in a genuine manner, simply within his or her social interactions, rather than removing the children from the "real world," placing them in a classroom, and teaching them multiculturalism from a book. Being "different," especially as a Muslim, is a nonissue in a homeschooling environment—a big plus, for instance, in a Muslim child's or a special needs child's self-esteem and confidence.

A homeschooled Muslim child's opportunities for socializing and friendships abound. There are countless exciting, educational—and often free—ways to enhance the homeschooling experience within Muslim communities: volunteering and community service, activities at the local library, classes at a community center, recreation at the YMCA, organized local sports leagues, Girl/Boy Scouts, cooperative learning groups, park play days, and field trips and workshops at local museums, historical sites, and points of interest—and, of course, the local mosque! The key is to search for these opportunities by researching and networking with other homeschooling families.

In fact, establishing relationships with local homeschooling support groups is seen to be crucial to homeschooling success. According to homeschooling philosophy, not only will these connections lead to additional social opportunities through field trips and classes these groups frequently sponsor, but this is often the best place to turn for advice from other homeschoolers—other parents who have been there and done that and may have useful insights and experiences. Local homeschooling families can also offer useful guidance on how to file legal paperwork and work with local school divisions. Support groups can be found by an Internet search that includes *homeschool* and the name of a city or geographic area, browsing flyers posted at libraries and recreation centers, and word of mouth. If a formal, organized group does not exist, simply meeting informally with a few other local families can also provide most group benefits. Finally, it is quite easy, via the Internet and flyers, to begin a new group.

Assessment

So how is a child's progress measured if she or he is homeschooled? How do parents know when the child has mastered a concept? An experienced homeschooler will tell you that you can find out simply by observing your child. You will be so in touch with your child's thoughts and activities day to day that you will not need external tools to "prove" what he or she knows or still needs to work on. Inevitably, however, most states do require parents to submit some sort of proof of their child's progress. The acceptable methods of measuring that progress vary from state to state. Generally, the most commonly used indicators of a homeschooled child's knowledge are standardized tests and evaluations.

Standardized tests are frequently made available to homeschoolers by their local school districts, which may invite homeschooled students to join their public school counterparts on their specified testing days. Parents can also order tests such as the California Achievement Test or the Iowa Tests of Basic Skills and administer the test themselves or hire a certified teacher to do so. Often, homeschool support groups will organize a group testing day for their members' children to be tested if desired. Just like some of their public school counterparts, however, many homeschooling parents tend to see the disadvantages and limitations of standardized testing, judging it to be an unfair way to evaluate a child's knowledge, and subsequently view it simply as a tool for complying with their respective state's proof of progress requirements.

Depending on the professional evaluator, written evaluations may include testing, review of a portfolio of the child's work, an interview with the child, or any combination of these. The evaluator then writes a letter attesting to the child's educational progress. Portfolios may include such things as book lists, writing samples, work sheets, and computer software titles. Compared to standardized testing, professional evaluations are seen by homeschoolers to provide a more holistic approach to measuring a student's knowledge. Ultimately, choosing which method of measurement to use should be based on which approach is required by state law.

Regulation

When state laws—or proposed legislation—do not appear to be friendly to homeschooling, chances are that state homeschool organizations have been formed in order to monitor legislation, speak with representatives, and mobilize homeschooling families to call or write their legislators with their opinions. These organizations present valuable opportunities for homeschoolers to network, attend conferences, socialize, and take action on issues important to the homeschooling movement. Because homeschooling is regulated at the state, not federal, level, legislative changes affecting homeschoolers can easily be supported—or countered—by families who choose to be involved in their state organizations. Some of the issues that come up frequently include changes to proof of progress requirements, tax credits for educational expenses, part-time enrollment in public schools, participation in public school extracurricular activities (such as fine arts and athletics), requiring public schools to make the SAT available to homeschool students, vaccination requirements, and driver education requirements. Families who choose to take political action on issues directly affecting their home education view their involvement as an opportunity to convey to their children—of all ages—the importance of the democratic and legislative processes, activism, civic engagement, and social responsibility as they live and witness all of these experiences firsthand.

At the national level, organizations such as the National Home Education Network and the American Homeschool Association provide homeschoolers the ability to network and discuss legislative and policy issues affecting homeschooling nationally.[11] They also provide general information about homeschooling as well as links to individual state homeschooling organizations. They are especially effective in supplying homeschooling families with news, information, and resources necessary to work toward protecting the freedom to homeschool.

Homeschooling Teens

Political activism is one of many hands-on ways to specifically engage homeschooled teens. Although most teens educated in this way have been homeschooled their entire lives, many are former public or private school students who decided, along with their parents, to withdraw from school and begin to homeschool at the high school level. Homeschooling teens definitely presents its own challenges and opportunities. At this stage in their education, teens along with their parents usually are already looking to the future and considering college and career choices. A homeschooler's preparation during this exciting time might include apprenticeships, internships, travel abroad, hands-on outdoor activities, and enrollment in a local community college. Administrative tasks, involving high school diplomas, transcripts, college entrance exams, scholarships, financial aid, and college applications, also become a high priority.

Like their public school counterparts, homeschooled teens who choose to attend college may attend college fairs and visit several university campuses. Colleges and universities are increasingly actively recruiting homeschooled students, offering scholarships specifically for them, and recognizing that they are generally more self-motivated and self-disciplined than their traditionally schooled counterparts. On a personal level, homeschooling during the crucial teenage years can enable parents and teenagers to rethink their changing relationship. The typical challenges, such as the need for increased privacy and independence, in parenting a teenager can more easily be developed in a home that has together time already built in. This, in turn, contributes to the emotional and mental health of our teens.

According to *Homeschoolers' Success Stories* by Linda Dobson, adults who were homeschooled as children have met with success as lawyers, law enforcement officials, entrepreneurial millionaires, best-selling authors, and professional and Olympic athletes.[12] Historically, 17 out of our 43 U.S. presidents were homeschooled, and the ranks of homeschoolers include such famous names as Andrew Carnegie, Joseph Pulitzer, Alexander Graham Bell, Ansel Adams, Leonardo da Vinci, Susan B. Anthony, Florence Nightingale, and Gloria Steinem.

Concerns

Naturally not every homeschooled child will achieve such success as these notable figures. The trails that these men and women blazed may offer little reassurance to parents who have chosen to homeschool but must still deal with criticism from well-intentioned family and friends, not to mention from their local grocery store cashier or postal clerk.

The concerns expressed most frequently about homeschooling often originate with individuals who are on the "outside" of the homeschooling movement, who lack a genuine understanding of the entire concept, and who have not witnessed it in practice. Individuals critical of homeschooling are generally only able to evaluate the process using their preconceived notions of what schooling and education should look like, based on their own personal educational experiences or, if they are professional educators, based on the educational philosophies and methods in which they were trained. As a result, their general observations are usually inapplicable because they represent approaches and techniques specific to children who are in a classroom setting for six to eight hours per day, five days per week, along with 20 to 30 other children of the same age.

Even so, many homeschooling families do indeed face—and successfully deal with—a good deal of criticism. Here are some examples of typical concerns:

1. *How can you teach subjects you don't know anything about?* For some parents, teaching a challenging subject might only require reading up one or two lessons ahead of their child. For others, networking

with other homeschoolers via state organizations and support groups is helpful. Just as one might hire a contractor to design and install a fence on one's property, a homeschooler can easily hire a tutor or a teacher to teach a course on advanced subjects such as calculus or subjects requiring advanced laboratory equipment such as chemistry. Many community colleges also offer dual enrollment to homeschoolers so that students can earn their high school diploma and college credit at the same time.

2. *How will they be ready for the "real world"?* This issue is a matter of perspective and background. Whereas those who believe the only real education can be gained in a classroom view homeschoolers as removing their children from the real world, homeschoolers see the confines of the *classroom* as actually removing children from the real world. While traditionally schooled children spend nine months every year, five days per week, six hours per day, in a classroom with 20 other children their same age—an environment not at all representative of the "real world"—homeschooled children spend every day of their lives with family and friends of varying ages out in the real world made up of real-life experiences—including "field trips" to such places as the zoo, the post office, the grocery store, a nursing home, museums, and so on. In other words, homeschooled children live in the real world every moment of their lives.

3. *What about socialization? How will they learn to interact with others?* It is a commonly held—and frequently expressed—stereotype that homeschooling families remove themselves from the world around them, living like hermits in their basement, unable to interact with or relate to other people, especially people different from them. A resourceful parent can easily tap into the extracurricular and enrichment activities mentioned earlier to make up for the all-important socialization that children miss by not being traditionally schooled. A homeschooling parent can also argue that public school children are not in school to socialize anyway, except for the maybe 15 minutes of recess and the 30 minutes of lunchtime they get each day. Because negative socialization also exists, being able to control the amount and quality of their children's socializing is an added perk of homeschooling. After all, Muslim families may argue, do we prefer our children to learn about the birds and the bees from us based on Islamic guidance or from their traditionally schooled peers?

4. *How will they learn to deal with challenges in life?* A homeschooled child may miss out on the class bully, but all children face challenges

from early childhood on. Homeschooling parents will argue that a classroom is not the only setting for honing conflict resolution skills or the ability to overcome obstacles and setbacks in life. Parents and children together become intimately familiar with a child's strengths and weaknesses—and wise parents will help their children take away lifelong lessons from these experiences. Alfie Kohn, an author and lecturer on human behavior, education, and parenting, calls this the "better get used to it" principle—the assumption that "the best way to prepare kids for the bad things they're going to encounter later is to do bad things to them now." But, Kohn argues, "people don't really get better at coping with unhappiness because they were deliberately made unhappy when they were young. In fact, it is experience with success and unconditional acceptance that helps one to deal constructively with later deprivation."[13] As an added bonus to homeschooling, conflict resolution takes place on an ongoing basis in families with more than one child. Sharing, taking turns, kindness, and courtesy are values that conscientious parents can easily engender in their children.

Although statistical data about Muslim homeschoolers are virtually non-existent, the significant growth of homeschooling among Muslim families in recent history has become obvious as they have become part of the mainstream homeschooling movement. Some homeschool conference organizers have been willing to dedicate space specifically for Muslim homeschoolers to offer daily prayers, as well as to send media professionals to Muslim families for interviews. The more active Muslims become in their local and state homeschooling organizations, the more the entire homeschooling community stands to gain. Muslims and non-Muslims can be united in their desire to educate children at home—and in their determination to cherish and to protect their freedom to do so.

Most important, Muslim families who choose to homeschool believe that this method is the best way to pass on to their children their uniquely Islamic ethics and values. By educating their children at home, they feel that they have the chance to improve themselves, their knowledge, their patience, and their family life. By focusing on their children's entire development, they say, they are carrying out their Islamic duty by contributing to the success of the future of the *ummah* and the world.

NOTES

1. Brian McNeill, "There's No Place Like Home(school)," *Connection Newspapers*, September 2, 2004, www.connectionnewspapers.com/article.asp?archive=true& article=36633&paper=69&cat=109, accessed January 11, 2007.

2. For information on the Kinza Academy, visit www.kinzaacademy.com.

3. For information on the Calvert School, visit www.calvertschool.org; for information on Oak Meadow, visit www.oakmeadow.com; for information on the Clonlara School, visit www.clonlara.org.

4. John Holt, *Learning All the Time: How Small Children Begin to Read, Write, Count, and Investigate the World, without Being Taught* (Boston: Addison-Wesley, 1989).

5. For information about Saxon Math, visit www.saxonmath.com.

6. For information about the Hooked on Phonics program, visit www.hop.com.

7. Charlotte Mason, *The Original Homeschooling Series* (Quarryville, PA: Charlotte Mason Research and Supply Co., 1993).

8. Fulton Public Library, "Homeschooling Resources," http://fultonpubliclibrary.info/homeschool.html, accessed April 6, 2007.

9. Jessie Wise and Susan Wise Bauer, *The Well-Trained Mind: A Guide to Classical Education at Home* (New York: W. W. Norton and Company, 1999).

10. Howard E. Gardner, *Frames of Mind* (New York: Basic Books, 1993).

11. For information about the National Home Education Network, visit http://nhen.org; for information on the American Homeschool Association, visit www.americanhomeschoolassociation.org.

12. Linda Dobson, *Homeschoolers' Success Stories: 15 Adults and 12 Young People Share the Impact That Homeschooling Has Made on Their Lives* (New York: Crown Publishing Group, June 2002).

13. See http://alfiekohn.com/.

6

"Guide Us to the Straight Way": A Look at the Makers of "Religiously Literate" Young Muslim Americans

Nadia Inji Khan

Just as loving parents have their children take vaccines, loving Muslim parents instill a healthy regimen of Islam for their children, hoping to safeguard their American offspring from perceived and real societal ills. Whether or not these parents, and the proxy institutions they enlist, are using an effective vaccine is another question. Many such institutions exist, though with slightly different ways of providing the "cure"—that is, a viable Muslim American identity. While their effectiveness varies, some vaccines may err in infecting their patient with the very disease they are trying to prevent. The same goes for Muslim religious institutions. This chapter investigates the various "vaccines" or burgeoning religious institutions that aim to "inoculate" young Sunni Muslim Americans with the religious background necessary to face the challenges of forming a sustainable hybrid identity.

Students of religion are often frowned upon by their societies in the Muslim world. Shaykh Hamza Yusuf, the founder of the first Muslim American seminary, Zaytuna Institute in Hayward, California, observes that because Islamic studies in the postcolonial world have been pursued mostly by the inept of society, the field has lost its esteem and legitimacy with Muslim peoples.[1] Najam Haider, a theology instructor at Georgetown University, states that "the *ulema* [religious scholars], after their failure to protect their countries from colonialism, adopted reactionary and pro-authoritarian stances that severely damaged their reputations. Many of those who claim authority today garner minimal support, and at worst misrepresent Islam because of their genuine ineptitude."[2] This lack of respect comes at a time when Muslim communities are most in need of their scholars in order to respond to ever more complex geopolitical situations. How will Muslim parents go about instilling religious values into their children—as an alternative to American culture or as a cautious fusion in the form of an American Islam?

Today, there is pressure on religious experts to seize authority from both extremes—Islamists and secularists—and regain prominence. Like the Islamists, jurists are expected to the use of the methodology of classical Islam, yet like the modernists jurists must be able to intelligently engage with contemporary American culture. In this chapter I will examine venues designed to create or at least inspire a new class of such jurists from the ranks of young Muslim Americans who are organically connected to American culture as well as authentically in tune with religious tradition.

First, I will look at the various motives students may have for pursuing a religious education: whether it is for a Muslim's idea of leisure activity, the solidification of social networks, facilitating identity construction, alleviating the paucity of credible Muslim American religious scholars, or simply to know God and His will. Second, I will briefly look at models of religious education, citing specific popular institutions, their history, their organizational structure, and their target audience. I will explore the physical setup of the classrooms with an eye on gender, pedagogical style, and curriculum.

Evidence is drawn from a nonscientific survey as well as a series of interviews. This chapter features models based on some of the more frequented venues cited. The institutions under consideration are generally part-time seminaries that either specifically target or attract young college-aged Muslims in the 18–24 age bracket.

Motivating the Student

Aar ya paar is a Sanskrit phrase roughly translated as "neither here nor there." For many Muslim youth, whether they are the children of immigrants allowed into America with the reforms of the sixties (first-generation American Muslims) or indigenous American children of converts, young Muslims in America find themselves living an aar ya paar existence, as their identities still linger between the two shores of the Atlantic. Practicing Muslim American youth may feel cut off from their coreligionists abroad. A practicing Muslim American, grown accustomed to hearing elders nostalgically describe an idyllic Muslim world, naturally wants to reconnect with a romanticized glorious historical past. Not only is an idealized past longed for, but so is today's motherland, home to the majority, in which the *adhan* (call to prayer) can be heard five times a day and where it is perceived to be easier and more "normal" to be Muslim. Sherman Jackson sheds light on the "in-betweenness" of many Muslim American youth when he observes that the young Muslims of America compose "a generation caught in the middle." He states: "[Y]ou [young Muslim Americans] are still trying to some extent to reconnect with an authentically felt Muslim identity and up to this point this Muslim identity is largely located 'back home....' That will not be the case for your grandchildren...if an Islamic Muslim identity is only located in the Muslim world, all the future of Islam in America is [over]—it's over."[3] With a religion that is still being "otherized," young Muslim Americans run the risk of suffering from perpetual foreigner syndrome.

Moreover, Muslim American youth find themselves on the assimilation path of those minorities before them. This requires them to negotiate their relationship with the majority culture, leading to hyperreflexivity in the way they view the religion that could potentially distinguish them. Because Islam currently enjoys a main stage in the media and in today's geopolitics, young Muslim Americans carry the responsibility for explaining themselves and their religion to their peers. This fact coupled with what some believe is the Quranic prescription to do *da'wah* (outreach) motivates students to learn more about their faith so they can properly represent it to others.

America today possesses a plethora of *Islams*—different ethnic varieties and ideological variants that compete for the hearts and minds of the Muslim Generation X. Such a situation is a crucible of confusion for young Muslim Americans. At times, students may misinterpret their teachers who seem to present their version of Islam as the *only* authentic one, making other interpretations and versions appear erroneous at best, blasphemous at worst. Anas Coburn, the director of Dar al Islam in New Mexico, describes the Muslim American landscape: "[W]e have Islamic Centers, media organizations, and political organizations, and educational organizations, associations of physicians, social workers, engineers and social scientists. There are Sufi organizations, Salafi organizations, and ideological organizations, like the Ikhwan al *Muslimeen* and the *Jamat* al *Islami,* all competing for attention in the North American Community."[4] Moreover, Muslim immigrants came unprepared for the double task of assimilating *and* inculcating their progeny, because they anticipated returning "back home."

Whether at home or in the mosque, at school or online, various efforts are taking place in America to educate Muslim youth about their religion. These efforts exist in full-time and weekend schools, classes offered in the *masajid,* online classes, and classes offered through university settings by either the Muslim Students Association (MSA) or university theology departments. There are *halaqas,* books, Sufi orders, cassette distributions, camps, retreats, podcasts, and sponsored trips abroad like those of the Chicago-based Nawawi Foundation.

Although American Muslim youth have various motivations for studying Islam, the greater their interest in Islam, the more they seem to desire an "authentic" immersion into "tradition," even if it means study abroad. Nascent institutions and domestic venues that feed these individuals' desire for knowledge give students different ideas based on pedagogical styles and diverse curriculums. Whether students are prepared to come back from their spiritual and educational journeys ready to join the teaching ranks of those who hope to shape Islam's American future is another matter. Some venues are designed to connect the tradition to American culture, while others still hope to cocoon youth within it.

These institutions are part of an intense marketing campaign, attempting to sell their religious perspective to their young and impressionable clientele. Inevitably, a young Muslim will find more than one version of "authentic Islam" being presented. While Islam has always been a religion characterized by intellectual cacophony (or, depending on how one views it, a multiple string orchestra), the plethora of "pure Islams" with which Muslim youth are confronted in America can become an issue if they are not given a framework of understanding that allows them to respect and accept inter- and intrareligious differences.

Common Sites for Religious Education

A variety of options have already been established to deal with the task of educating young Muslim Americans. First, there is Sunday school. Although children of practicing Muslims in America may not attend the fledgling Muslim full-time schools, most have had some Sunday school experience. Second, a more informal yet popular approach to education is the halaqa, the Muslim equivalent to a Bible study group. Third, cyberspace functions as an educational venue. Fourth is the MSA, found in almost every university and even increasingly in high schools across America. Each MSA emphasizes da'wah (outreach) both to non-Muslims and to less practicing Muslims on campuses. Although there is a national overseer of the Muslim Students Association, the activities of this group are quite decentralized and can vary tremendously from one campus to the next and even from class to class within the same campus. Fifth, it is true that most knowledge of Islam is acquired first in the home, what one respondent referred to as the "School of Mom." The overwhelming majority of individuals in the survey identified their knowledge of Islam as coming from home. In addition to the fact that their parents may lack proper qualifications, however, the children of immigrants may find it difficult to relate to mothers and fathers who have never faced the challenges of growing up as a minority in American culture. When children are taught Islam by immigrant parents and Sunday school teachers, the religion is blurred with cultural practice. It becomes the task of a young Muslim American to then study Islam in depth in order to distinguish cultural practices from authentic religious statutes.[5] The hope is to find teachers who are better qualified than the average parents or Sunday school teachers, who are often at a loss when youth bring complex cultural issues and the questions of their non-Muslim classmates home or to the mosque.

Issues of Identity Construction Influence the Way Young Muslims Practice Islam

The ability young Muslim Americans have to refute their parents by using their knowledge of Islam is an ever-refined tool employed by many clever young Muslims who find it one of the only effective ways of challenging immigrant parental controls. When they are battling with their parents over what they are allowed or not allowed to do, American Muslim children often can use their knowledge of scriptural interpretation to help win the argument. Sherman Jackson has taught Muslim American students to be wary of the Arabization of Islam and the subsequent difficulties of assimilating in non-Arab contexts.[6] While the issue of committing cultural apostasy in order to be a practicing Muslim is always there, knowledge of Islam proves to be a useful tool for rebellion against parochial parents.

Religious education has the capacity to influence hybrid identity development, for it facilitates ways for young Muslim Americans to see themselves as both Muslim and American. It has been argued that students in Muslim full-time schools have a higher sense of self-confidence than their coreligionists in public and non-Muslim private schools, but others worry that this trend is contributing to the minority's isolation. Venues of religious education for Muslims in America not only teach Muslims about Islam but also are important sites in which identity construction occurs. As Shabana Mir comments, Muslim student communities create a "third space" where they can produce "discourses as sites of resistance and negotiation."[7] A recent advertisement for MSA regional conferences boasts that the event is "not only a way to gain more knowledge about our *deen*, but also is a time for brothers and sisters to unite…!"[8] Religious education institutions are teaching necessary information and are providing young people with social networks connecting them to other religious young Muslims. As one respondent noted, however, "[T]here is still considerable ambiguity as to what the Sunnah of our Prophet is in relation to what we are actually doing here in North America, not to mention the rest of the Muslim world who seem set on imitating the West.... There is little social life here for Muslims and it seems that in order to have one you must look to the *kufar* [disbelievers] for it. The *adab* [character] of the first community is only somewhat visible on *Jum 'ah* [Friday prayers] and on *Eids* [Muslim holidays]. Unless you are in a *Tariqa* [Sufi order] you have little mingling with the believers."[9]

Programs like the Nawawi Foundation in Chicago offer "continuing education" classes to full-time professionals and students. The Nawawi Foundation also hosts an annual trip to areas overseas in which Muslim societies have historically thrived. These trips abroad highlight another important function of religious programs, namely, that they provide recreation. Such trips are indeed a "luxury" for those who can afford them. Besides the Nawawi Foundation, many of the camps, retreats, and programs do incorporate recreational and social activities into their agendas, fortifying the social networks they provide and providing an avenue for Muslim Americans to connect with one another, potentially even to find spouses.

Muslim Americans have a variety of intentions and motivations that drive them into religious studies programs. These may include pursuing a religious education for its own sake, educating oneself to prepare for outreach in times when dialogue is needed, developing hybrid identities, or deciphering inapplicable culture from applicable religion. One survey respondent noted, however, that "when evaluating the topics and methods that one receives in such [a religious] education, it's also important to ask, why one would even feel motivated. *Truth be told, only a minority of Muslim American youth are seeking such knowledge*" (emphasis added).[10]

Though not every Muslim American can be considered practicing or interested in religious studies, and though there is a smaller number of Muslim Americans interested in Islam as part of their "continuing education," there are those who desire full religious training. There is a significant number of Muslim American students working toward a Ph.D. in Islamic studies or its "traditional" equivalent. These students must find a course of study that will gain them legitimacy in the fledgling Muslim American community. The majority, however, have no intention of emerging from study as a religious scholar. For those students who want to master an understanding of Islam as a faith, attending mere academic programs does not suffice. Where, then, can they go?

Many students complain that they lack a *minhaj*, or curriculum. In the absence of a Muslim American university they have no guidance available to instruct them on what books to use or what instructors to follow. This kind of guidance is necessary if America is to see its own class of trained *mujtahids* (jurists of Islamic law).

The good news is that various curricula are increasingly becoming available. This chapter will highlight four potential programs that young Muslim Americans from stable economic backgrounds, with adequate interest, and with access to Muslim conferences or the Internet are likely to encounter. Although heretofore the common answer to young Muslim students who ask where they should learn Islam seriously has been "overseas," other options are slowly becoming available domestically. The models addressed in this chapter, both in the United States and abroad, are those of Al-Maghreb, the American Learning Institute for Muslims (ALIM), the traditional model (which will include Zaytuna Institute and the Rihla), and a sample of study programs overseas. This is roughly the order of how much these models aim to "immerse" the students into Islamic studies and a Muslim-centric environment. Going overseas is classified as the utmost "immersion" experience, though those that return are faced with the task of applying the theories they have learned abroad to practice here in the United States.

The Al-Maghreb Model

In the year 2000 Br. Muhammad al-Shareef spoke at an MSA National East Zone USA Conference. Many in the audience liked what they heard. Shareef had observed that halaqa attendance seemed to decline as students got bored with long sessions and decided that a different approach was necessary to educate Muslim Americans. So in 2002, in College Park, Maryland, he set up forums for his students to communicate with each other, starting with studying the exegesis of *juz amma* (the last thirtieth of the Qur'an). His model spread to other cities, and in 2003 a new institute was born, called the Al-Maghreb (the Web site spells it "Al Maghrib"), with headquarters in Houston. Since then the institute has slowly spread across America, first with pilot classes and then setting up *qabilahs* (tribes) in various cities. Each of these qabilahs has appointed its own *ameer* and *ameera* (male and female leader) who oversee logistics and advertising in the areas. Online forums on the site help to coordinate these efforts. Today there are thirteen *qabilas* [tribes] in the United States and two in Canada.

The founders of Al-Maghreb know that it is easier to keep students engaged in segments of two weekends in their "double weekend accredited model" rather than over six months of a never-ending halaqa. One volunteer likened their approach to the executive education that business schools provide, training busy professionals on the weekends in short segments. Rather than training busy executives, Al-Maghreb trains busy students, who can now complement whatever they study or work on in their daily lives with a more serious study of Islam. Al-Maghreb can measures its success in the fact that other institutes like Zaytuna and ALIM (see below) are mimicking this model with the Minara Program and the winter program, respectively. Scholars are allowed to take their classes "on the road," significantly influencing Muslim American discourse along the way. Al-Maghreb's focus on students, described by one respondent as "those not so solid in the *deen*," catches those who have not been to the ALIMs and Zaytunas.

What does an Al-Maghreb class look like? Classrooms are designed according to an L-shape model in which men are in the front row with an aisle separating them from the women, who are seated from the front row receding to the back. No physical barrier separates the sexes. Al-Maghreb uses the "*qiblah* policy," which is that when a sister is asking the instructor a question, the brothers must maintain their gaze "toward the qiblah (direction of prayer to Mecca)."

There is a general misconception that the Al-Maghreb Institute caters only to those with Salafi (literalist) convictions. This may be because many of Al-Maghreb's instructors are trained from the University of Medina in Saudi Arabia, and many of the instructors born and raised in America have studied overseas in Saudi institutions, which tends to create a cultural barrier between them and their students. Some instructors, however, have been successful in overcoming this barrier. Although the jurisprudence taught at Al-Maghreb is from the Shafi'i school of law, the school does not explicitly teach the *madhahib* as a more traditional institute would. The confusion arises when students without exposure to other schools of law are not taught that opinions other than those presented by the Al-Maghreb Institute exist. One respondent explained that Al-Maghreb refrains from teaching Islam's different schools of law because the target audience has little or no exposure to Islamic studies and would find it confusing. The same respondent categorized the instruction as "more than what you would get at a halaqa, but not at an academic level." While the different madhahib are not discussed, however, *aqidah* (creed) is strongly emphasized. The materials used at the institute are prepared by the instructors. A juristic text may quote Ibn Baz, whereas in "*Fiqh* of Love" the text *Tawq al-Hamama* (The Winged Dove) by Ibn Hazm is used.[11] No knowledge of Arabic is required in classes. Al-Maghreb places no emphasis at all on the concept of an "American Islam." Most of its instructors were trained in religion overseas and do not see the need for such a culturally attuned Islam. Although the focus of the classes may not be on American Islam, the marketing of the institute has been extremely effective to an American audience.

The ALIM Model

Another popular institute attended by young Muslim Americans is the American Learning Institute for Muslims, first held in 1999 at Madonna University in Livonia, Michigan, during summer vacation. ALIM's mission statement is "empowering Muslims through education." One respondent claimed that "ALIM provides substantive knowledge in all relevant aspects of Islamic sciences but goes beyond these basic building blocks to teach critical thinking mixed with the elements of true Muslim character as applied to these subjects. This leads to basic Islamic literacy, which allows for the development of empowered Muslims through meaningful discourse and true intellectual and spiritual development."[12]

The ALIM program began as an MSA National initiative started by college students who felt "illiterate" with regard to their religious education and yet felt a constant need to explain themselves to fellow Americans and less practicing Muslims in their own ethnic communities. They approached those who became the core faculty with their concerns. These scholars affirmed the need for such an institute to be put into place and complied with the students' requests. One visiting scholar provided the raison d'être of the program:

> Unfortunately our educational system is very poor, which
> is why ALIM [was initiated. What we are teaching] is basic
> knowledge.... What happens is that Muslims get to college and
> they take some Islamic civilization classes, [realizing they] have
> never even heard what was skeletal [knowledge]. Overseas, Muslim
> kids go through Islamic school, [in] other Muslim countries there
> are sixteen and seventeen year olds that have studied with different
> shuyukh.... This is why we need to educate ourselves so that we
> aren't easily deceived or confused by people who have some knowl-
> edge that we don't have [and then the student's faith is shaken].
> None of this undermines the Qur'an at all in fact it is what should
> make us feel even more confident when you study this [the
> science of the Qur'an].[13]

ALIM's core scholars include Sherman Jackson, Muneer Fareed, and Ali Sulaiman Ali. Rotating throughout the program are guest scholars such as Umar Faruq Abd-Allah, Imam Nur Abdallah, Shaykh Abdallah Adhami, Taha Jabir al-Alwani, Jamal Badawi, Yusuf Talal Delorenzo, Mohammad Fadel, Shaykh Abdullah Idris, Mokhtar Maghraoui, Ingrid Mattson (current Islamic Society of North America president), Amina McCloud, Sulayman Nyang, Tariq Ramadan (before his visa was revoked), Imam Zaid Shakir of Zaytuna Institute, and Imam Siraj Wahaj.[14] ALIM deliberately tries to bring individuals from a variety of different spiritual persuasions to enrich the intellectual experience of its students.

The 2006 curriculum at ALIM included "Aqida" (Creed), a panel called "Artistic Expression in Islam," "Comparative Religion," "Diseases of the Heart," "Jurisprudence," "Hadith Critiques," "History of the Caliphate," "History of Law," "History of the Qur'an," "Islam in America," "Shi'ism," "Tafseer" (Quranic Exegesis), and "Usul al-fiqh" (Principles of Jurisprudence). In addition, various panel discussions took place in the form of evening lectures open to the general public. ALIM seeks to inculcate in its students a sense of "Islamic literacy" rooted in the past but in tune with the present. An advertisement for a lecture by Sherman Jackson says that he "popularized the term 'Islamic literacy' to refer to the basic awareness of Islam that every Muslim needs not just for individual observance but to exercise broad, critical judgment about how Islam ought and ought not to be applied in practice. Islamic literacy imparts standard knowledge of Islam, while empowering Muslims to challenge questionable interpretations of their faith and insist upon good, common sense.... Ultimately, Islamic literacy in America must seek to empower us to bridge the racial, sectarian, and class divisions that divide us today."[15]

ALIM is more successful than other such venues in presenting Islam in a way that resembles the presentations of the religion in the Western academy. Most instructors are professors in their day jobs, thus Muslim American students are accustomed to their teaching styles. At ALIM students find that the *sahabah* were not the paragons of virtue and excellence described in local halaqas and Sunday schools but, in fact, were human and made mistakes. Therefore Muslim American students can more easily aspire to be like them. Here students find that the compilation of the Qur'an is more complicated than what was previously assumed. Students are exposed to the debates that puzzled mujtahids, debates that may never have been entertained in their local mosques. ALIM's instruction can be painful for many students. Through cautious dismantling of Sunday school dogmas, the ALIM faculty cleans out mental cobwebs of misconceptions. Such cognitive spring-cleaning forces students to shed former beliefs and make room for new perspectives on the faith, but giving up long-held ideas can be traumatic. Professors tend to deconstruct the romantic attachments many students hold with regard to Islam. Despite the nurturing environment, ALIM's course of study can be spiritually overwhelming for many students. Because old conceptions of the faith are broken, it is not uncommon to hear of individuals falling into spiritual crises during their stay.

At ALIM we studied radical Islamic movements, modern movements, Madhhabs [traditional schools of thought in Islamic jurisprudence], and how Muslim intellectual history developed as a dynamic rather than a static process. Many students did not even know the word *Madhhab* before they attended ALIM. Some realize how desperately "illiterate" they are. ALIM brings people from all over the United States to one place. It is a rare occasion when Muslim Americans from other parts of the country engaged in MSA work at high levels of the organization congregate. After ALIM comes to a close, students keep in touch through a listserv of graduates through which they debate points, share ideas, keep in touch, and post job opportunities; listservs provide a steady source of a running Muslim American commentary and debate on the news. Instructors incite students to think critically about our religion, something that rarely happens in local halaqas, Sunday school, or even Muslim homes. Professors often share lunch with their students as classroom debates spill into dining halls.

Both men and women are welcome at ALIM, divided in classes on each side of the aisle. Professors deliberately alternate sitting with male and female students during lunch, a phenomenon rarely, if ever, found in other programs. Many female students wear the hijab, and male students often grow their beards, wanting to signal their allegiance to Islam. ALIM proves to be bitter but needed medicine, providing a sense that for Islam to survive in America it has to take root and be an American Islam, a cultural norm rather than an exception.

ALIM is one of the few Muslim organizations that cannot be associated with a particular ideology, since all ideologies are equally presented and equally scrutinized. One goes back home with a critical outlook, equipped not with a plethora of detailed information but, rather, with the tools to understand where various Muslims are coming from and how their different orientations might color the ways in which they preach and practice. What ALIM tries to do is give students a sense of what is authentic and what is not, to be able to learn how to digest the various Islams available on the Internet, in the nascent institutions, in the Sufi orders, and in the masajid. Students are taught to make an informed *fatwa* (legal ruling) from their own hearts, taking the good from all that is offered to them and forbidding the evil, without needing to swallow any type of Islam or *jumma'ah khutbah* whole.

The goal of ALIM is to expose us to the many facets and vantage points within Islam—the Shiite perspective, the Salafi perspective, Ikhwani, Sufi, the whole gamut—much to our confusion. Each day we would meet another scholar with a completely different take on things than the one that came previously. We saw how complex it all is and yet how important it is to be more tolerant of the differences found in our communities. After ALIM we knew that we were less likely to scold the Muslims next to us about leaving their hands to the side in their prayer, for who knows, now we knew that they could be either truly observant Muslims, Maliki, or Shiite and not the heretics we might originally have thought. It was shock treatment.

At ALIM there are no mandatory *zhikr* sessions. In addition to the five daily prayers, one hour is devoted to voluntary Qur'an and contemplation time. Being on a college campus, nothing was unfamiliar to us as students. We ate halal hamburgers, had access to the Internet and cell phones, roller-skated in the parking lot, and went running around the campus after classes. We could even talk to boys as long as it was in the lounges and not at odd hours. A relaxed atmosphere, it was within the confines of Islam's guidelines by all respects but still utterly American.

The Traditional Model

At this critical moment in our history, the *ummah* has only one realistic hope for survival, and that is to restore the "middle way," defined by that sophisticated classical consensus which was worked out over painful centuries of debate and scholarship. That consensus alone has the demonstrable ability to provide a basis for unity. But it can only be retrieved when we improve the state of our hearts, and fill them with the Islamic virtues of affection, respect, tolerance and reconciliation. This inner reform, which is the traditional competence of Sufism, is a precondition for the restoration of unity in the Islamic movement. The alternative is likely to be continued, and agonizing, failure.[16]

A palm card for Deen Intensive shows a candle in a lamp, a reference to the description provided in Surah Nur: *"light upon light, God shines his light to whom he wills"* (Qur'an 24:35).[17] This palm card advertises for the Rihla program, but more than the palm card, what attracts individuals is ultimately the fact that it is graced with the name of Shaykh Hamza Yusuf.

Rihla is an Arabic word for "the journey." This name refers to the spiritual journey Sufism espouses. Rihla engenders a spiritual regimen, a background in Sufism, and a dose of what it is like to have a traditional Muslim education of the kind usually found overseas. Shaykh Hamza himself studied under one lamp in an isolated village of Mauritania with Murabit Al Hajj. Because of safety concerns American Muslim females may not be able to travel to this place still untouched by modernization, so the Rihla staff makes it a point to bring that environment home in an authentic way. The grounds on which classes are held are void of any icons, cell phones, or pagers. As soon as the student leaves the airport he or she is immersed in a traditional setting. And the focus is on matters of the heart. Of course, shari'ah is also given its respected due. Rihla students are expected to choose a Madhhab and are briefed on the topic of Madhhabism in readings given to them before they arrive.[18]

One common site for traditional programs is at Dar al Islam, in Abiquiu, New Mexico. According to its Web site Abiquiu was founded in the 1980s. It "began with a meeting, at the Ka'aba in Mecca, of an American-educated Industrialist with an American-born Muslim. Their dream was to establish a Muslim Village as a show-case for Islam in America. Northern New Mexico was chosen as an inspiring location. World-renowned Egyptian Architect Hassan Fathi designed a masjid (mosque) with an attached madrassa (school) in traditional North African style. But even as construction continued, it became clear that a village of exemplary Muslims is not something to be engineered."[19]

Instead of a Muslim American utopia, however, Dar al Islam turned into a place to host gatherings of traditional scholars teaching a classical understanding of Islam to America. The first "powwows" held in Abiquiu were attended by Imam Zaid Shakir, Shaykh Hamza Yusuf, Shaykh Abdullah al Qadi, and Shaykh Nuh Keller. According to the Deen Intensive newsletter, "[T]hese scholars...represent an approach to Islam which is based on a solid, traditional, mainstream scholarship. This is, of course, nothing other than authentic Islam informed by knowledge and wisdom as it has been articulated and practiced by its great scholars for 1400 years."[20] The traditional approach provides not only the knowledge to practice Islam in a clear, authentic manner despite the complex circumstances in which we find ourselves; it also provides the impetus to engage in the crucial process of transforming one's character. It is the realization that knowledge can lead to making one a better human being that is a large part of the appeal of Deen Intensives.[21]

As the sun set over the picturesque valley of Dar al Islam, we were called in for a simple home-cooked meal, low on meat as the program suggests. Students were shown to their room, a large hall in the adobe structure that was designed to house 20 female students of a variety of ages, backgrounds, and ideological persuasions. The "brothers" were accommodated in large tents called yurts with outside showers. All students were instructed to follow a strict schedule. We were wakened before dawn to pray *Fajr*, after which we would stay up for the morning *awrad* (recitations) of the Qur'an and involuntary supplications that would be recited by all, in a group setting. We then had the pleasure of attending a class with Abdul Hakim Murad on his *Contentions,* one-liners covering various topics. His Cambridge education was apparent in his verses, which flew quickly over some students' heads, especially at that hour in the morning. Students were inspired to come up with contentions of our own, debating his. After breakfast we were ushered into classes of *tajweed* (recitation), working to perfect our Quranic recitation in front of Shaykh Jamal Zahabi of Syria. Tajweed classes were also held in the mornings at ALIM, but they were very different at Rihla, where we sat outside after sunrise in the desert, with no cell phone connection, with no access to the Internet, and in quasi-isolation from even the closest convenience store. In fact, according to a newsletter that Deen Intensive, the foundation that hosted the Rihla, publishes, a retreat-like setting is a staple attribute of the programs. The most important aspects of a Deen Intensive program are said to be a retreat setting, time for plenty of *'ibadat* (prayer), instruction based on well-accepted scholarly works, and instructors who are inspirational and who learned what they teach from a teacher rather than from a book.[22]

Instead of cell phones, Rihla gave us hikes with friends; instead of the Internet, it gave tests in *fiqh;* and instead of music, it gave us *qasidas* (classical Arab songs). We were being divorced from all facets of our daily schedules so that we could evolve spiritually and break bad habits; even the schedule was meant to revolutionize the way we live, which it did. A quiet setting in nature is said to be conducive to reflection, forming what has been called a "frame interrupt." The idea is that we all have habitual ways of behaving when in the various settings or "frames" of our daily lives.[23] Learning is maximized when one is in a fresh setting, when one's ordinary "frames" have been interrupted.

During our tajweed, many students were humbled at their poor pronunciation, making them want to drop out of whatever they were doing in their lives and flee to Syria today to study with the *Qubaysiyya* [a Syrian-based woman's Sufi group founded by Munira al-Qubaysi] so that they too could chant the Qur'an as sweetly as the *shaykh* does. After tajweed students were allowed to nap or to opt for a nature hike with an always-smiling Imam Zaid who would focus our attention on God's splendor in New Mexico's majestic valleys as one student might comment to the other on how many of the jinn reside in this place. Being in the desert one felt close to the stories of the Prophets, dodging invisible scorpions, doing laundry by hand with water and soap as no machines were available, washing dishes after class as some counselors joked that this was a way to humble the students before their teachers. Rihla legislates on each facet of a student's life in order to utterly transform the way he or she lives afterward. Classes would be complemented by nights spent gazing at the stars, watching shooting stars and meteor showers, all to reconnect modern urban-dwelling students with the cosmos and ultimately with the divine.

The basic idea of Rihla is brief but total immersion in the study of sections of traditional texts under the direct guidance of scholars. Instructors are outstanding role models, with exemplary character, deep understanding of each text, and an ability to convey meaning to contemporary students. Hakim Archuletta, a visiting instructor to Rihla, gives the history: "[Following] the 1994 Dar al Islam Powwow, we began to carry out the programs we call Deen Intensives.... As word of the programs spread among young Muslims across North America and England, the demand for more of these intensive programs grew. Very soon there were not enough Hamza's and Shaykh Abdullah's to meet the demands. Today, the concept of the Deen Intensive has become a meme imbedded among the Muslim students in North America."[24]

Rihla staff are particular about their teachers, emphasizing a kind of uniformity in what is being taught that differs somewhat from the diversity of opinions presented at ALIM.[25] The rules on class attendance are strict; tardiness requires going after class and apologizing to the shuyukh. What to me was most stark at Rihla was the way in which the shuyukh were approached, as just that, not professors but traditional shuyukh. These men are regarded as "heirs of the prophet," thus there is an emphasis on adab, on respect to the teacher, not unheard of at ALIM but not nearly as emphasized.[26] Students are required to sit on the floor in a schoolhouse for their classes, the traditional way that knowledge of Islam has been transferred since revelation, from teacher to student, from an inheritor to a potential heir. This potential heir must be bred, appropriately cultivated, and groomed for reception of classical texts.

Classes are conducted in a one-room schoolhouse, where genders were kept separate by a curtain that went down the middle of the room. Although questions are allowed in smaller class settings, in larger class settings questions must be written and passed under the curtain dividing men from women, screened, and passed on to the scholar. Scholars have office hours for private questioning. The instructor sits on a raised platform with the students at his feet. We tried not to stretch our legs out in front of us out of respect for the shaykh. Sometimes we had to fight back yawns, not because of boredom but because we were often quite sleep deprived from the rigor of the schedule. It was material we had never heard of: classes included fiqh with separate classes for the Shafi'i (taught by Imam Zaid), Maliki (taught by Sidi Walead Mossad, a chaplain at Rutgers), Hanafi (taught by Sidi Naeem, a white convert), and Madhhabs; "Aqidah" was taught by Sidi Jihad Brown, another convert who studied in Syria with Imam Zaid; "Hadith Commentary" was taught by Sidi Walead; the

Hikam of Ibn Ata'illah was taught by Imam Zaid; and the *Maktubat* of Ahmad Sirhindi was taught by Sidi Naeem, who explained the concepts of *fanaa* (extinction) and *baqaa* (permanence) and other selected topics such as T. J. Winter's *Contentions.*[27]

Although hijab technically is required at ALIM, the rule is contested by some in each new class. At Rihla hijab is absolutely necessary. The presence of any logos was banned from our clothing, and jeans were strictly forbidden. The sexes were strictly segregated, with dialogue between them strongly discouraged unless it occurred in class between student and teacher or among organizers and participants when absolutely necessary. Whereas at ALIM all students take their food and sit in the same cafeteria, students at Rihla are seated with their respective genders far apart so that the students can focus only on what they came for, the pursuit of religious knowledge, with all potential distractions eradicated. Matrimonial arrangements are left to the end of the program to minimize distraction during classes.

After lunch we would go for another long stretch of classes until the *Isha* prayers, after which qasidas would be sung in union as male and female participants sat in large circles on both sides of the curtain, reciting in unison. This would be followed by recitation of the Qur'an, also in a group. To those who were more Salafi minded, this recitation and singing out loud in unison seemed blasphemous. They would often crawl off to sleep when qasidas were sung, not able to stomach this *biddah* (innovation). When the evening ceremonies were over, around 11:30 P.M., we went to sleep. At 4:30 in the morning we were wakened again, and this cycle of spiritual boot camp and at the same time spiritual ecstasy would continue. It is this relationship between student and teacher and the conviction that what is being transmitted is the truth that sets traditional education apart from the modem educational process.

Once our Rihla was over, some students experienced a kind of spiritual withdrawal. No longer under the pressures of a strict schedule or under the guidance of such righteous teachers, we felt our spiritual energies wane. Sometimes students feel compelled to return to traditional programming in order to salvage what they think they are quickly losing while caught up again in all the trappings of Western universities. This is often a critique of rihlas, traditional programs and even overseas experiences in which Muslim youth go from America either to isolated locations within America or abroad in order to reconnect or find themselves spiritually, only to find that such a reconnection is unsustainable once the retreat is over.

At both ALIM and Rihla many of the key instructors, regardless of persuasion, are themselves converts, either white or African American, while the majority of the students are immigrant, of South Asian or Arab background.

The converts can be as "traditional" as they like and still seem very "relevant" in their understanding of the American context. It is easier for students to take instruction from Muslim Americans who possess the honorific title "students of knowledge" than from immigrant Sunday school teachers. Regardless, Muslim youth learn to develop their eyes and ears for the type of Islam they prefer. This visual "eye" and intellectual "ear" can only be developed with exposure.

Zaytuna Institute

A formerly clean-shaven Muslim brother starts to leave on some facial hair; an uncovering Muslimah decides to keep her scarf on a little longer after leaving the mosque; an "Eid Muslim" stays after jummah and performs supererogatory prayers; a non-Muslim converts. When these individuals are asked, "What has gotten into you?" the response is: "Zaytuna!" Many students who return from Zaytuna's Minara Programs or Deen Intensive collaboratives or merely have been listening to CD sets or podcasts that the institute produces exhibit dramatic change after such experiences of "*imanic* recharge."

The Zaytuna campus seems to have its own fountain of *barakat* that spills into the hearts of those who visit it. The physical setup of the Zaytuna Institute seems to be replicated at Rihlas and Deen Intensives. Many of the same students frequent programs held by both organizations, which showcase many of the same teachers. The Zaytuna Institute is right outside San Francisco in Hayward, California. The layout of the campus is small yet kept in pristine condition. There is a complex where *wudu* or ablutions can be done for both men and women. This area starkly contrasts those found at other masajid, in that the bathrooms are kept separate from the areas in which ablutions are performed, with the spatial emphasis on ablutions, the place of which is given space, kept clean, and with an almost aesthetic appeal seems to reflect and underscore the priority in real estate to ritual purity, a prerequisite to spiritual purity. The aesthetic appeal of Zaytuna's campus, products, and even the composure of the people who call it home highlights the institute's efforts to synchronize excellence inwardly, spiritually, and esoterically and outwardly, aesthetically, and exoterically. During my visit to Zaytuna, I was struck by the tranquility of the place: one could hear traces of the Qur'an recited by children regularly in the Imam Warsh School of Qur'an Memorization and books of supplications that are sung like the "Burda sharif" and other *qasa'id* [plural of qasida, Arabic Sufi hymns]; an imam silently came and recited the adhan (call to prayer) in the Warsh fashion most associated with the Maliki school.[28] Everyone who seemed like a local was dressed in traditional garb of *thobes* and the *jalabiyya*. The

Zaytuna masjid does have a partition, but unlike partitions in most mosques it is also pleasing to the eye, a mahogany carved lattice that screened the women from the men. Because the masjid is used as a classroom space as well, there is a stage immediately in front of the end of the partition that enables both men and women to see the teacher equally, the partition dividing the room in half (fig. 6.1). The raison d'être for the partition in this structure seems to be so male students can focus during class on the sacred texts rather than the sisters while still allowing female students to interact with their male instructors.

The institute has a "quasi-monastic" aura. This is reflected in the dress code it suggests for the children in the memorization school, identical to requirements for dress found at the Rihla program: "All students are required to wear proper Islamic clothing. Clothing must be loose fitting. Students are not allowed to wear t-shirts with logos or any type of jeans. If they do they will be taken out of class and sent home. Also, avoid wearing any brand-name clothing." Boys are required to wear "[l]ong trousers and long-sleeve shirts (or traditional ethnic clothing)" and "should also wear kufis." For girls, "ankle-length trousers or skirts [and] long-sleeve shirts (or traditional ethnic clothing) are required. Girls are required to wear head scarves that cover all their hair."[29] In delineating the level of commitment necessary for students who wish to participate in Qur'an classes, apart from the obvious need for students to regularly maintain their memorization, students are also encouraged to "avoid activities that take away from the preservation of the memory such as watching television and eating foods that are harem or unhealthy." Again in this suggestion by the program one finds continual emphasis on keeping inward and outward states intact, protecting the avenues of the heart—the eyes, the ears, the tongue. These are kept in check through dress requirements, vigilance regarding what students are consuming via mass media, and such cautions as making sure

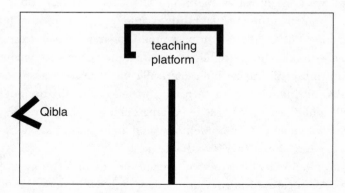

FIGURE 6.1. Floor map of the Zaytuna Institute.

that potential impurities—television, brand marketing, the distraction of the opposite gender—are concealed from the students' eyes and ears so that they will also be kept from the students' hearts and a higher focus can be achieved. The hope is that once the heart of the student is purified, the student will take charge of his or her tongue and limbs, freed from being a "slave to desire" and thus newly distinguished by one's fine adab, one's refined character.

The advertising theme of the Minara Program sponsored by the Zaytuna Institute is "Agenda to Change Our Condition," which is reminiscent of a Quranic verse that can be translated as: "God will not change the state of a people unless they change themselves" (13:11). Subsequently, Zaytuna's emphasis on individual spirituality and purification of the soul, concepts expanded on in the "science" of *tassawuf,* are grounded in the Qur'an. It is argued that such esoteric focus is necessary in order to improve the lot of not only Muslim Americans but Muslims worldwide—the hope being that coreligionists abroad will follow this American example. Muslim youth who may feel marginalized or helpless with regard to current geopolitics but who also see themselves as Americans and do not wish to engage in violence in order to solve the political problems that plague the *ummah* (community) today find refuge and a solution in Zaytuna. Zaytuna teaches such students that the real crises facing contemporary Muslims are spiritual crises, not political ones. The theory is that if Muslims can collectively improve their spiritual, esoteric states, the political, exoteric states will fall into place as a corollary to inward purification without the unnecessary shedding of any blood.

Founded in 1996, the Zaytuna Institute was established for Muslim Americans and Westerners in general, contributing to "reviving the tradition of sound Islamic teaching institutions."[30] One of its founders is Shaykh Hamza Yusuf. He was recently quoted in the *New York Times* as insisting that "if more Muslims were schooled in their faith's diverse intellectual streams and had a holistic understanding of their religion, they would not be so susceptible to the Osama bin Ladens who tell them that suicide bombers are martyrs."[31] The institute is named after a renowned seminary in Tunisia and is the first full-time Muslim American seminary, "where they hope to train a new generation of imams and scholars who can reconcile Islam and American culture."[32] Although it currently is in its pilot phase and thus only teaches six students, the enrollment is soon expected to double. One survey respondent characterized Zaytuna as follows: "The mission of Zaytuna is to provide Islamic education to the American student. [Zaytuna differs from other venues available to the American student in that] it has no immigrant slant to it that is powerful. [What one gets at Zaytuna that one cannot get anywhere else is] the ability to learn from someone who is very smart and has studied history, medicine, literature, etc., someone who has studied all [of] that and can then apply [these disciplines] to teach Islam is very powerful."[33] Another respondent commented that Zaytuna's goal is "the spread of traditional Islamic knowledge in a form and manner that is relevant to Muslims living in the West today. I really felt that Zaytuna understood and made itself relevant to Muslims living in the US. The institute targets Sunni Muslims of all ages who are interested in a practical understanding of traditional Islam."[34] Practical indeed, Zaytuna has launched a podcast free of charge as well as CD sets. In addition to local classes, it also telecasts classes and has begun publishing a quarterly titled *Seasons*, which Shaykh Hamza Yusuf has poignantly coined an *"aca-devotional* journal." One student who has frequented traditional institutions like Zaytuna and benefited from them nonetheless offered this critique: "Well, I'd say that one problem with the top-down traditional model is that it can lead to students parroting what their teachers say, without really understanding or experiencing it for themselves. Furthermore, this can lead to a type of 'groupie' mentality where you either toe the party line, or you're out. This problem is magnified because it is such a stark contrast to the general feeling in American education (or at least in my experience) of being encouraged to express my own opinions and to share my own experiences."[35]

Once home, students find themselves unable to connect what is learned "traditionally" to the realities of modern American life. They retreat back to fellow participants through listservs and regional conferences, gaining a repu- tation for having a "groupie" mentality, adding to a perception of elitism in these types of institutions. Students feel that they have to leave behind their "objectifying" natures if they hope to benefit from traditional immersive expe- riences. As one commented, "Many of the currently popular institutions teach passively, meaning that the students are 'consumers' that enter, take in, and leave. There is little effort from what I've noticed to thoroughly understand and critically examine the application of what is being taught," although he cited ALIM as an exception.[36] Still, the Zaytuna Institute is a bastion of hope for Muslim Americans, especially with its new curriculum and seminary program from which new classes of Muslim American scholars will be raised domesti- cally rather than overseas.

The Overseas Model

> *My knowledge is with me wherever I go, and it is not in my trunk at home.*
> —Imam ash-Shafi, founder of the Shafi Madhhab
> (one of the four orthodox schools of law)

Due to heightened interest in Islam in light of current events, the number of Islamic studies and Arabic programs is on the rise in America—in places like the University of Michigan at Ann Arbor and the University of Chicago for the former and Middlebury College for the latter.[37] However, it may still be true that an intensive study of Islam and Arabic is still most easily (and most economically) attained overseas. Informal social networks, recommendations from teachers/mentors, and the Internet can be used by Muslim Americans to determine appropriate areas to study abroad. Some may choose to study in secular institutes or universities in the Middle East (programs specifically with an Arabic language-acquisition focus), while others prefer institutes with a more religious environment in which to they can learn not only Arabic but Islam. Programs may take shape in more formal settings like in universities or institutes in addition to informal settings where a student may study with specific teachers individually and attain an *ijazat* (certificate to teach) by the time the teacher feels confident in the student's ability to teach a given text. Programs in Yemen include opportunities to study with Habib Ali al Jifri in Hadramawt and his followers, the Badr Language Institute for Arabic in Tarim, Dar al-Mustafa, and Dar al-Zahra.[38] In Syria, there is the acclaimed Abu Nour Institute, Jamia al-Fath, the University of Damascus, various Arabic programs such as the Center for Arabic Study Abroad (CASA), and the opportunity to study with specific individuals in a tariqa like that of the Shadhilis or the Qubaysiyya.[39] Mauritania (where Shaykh Hamza received part of his training in the home of Murabit al Hajj), London, Pakistan, and South Africa have their own madrassas and branches of Dar al Uloom as well as the various *turuq* networks.[40] Morocco hosts Arabic programs like the Arabic Language Institute in Fez (ALIF) in addition to Al Akhawayn.[41] Egypt is home to Arabic language centers as well, such as Fajr and Diwan, among many others, along with CASA based in the American University in Cairo and, of course, for Islamic studies, Cairo's Dar al-Ulum and Al-Azhar University.[42]

Students used to traditional environments, who face withdrawal when removed from them, often thirst for seeking knowledge overseas. Moreover, traditional institutions often stress the need for Arabic skills if students hope to progress. These students are drawn overseas not only for language studies but also for the ultimate immersion experience. Aasil Ahmed, who studied overseas at ALIF in Morocco, commented on these phenomena: "Many Muslims are looking to find alternatives to traveling overseas for good education in Arabic and Islamic Studies. Students looking to enter Academia generally have to go overseas because quality of Arabic education in the United States is weak. Students wishing to go overseas for religious knowledge and spiritual awakening either get caught up in a lifestyle which is not-sustainable in the

West, or they come back and are unable to bridge the gap between their life in the Muslim world and their life in the West."[43] An issue with the overseas model is the sometimes undue sacredness attributed to the experience, with some prestige value in America, which led one survey respondent to ask, "Why are American Muslims perceived as 'second-class Muslims'? I don't think it's necessary for a person to study overseas in order to teach and practice Islam in the United States!"[44]

In many respects, Qasid Institute in Amman, Jordan, is the perfect match for many Western Muslims. This choice is ideal because the institute itself was initiated by Western Muslims, who themselves saw the need for a school devoted simply to classical Arabic. Classrooms at the institute are gender segregated. Lounges are also segregated, with one for male students and another for females. A partition to rest on the desks is available and used at the discretion of the instructor. Due to the Sufi bent of many of the students and faculty at Qasid, many female students wear *niqab,* and even those who normally do not choose to do so in order to fit into the conservative atmosphere as well as to purify their intentions when learning and allow both students and instructors to concentrate on nothing other than subject matter. Another reason many women choose to wear niqab during their stay and encourage their female classmates to don the face veil as well is because the neighborhood in which students reside is so small, privacy is often at risk, and the niqab alleviates privacy concerns, allowing women to walk within the neighborhood's winding streets unnoticed.

Most students, however, did not simply come to Qasid for the sole pursuit of language acquisition. Rather, an important neighbor of the institute is the headquarters of Shaykh Nuh Ha Mim Keller, who resides there with his *mureeds* (aspiring spiritual disciples).[45] His presence makes the neighborhood a headquarters for the followers of the Shadhili Tariqa. His *zawiyya* is conveniently located a brisk walk from Qasid. The neighborhood is infused with his aura. Students thus not only have access to a bastion of classical Arabic, its tajweed, *tafseer,* and other specialized Islamic studies classes, but also have the opportunity to attend classes in *tasawwuf* (purification)—be it attending *hizb al-bahr,* a *hadra* (collective supererogatory rituals), or attending classes for "Ihya ulum-ud Din" (Revival of the religious sciences) as well as private and open forums for potential mureeds (pledged Sufi adherents) to question the shaykh. More than housing the Shadhli Tariqa, the neighborhood serves as a hub for scholars and serious students to frequent from all over both the Western and Middle Eastern worlds. It is also the home base of many of the scholars who offer classes through SunniPath.com.[46] It is home to local stores like Shukr whose fashion line caters to the Sufi and conservative minded, providing Western clothing that meets traditional standards and tastes. Moreover, many of the writers for *Islamica* magazine find their place in the neighborhood, as does the Jordanian secret police, the *mukhabaraat* who supposedly have an office conveniently located within this quiet neighborhood called Hayy al Kharabshah, tucked away in the outskirts of Amman.

Accessibility Concerns: Race, Class, Gender

This chapter has attempted to cover four models of religious institutions frequented by Muslim Americans. What it has not done is address the accessibility concerns and possible differences in access of these models for various races and classes and the potential gap in access between genders. Whereas the Al-Maghreb Institute costs around $165 per student, ALIM and Deen Intensive programs can cost thousands. Studying overseas can be even more expensive. It is often difficult for economically disadvantaged young people to have access to these programs.

One cannot help but wonder what the future implications of disproportionate access to religious knowledge will be and whether this disproportion affects the type of religious education various socioeconomic classes and different racial groups receive. One undergraduate student commented that

> much of it is based on *family situation*. . . . A large number of inner-city
> youth of various ethnic origins work to support family, or study in
> community colleges just to get by, and often these find opportunity
> in *tablighi,* or *Salafi* groups. In particular, African Americans (who
> make up a significant percentage of the Muslim American popula-
> tion) often do not partake in such conferences, organizations, etc,
> but little attention is paid to their education. Too often I feel that we
> give too much credit to the well-known programs and organizations
> and assume that they are the primary educators of youth, college, and
> high school, today. [Are such programs] even the most visible? Maybe
> [these programs are known only in a] certain crowd of high economic
> status, [which] somehow at one point became inter-linked, who *see*
> these groups as the most visible.[47]

Others surveyed shared the "separation between colors" concern, lamenting that "there is not enough teaching for our African-American youth."[48] Not only are African Americans underrepresented, but so are those of lower economic brackets. One popular blogger, Ali Eteraz, critiques what he calls the "glossy books," the "moderate Muslims" apt to print well-designed reading material, deeming that

public speakers who stand on the "Muslim" platform are largely
preaching to the converted...engaged in a struggle between themselves to be *the* voice of Muslims....[Traditionalist public speakers]
are talking to people who have relatively stable incomes, have a good
("secular") education, are literate....They have the time and luxury
to attend these events, buy books representing the *broader tradition,*
and purchase *online courses.* That is, they can be won over against
extremist propaganda, which itself often emanates from the mouths
of similarly well-educated middle class types, who have the luxury
to play armchair *hirabi,* and have the skills to wax lyrically about the
phony *sunna* of Osama bin Laden.[49]

Although some have claimed that "traditional" institutes are in fact not
"traditional" enough, others deem that such institutes have made a "god out
of tradition." What is certain is that these institutes are filling a gap in the
spiritual and religious lives of Muslim Americans through their guidance and
leadership on how Muslim youth may best live their lives as minorities in peace
with their societies and at peace with God.

Conclusion

America has not seen the likes of an American Azhar or a Karaouine develop
yet.[50] In fact, the plethora of nascent venues leaves some "students of knowledge" confused. Some choose to stick with one organization, taking what they
can from it, while others try to be exposed to as wide a range of teaching as
possible.

Shaykh Hamza Yusuf comments on the numerous groups who claim that
they constitute *ahl us sunnah wal jammah,* comparing this honorific title to the
trope of Leyla, just as "[e]veryone claims he was intimate with Leyla, but Leyla
denies them all."[51] It is in the pursuit of Leyla that young Muslims now find
themselves.[52] One respondent highlighted the issue when stating that since
"each organization presents Islam in light of their ideology, I try to take what
is good and leave what I don't know."[53] It is in the face of religious cacophony
that many Muslim youth resort to prophetic advice, that is, to ask your heart for
a fatwa [legal decision]. Having an entire generation taking their own fatwas,
however, makes building strong communities difficult and leaves us with the
desire for an authoritative institution recognized by what many see as the need
for a "critical majority."

There is a tendency for students to almost immortalize their scholars, leading to a cultishness that threatens Islamic discourse in America. For the most

part Zaytuna students only mingle with Zaytuna students, and Al-Maghreb students only interact among themselves. Students believe that whatever their respective institutions say must be true. This narrowness of understanding will hurt Muslims in making progress toward viable institutions. The rise of various institutions aimed at teaching young Muslims ought to be a phenomenon welcomed for bringing healthy intellectual competition, not feared for sowing further divisions. In anticipating the founding of a full-fledged Muslim American seminary, one hopes that it will prove instrumental in teaching Muslims how to be contributing citizens, and in so doing, such places will serve both Muslims and Americans at large.

NOTES

The term *religiously literate* has been adapted from Sherman Jackson's lectures.

1. Hamza Yusuf, "Who Are the Rightly Guided Scholars?" (speech presented and converted into a cassette tape, released by Alhambra Productions, San Ramon, CA, 2006).

2. Najam Haider, e-mail message to the author, March 25, 2007.

3. Sherman Jackson, "Seerah" (lecture presented at the American Learning Institute for Muslims, Livonia, MI, 2006).

4. Anas Coburn, "The Context of Dar al Islam Activities," *Deen News*, summer 2000: pp. 4–5.

5. Christine Johnson, "Staying on the Straight Path" (Ph.D. dissertation, University of Bergen, 2006), p. 261. Johnson comments that one young female respondent "used to find certain things in Islam problematic, until she learned, by acquiring more knowledge of 'true Islam,' that these were in fact not Islamic but cultural traditions. When she spoke to me about the uneasiness she once felt towards some aspects of Islam, regarding for instance the position of women, she interpreted her own criticism as a lack of knowledge, 'I do not see anything negative in Islam itself. But I do see a lot of negative things in Muslims.'"

6. Jackson is a professor of Afro-American studies at the University of Michigan at Ann Arbor. He recently published *Islam and the Blackamerican: Looking toward the Third Resurrection* (New York: Oxford University Press, 2005). He is also cofounder of the American Learning Institute for Muslims.

7. Shabana Mir, "Constructing Third Spaces: American Muslim Women's Hybrid Identity Construction" (Ph.D. dissertation, University of Indiana, 2006), p. 60.

8. Muslim Students Association, Ezrepusa, "MSA NATIONAL EAST ZONE CONFERENCE!!" e-mail to the author, March 25, 2007.

9. Khadijah Khan, online survey by the author, survey results, Washington, DC, December 25, 2006.

10. Anonymous respondent, survey by the author, December 2006. (Respondents promised anonymity.)

11. Abd-al-Aziz ibn Abd-Allah ibn Baaz (d. 1999) was the former grand mufti (jurisconsult) of Saudi Arabia.

12. Ali Haque, online survey by the author, survey results, Washington, DC, December 25, 2006.

13. Ingrid Mattson, "History of the Qur'an" (lecture given and recorded at the American Learning Institute for Muslims Summer Program, Livonia, MI, July–August 2006).

14. Umar Faruq Abd-Allah (Wymann-Landgraf) is an American Muslim scholar and the founding chair and scholar-in-residence of the newly founded Nawawi Foundation, a nonprofit educational foundation. He has recently finished writing a biography of Mohammed Webb (d. 1916), an early American convert to Islam, titled *Muslim in Victorian America: The Story of Alexander Russell Webb* (New York: Oxford University Press, 2006).

Shaykh Nur Abdallah served as the chairman of the Fiqh Council for the Islamic Society of North America (ISNA). He was also a former president of the ISNA (www. alimprogram.com/scholars/abdullah.shtml).

Shaykh Abdallah Adhami is a certified narrator of hadith. His work focuses on the "legal, ethical and spiritual dimensions of the linguistic implications of *shari'ah* texts. His works also strive to relate the eternal relevance of the essence of *shari'ah* laws as a vehicle to enhance modern lived experience" (www.sakeenah.org/sabio.shtml). He is well known for his work on gender relations in Islam.

Taha Jabir al-Alwani has a strong background in Islamic jurisprudence: "Dr. al 'Alwani participated in the founding of the International Institute of Islamic Thought (IIIT) in the USA in 1981, and is now the Institute's President and a member of its Board of Trustees. He is a founder-member of the Council of the Muslim World League in Makkah, . . . and President of the Fiqh Council of North America since 1988" (www.islam-democracy.org/alalwani_bio.asp).

Jamal Badawi was featured in a "352-segment television series on Islam, shown in many local TV stations in Canada and the USA and in other countries as well. Audio and video copies of these programs have been widely used in many countries. . . . He . . . is the founder/chairman of the Islamic Information Foundation, a non-profit foundation seeking to promote better understanding of Islam by Muslims and non-Muslim" (http://onlineislamicstore.com/jamalbadawi.html).

Yusuf Talal DeLorenzo is a specialist in Islamic banking and finance. He is a former adviser on Islamic affairs to the Government of Pakistan and a "[m]ember of the Shari'ah Supervisory Boards of Islamic financial institutions worldwide, including the *Dow Jones Islamic Markets*" (http://muslim-investor.com/mi/bio-delorenzo.phtml).

Mohammad Fadel "worked on his PhD in Near Eastern Languages and Cultures at the University of Chicago (Illinois), where he completed a dissertation focusing on Islamic legal processes during medieval times. . . . He previously worked with the United States Court of Appeals Fourth Circuit, and the United States District Court. He has taught Arabic at [many universities] . . . and is a past president of the Association for Arab-American Understanding and a member of Muslim Voices for Peace. . . . Among topics covered in his publications are Islam and Democracy, Islamic Scholastic Theology, and Analogical Reasoning in Islamic Jurisprudence" (www.alimprogram.com/scholars/fadel.shtml).

Sheikh Abdullah Idris Ali served as ISNA president from 1992 to 1997 (www.alimprogram.com/scholars/idris.shtml).

Imam Mokhtar "received his Islamic education in Algeria before coming to the U.S. He has been an Imam in the state of New York and is a Central Shura Member of the Islamic Circle of North America" (www.alimprogram.com/scholars/mokhtar.shtml).

Ingrid Mattson "is Professor of Islamic Studies and Director of Islamic Chaplaincy at the Macdonald Center for Islamic Studies and Christian-Muslim Relations at Hartford Seminary in Hartford, CT.... In 1995 she served as advisor to the Afghan delegation to the United Nations Commission on the Status of Women.... Dr. Mattson earned her Ph.D. in Islamic Studies from the University of Chicago in 1999. Her research is focused on Islamic law and society" (www.isna.net/ISNAHQ/pages/Ingrid-Mattson-President-US.aspx).

Amina Beverly McCloud "converted to Islam in 1966. A professor of Islamic Studies at DePaul University in Chicago, she studies Islam and Muslim life in the United States. In *Muslims*, a recent documentary on PBS's *Frontline*, McCloud facilitated a debate between Muslims and non-Muslims in Palos Heights, Illinois, over the placement of a mosque in the community" (www.alimprogram.com/scholars/mccloud.shtml).

Sulayman Nyang "teaches at Howard University in Washington, D.C. where he serves as Professor of African Studies. From 1975 to 1978 he served as Deputy Ambassador and Head of Chancery of the Gambia Embassy in Jeddah, Saudi Arabia.... He also serves as co-director of Muslims in the American Public Square, a research project funded by The Pew Charitable Trusts" (http://pewforum.org/events/0410/nyangbio.htm).

Tariq Ramadan "resigned from the post of Professor of Islamic Studies at Notre Dame University (Classic Department) and Luce Professor at the Kroc Institute (Religion Conflict and Peacebuilding)" after his visa to the United States was revoked: "He is active both at the academic and grassroots levels lecturing extensively throughout the world on social justice and dialogue between civilizations. Professor Tariq Ramadan is currently President of the European think tank: *European Muslim Network* (EMN) in Brussels" (www.tariqramadan.com/spip.php?article11).

Imam Zaid Shakir "accepted Islam in 1977 while serving in the United States Air Force.... In 2001, he graduated from Syria's prestigious Abu Noor University and returned to Connecticut, serving again as the Imam of Masjid al-Islam, and writing and speaking frequently on a host of issues. That same year, his translation from Arabic into English of 'The Heirs of the Prophets' was published by Starlatch Press. In 2003, he moved to Hayward, California to serve as a scholar-in-residence and lecturer at Zaytuna Institute, where he now teaches courses on Arabic, Islamic law, history, and Islamic spirituality. In 2005, Zaytuna Institute published 'Scattered Pictures: Reflections of An American Muslim'" (www.newislamicdirections.com/nid/about/).

Siraj Wahaj, imam of Masjid Taqwa in New York, "received Imam training at Ummul Qura University of Makkah in 1978 and has gone on to become a national and international speaker on Islam. Imam Wahhaj has been Vice President of ISNA

U.S.... Imam Wahhaj has appeared on several national television talk shows and interviews especially about his anti-drug campaigns. He received high praises from the media and NYPD for initiating anti-drug patrol in Brooklyn, New York in 1988. Among other achievements, Imam Wahhaj was the first person to give an Islamic invocation to the United States Congress" (http://onlineislamicstore.com/audio-lectures-speeches-single-tapes-imam-siraj-wahaj.html).

15. Nawawi Foundation, "Nawawi Class: Essential Elements of Islamic Literacy," e-mail to the author, January 3, 2007.

16. Quote from Timothy James Winters. Also known as Shaykh Abdul Hakim Murad, he has been a visiting instructor on Nawawi Foundation trips, as well as at the Rihla in New Mexico.

17. Surah 24:34, *Al Nur* (The light), Abdullah Yusuf Ali, *The Holy Qur'an* (1989).

18. Various authors, "Deen Intensive Reading Packet," *Rihla Deen Intensive 2004*, www.madinah.org/dip_rea-pack.htm, accessed April 2, 2007.

19. "Our Story," Dar al Islam, www.daralislam.org/AboutUs/OurStory.aspx, accessed April 2, 2007.

20. Anas Coburn, "Methodology of Deen-Intensive," *Deen Knowledge*, summer 1999: pp. 3–4. On "traditional," Abdel H. Honnerkamp writes, "The inherent unity of traditional education is not explicitly in sitting in circles and studying the *mutun of fiqh* and *ahadith*. Traditional learning rather escalates into something much greater that leaves no aspect of the world we live in untouched by its sacredness, and that is in a sense what makes it so totally traditional." See "The Traditional Learning Methodology," *Seeds of Knowledge*, 2000: pp. 1–3.

21. Hakim Archuletta, "The Development of Deen Intensives," *Deen Knowledge*, summer 1999: pp. 1–2.

22. Author unknown, "What Is Traditional Islamic Education?" About SunniPath, 2003–2006, www.sunnipath.com/about/faqs.aspx#4: "This traditional model of education ensures that students have respect for their teacher, their teacher's teachers, and so on all the way back to the Prophet (God bless him and give him peace). Iconoclastic tendencies in the modern Muslim mindset that have filled our homes with disrespect, our mosques with argumentation, and our societies with intolerance are a direct result of our departure from traditional methods of education. Direct aural instruction from a teacher also ensures that sacred knowledge is properly understood and applied: unlike books, teachers bring sacred knowledge to life by interacting with their students and providing living examples that can be emulated."

23. Coburn, "Methodology of Deen-Intensive.".

24. Archuletta, "The Development of Deen Intensives," pp. 1–2.

25. Rihla instructors include Shaykh Hamza Yusuf, Shaykh Jamal Zahabi, Shaykh Abdal Hakim Murad, Imam Zaid Shakir, Shaykh Walead Mossaad, Shaykh J. Hashim Brown, and Shaykh Naeem Abdul Wali.

26. Ibn Rajab al-Hanbali, *Heirs of the Prophets,* trans. Zaid Shakir (Chicago: Starlatch Press, 2001). The book expands upon a hadith of the Prophet: "The scholars are the heirs of the Prophets."

27. Deen Intensive, letter to the author (Rihla Student Welcome Packet), July 1, 2004.

28. Imam Warsh School of Memorization, "Qur'an School" (Hayward, CA), www. zaytuna.org/quranschool.asp, accessed April 5, 2007.

29. Ibid.

30. "About Zaytuna Institute," Zaytuna, www.zaytuna.org/about.asp, accessed April 2, 2007.

31. Ibid.

32. Laura Goodstein, "U.S. Muslim Clerics Seek a Modern Middle Ground," *New York Times,* June 18, 2006.

33. Omar al-Kandari, online survey by the author, survey results, Washington, DC, December 22, 2006.

34. Anonymous respondent, survey by the author, December 2006. (Respondents promised anonymity.)

35. Mariam Sayyid, online survey by the author, survey results, Washington, DC, December 22, 2006.

36. Online survey by the author, survey results, Washington, DC, December 2006.

37. The University of Michigan at Ann Arbor has an old program in Near Eastern studies; it also houses rare Arabic documents from the Muslim world, as well as the Near Eastern Studies Colloquium. Sherman Jackson teaches at this university, which also has one of the largest Muslim student associations in the country.

The University of Chicago has been home to influential Muslim minds like Fazlur Rahman, Umar Faruq Abdallah, Ingrid Mattson, Amina Wadud, Michael Sells, and Shaykh Nuh Keller. It is an important site for higher education in Islamic studies and attracts many Muslim students interested in Ph.D.s in the field. Middlebury College is known for its high-caliber language programs, Arabic included.

38. Yemen hosts many places to study Arabic alone in both "secular" and "traditional" settings, including the Yemen Language Center (www.ylcint.com/) and the Sana Institute for the Arabic Language (www.sialyemen.com/). Shaykh Habib 'Ali Zain al-'Abideen al-Jifri traces his lineage back to the Prophet through 'Ali Zain Al-'Abideen, the son of Imam al-Hussein, the son of Imam 'Ali ibn Abi Talib and the Sayyidah Fatimah, the daughter of the Messenger of Allah (pbuh). He has collected *ijazas* from well-known scholars with authentic chains of transmission back to the Prophet Muhammad (pbuh). He lectures and travels widely.

Badr Language Institute is located in Tarim, Yemen, and often provides students who wish to study with the Haba'ib a chance to spruce up their Arabic skills, which it is necessary to attain beforehand. Dar al-Mustafa in Hadramawt, Yemen, is for male students seeking a "traditional" Islamic education. Dar al-Zahra is also in Hadramawt, Yemen, but is for female students seeking a "traditional" Islamic education.

39. Abu Nour Islamic Foundation, in Damascus, Syria, is oft frequented by Muslim Americans serious about pursuing Islamic studies in a traditional fashion (www. abunour.net). Imam Zaid Shakir is among those who studied there.

Jamia al-Fath is a center of traditional learning of Islamic sciences in Syria. The University of Damascus is the largest university in Syria and offers introductory Arabic classes for Western students. And CASA is based in both Syria and Egypt and is one of the most well regarded Arabic programs in the Western academy. There is less focus in this program, however, on classical Arabic in favor rather of the modern standard (www.utexas.edu/cola/centers/casa).

Various institutes exist in Syria to serve the needs of Arabic students who are looking for training in classical rather than modern Arabic, the difference mainly being in what texts they use to learn from. Some examples include Dalalah Institute and the Institut Français d'Etudes Arabes de Damas. Female students have the option of studying with the Qubaysiyya, a female tariqa that teaches women how to read Qur'an properly, jurisprudence, and Qur'an memorization, among other things. Private tutoring is also an option for all and relatively cheaper in Syria.

Munira al Qubaysi initiated a female tariqa, a Naqshbandiyya offshoot, which is called the Qubaysiyya after her. It is an active network of female adherents in Syria and regularly targets the daughters of the influential, thus yielding considerable social capital in the region. See Olivier Roy, *Globalized Islam: The Search for a New* Ummah (New York: Cambridge University Press, 2004).

40. Murabit al Hajj is a well-respected Muslim scholar who resides in the harsh village areas of Mauritania. He works to preserve the "traditional" way of acquiring knowledge of Islam and is a sought-after teacher by Muslim Americans, especially because Shaykh Hamza Yusuf was once his student.

Dar al Ulum is translated as "House of Sciences" (usually referring to religious sciences). The term is used to refer to a seminary. *Turuq* is the plural of *tariqa*, a Sufi order.

41. The Arabic Language Institute in Fez is frequented by both Muslims and non-Muslims interested in Arabic language in Morocco. Al Akhawayn University is located in Ifrane, Morocco, and offers Arabic studies to Westerners (www.aui.ma/).

42. Fajr Center also caters to Muslim American students studying Arabic abroad in addition to centers named Iqra, Qordoba, and the Nile. Diwan Center has been an institute used for studies in the Arabic language by the likes of Imam Suhaib Webb as well as other Muslim American students studying abroad for the purposes of Islamic studies vis-à-vis the Arabic language.

43. Aasil Ahmed, e-mail message to the author, March 25, 2007. See also Roy, *Globalized Islam*.

44. Anonymous respondent, survey by the author, December 2006. (Respondents promised anonymity.)

45. Shaikh Nuh Ha Mim Keller is an American Muslim translator and Islamic law specialist. He has studied traditionally in Syria and Jordan as well at the University of Chicago and the University of California at Los Angeles. He leads many followers as a sheikh of the Shadhili Tariqa. He is currently based in Amman, Jordan.

46. SunniPath, http://sunnipath.com, accessed April 5, 2007.

47. Huda Deyaf, e-mail message to the author, December 31, 2006.

48. Anonymous respondent, survey by the author, December 2006. (Respondents promised anonymity.)

49. Ali Eteraz, "States of Islam," http://eteraz.org, accessed May 16, 2007.

50. Al-Azhar was among the most prestigious sites of Muslim learning; it is known as the second-oldest university in the world. The University of Al Karaouine is thought to be the world's oldest learning institute, founded in Fes, Morocco, in 859.

51. *Ahl us sunnah wal jammah,* "the people of the Sunnah and the (scholarly) consensus," is regarded as the way of the Muslim orthodox.

52. Yusuf, "Who Are the Rightly Guided Scholars?"

53. Anonymous respondent, survey by the author, December 2006. (Respondents promised anonymity.)

7

Screening Faith, Making Muslims: Islamic Media for Muslim American Children and the Politics of Identity Construction

Yasmin Moll

Muslim diasporas in the West, as with other diasporic communities, have had to grapple with fundamental and complex issues of identity, citizenry, and minority rights on a variety of different levels (the local, the national) and in a variety of different spheres (the social, the economic, the political).[1] The specificity of the Muslim diasporic experience, however, unfolds against a post-9/11 highly charged backdrop of social marginalization, political disenfranchisement, and popular vilification.[2] Examining the contours of this particular experience of "being in the West" as it is articulated, (re)imagined, and constructed through media programs for Muslim American children is the aim of this chapter.

The first Muslim "communities" in the West were composed of mostly immigrant working-class laborers who came in search of economic opportunities and with the idea that they would eventually return to their home countries once they had "made it" financially.[3] As self-perceived and, indeed, expected sojourners, there was little to motivate them to participate in, or deeply interact with, their host society. Even if they had chosen to participate politically or socially in the formal institutions of their host states, they were ill equipped to do so due to their generally low levels of education and lack of fluency in the host language. It was therefore up to the children and grandchildren of these first Muslim immigrants, living in the West by "permanent choice," as it were, to think critically about their place as Muslims in a Western society and attempt to come to terms with that society's dominant institutions, customs, and values. As Muslim communities become increasingly established and organized, and as more immigrants acquire citizenship and their progeny become second-, third-, and fourth-generation "Muslim Westerners" rather than newly arrived immigrants, their power not only to create more space for themselves in the social, political, and economic spheres but also to fundamentally change the nature of that space will grow.

Central to the Muslim experience in the West is the challenge of negotiating between competing and often conflicting identities. The seemingly entrenched secular public ethos of Western liberal democracies poses special problems for those Muslims who view Islam not only as a religion but also as "a way of life" encompassing both spiritual belief and practice and also social, economic, and political concerns.[4] Muslims in the West have formulated differing responses to this challenge. Some have chosen to simply ignore it, assimilating completely into the hegemonic culture of public (albeit in some countries such as the United States, distinctly Christian) secularism. Others have retreated into virtual Islamic ghettos, living as if the rest of society simply did not exist—or if it did, it existed only as an example of what not to follow. A significant section of the Muslim community, however, has adopted a midway approach. They seek to publicly affirm their Islamic identity within the Western context and through interaction with it rather than in spite of it, (re)defining and (re)constructing in the process what it means to be "Western" as well as to be Muslim. An important way in which such redefinitions take place is through the production of "Islamic media" in the form of magazines, newsletters, and more recently, videos, audiotapes, DVDs, and CDs.

This chapter addresses the phenomenon of Islamic media production for children in a Western country that has an important Muslim presence—the United States.[5] This phenomenon is symptomatic of the desire on the part of the Muslim community in America to ensure that the coming generations of Muslims do not get lost in the so-called American "melting pot," which strives for the homogenization and assimilation of all minorities and immigrants into the hegemonic culture, as defined and practiced by the white, Christian majority. Analyzing Islamic media production is important, in that it has the potential of shedding added light on the dialectics of identity (re)construction of Muslims in the West and their resistance to pressures to conform or recast that identity within the dominant (and for them, alien) sociocultural modes.

The starting assumption for this study is that identity is not "inherent," "primordial," or "essential" but, rather, "constructed." The social construction-ist approach to identity "rejects any category that sets forward essential or core differences as the unique property of a collective's members" and argues that "every collective [is] a social artefact—an entity remodeled, refabricated and mobilized in accord with reigning cultural scripts and centers of power."[6] Thus, Islamic American media "construct" a sense of Muslim American identity through their choice of which aspects of the Muslim experiences to highlight, which "stories" to tell, and who is allowed to tell them. Throughout this pro-cess, several themes and subthemes are consistently and repeatedly presented and highlighted, leading to the formation of what can be termed a dominant discourse. At the same time, this discourse runs counter to that other, far more dominant and visible discourse on Islam/Muslims, the one most people en-counter daily in the mainstream American (and Western) press and through which runs, as numerous studies have documented, an undercurrent of latent Orientalism.[7] Muslim minority media attempt to deconstruct mainstream dis-course through a construction of their own discursive alternative, in an almost defiant act of "auto-interpretation" or "talking back."[8] If Orientalism is about an other defining the Other for itself, this discourse is about defining the Self, for both itself and others. These media show us how some Muslim Americans see themselves and would like others to see them, thus moving them beyond the subjugation of what Werbner calls "external definition."[9]

Islamic media production for Muslim children in America represents an important factor in the intersubjective process of identity construction and Is-lamic socialization. The pedagogical agenda and intent of these productions seek to build a particular vision of reality and construct a particular Islamic identity (the "right" Islamic identity), leading to the construction of a very styl-ized and exclusive image of the Muslim Community, History, Woman, Family, and Values. Therefore, as Linda Steet puts it in her discussion of the repre-sentation of Arabs in *National Geographic,* it is fundamental to ask what are "the conscious choices made in structures of representation" in order to better understand the underlying motives/ideology of those who generate these struc-tures, since they "constitute versions of reality in ways which depend upon the social positions and interests and objectives of those who produce them."[10]

This study analyzes eight video programs and animated pictures geared to Muslim children between the ages of two and nine that were made approxi-mately within the last decade. The programs are compared and contrasted in an effort to find recurring themes and images as well as pinpoint an underlying hegemonic articulation of Islamic ideals and traditions that is imperative to a particular construction of American Muslim identity.[11]

This chapter addresses the motivations underwriting the production of Islamic media as well as their substantive content. In addition, the underlying tensions found in these productions between the different "concentric" circles of identity that Muslims in America occupy (Texan-American-Pakistan-Sunni-Muslim, for example) as well the tensions between the different worlds (views) they have to negotiate on a daily basis (Islamic versus Western) are addressed.[12]

Making TV "Halal": American Television and Muslim Discontents

Muslims, like many Americans, worry about the effects the daily consumption of television has on their children and families.[13] However, while most secular critics of television merely want to "clean up" TV by removing offensive sexual and violent scenes or ensuring that such scenes are not aired at a time when children are likely to be watching, "the perceived moral laxity [of American culture] has promoted many Muslim parents to search for alternative schoolings and social activities for their children."[14] One of these alternatives is creating a type of "Islamized" television, whereby media is produced *by* Muslims *for* Muslims and given an explicit Islamic content.[15]

There are two primary motivations for this "Islamization" impetus. First, some Muslim parents have a very real fear that their children, through the influence of daily interaction with non-Muslim peers and through the influence of the secular Western education they receive in public schools, will grow up to either reject Islam or be ignorant of Islamic values.[16] Thus, they see Islamic media as a way of providing children a fun and educational Muslim alternative to the (non-Muslim) fun they have with their friends and the (non-Muslim) education they receive in school. Jawad Jafry, the director of the successful *Adam's World* series, which features Adam the Muslim Muppet, expressed this view in an interview: "In a small way, I hope that shows like Adam's World can create a much more wholesome experience for children. If an Islamic children's series can become a viable alternative, then we will have played an important role in laying a better foundation."[17] Thus, Islamic media productions appropriate Western technologies of representation to mount a critique of the West as part of the drive for self-empowerment and the strengthening of identity discourses.

Furthermore, in addition to the motivation of counteracting the assimilating tendencies of mainstream television through its reflection of the hegemonic culture and norms, Muslims have a second motive for supporting

Islamic media production that is intimately linked to the way Muslims *specifically* have been depicted in mainstream American popular culture. Jack Shaheen's meticulous documentation of the image of Arabs and Muslims in American popular culture through the media of television, film, books, and the press shows how these minority groups are projected as an alien "Other," embodying negative characteristics such as unfettered violence, antidemocratism, and irrational hatred.[18] Indeed, the TV serials he surveyed "show all Arabs, Muslims, and Arab-Americans as being at war with the United States."[19] If we take the United States as normatively embodying the ideals of democracy, liberty, and peace for Americans, this means that Arabs and Muslims are at war with these ideals and therefore condone tyranny and violence. In other words, "Hollywood's Arab Muslims...threaten our freedom, economy and culture."[20] These findings demonstrate how Orientalism (in Edward Said's sense) is still very much alive in Western popular and mediated imaginaries and how the space for "alternative" viewpoints on Muslims/Islam within the mainstream media is small to the point of being inconsequential. Muslim Americans thus aim to create their own alternative spaces through the establishment of alternative media.

Shaheen's focus on images in the (mass) media is not arbitrary. He recognized that "by influencing public norms, perceptions, expectations, hopes, fears, desires and angst about diversity, the mass media play a powerful role in the social construction of knowledge about race, ethnicity, religion, gender, culture, sexual orientation and other aspects of diversity."[21] Members of minority groups are particularly susceptible to this media power of knowledge construction. Indeed, children from minority and low socioeconomic backgrounds are more prone than white, middle-class children to having their conceptions of reality shaped by the small screen, as they are more likely to believe that the world portrayed on television faithfully mirrors the "real" world.[22] This is because U.S. television presents a predominately Anglo-Saxon and middle-class world, and "portrayals of a social milieu unlike the child's own...[will] have greater power to shape the child's view of that milieu."[23] Muslims as a minority are therefore understandably justified in being sensitive to the potential effects negative representations of Islam (with a simultaneous positive representation of other religions/groups) could have on the self-perception of their children.

In a general study conducted on the effects of the media on social behavior in children, it became clear that members of racial minorities are projected as poor and powerless by U.S. television, leading to these images becoming "internalized" by children belonging to all ethnic groups.[24] However, another study has shown that television also can be used to counteract these very tendencies. For example, research done on *Sesame Street*, a popular educational television show for young children that presents minority groups in a "nonstereotyped" fashion, demonstrated that minority children who viewed the show gained markedly in terms of self-esteem and ethnic/cultural pride.[25]

The Islamic media productions take on the aims of shows such as *Sesame Street* but with a very specific target audience in mind—Muslim children. Since even "positive" mainstream educational programs such as *Sesame Street* typically do not feature Muslim characters, Islamic media thus fills an important representational gap. It speaks to the concerns of one Mexican American media researcher who asked: "Where, I wondered, was someone on TV who looked like me? Where were my family and friends?...Who were Cinderella and Snow White to me? I liked them, but they didn't look like the folks I knew."[26] The promotional blurb accompanying an *Adam's World* episode states that "children's audiences of this video will see other Muslim kids in action, doing Islamic things like praying, reading Qur'an, etc." In this way, Islamic media seeks to instill pride in Muslim children in their Islamic identity, with the aim of transforming identity from a potential source of embarrassment to a source of empowerment.

Dominant Themes in Islamic Children's Media

A close analysis of a sampling of Islamic media productions reveals several recurring themes, from the diversity/unity of Muslims to the greatness of an Islamic past to the importance of the family. These themes are never explicitly presented as such—the categorizations are my own. These themes were articulated in the majority of videos I watched, with secondary themes woven around them. It is important to note that the boundaries between these themes are quite porous, allowing them to reinforce one another.

Muslim "Melting Pot" or Muslim "Salad Bowl"?

According to the producers of *Adam's World,* the children featured in the series represent over 40 different ethnicities. There is an effort to present an outward, "physical" diversity in each episode, which features children who "look" South Asian, Arab, East Asian, or African American.[27] The ethnically diverse Muslims portrayed in these productions are a direct reflection of the diversity of the Muslim community in America. Muslim immigrants in America come from a myriad of different countries and regions.[28] The existence of such diversity within the Muslim community challenges Muslims "to attempt to build the bridges within the Muslim communities necessary to spare the Muslim

Americans the racial divides that presently split the other Abrahamic religions into multiple ethnic/racial islands."[29] Islamic media attempt to do just that by featuring Muslim children who, despite their differing origins, all play, pray, and have adventures happily together. This is well illustrated in the *Muslim Scouts* series, which shows a close band of four young Muslim boys of varying ethnicities who go around the (Muslim) world "fighting injustice."

The theme of the diversity/unity of the American Muslim community is carried over in representations of the larger Islamic *ummah*. In *Adam's World,* there is a recurring segment in each episode where Adam travels with the aid of a "transvisualizer" (a nifty space-age travel machine taken from the *Star Trek* series) to different Muslim countries such as Turkey, Egypt, Jordan, and Malaysia. Adam then proceeds to showcase the food, history, customs, and language of these countries. However, what is always stressed is the fact that despite cultural, historical, or linguistic variations, the inhabitants of these countries are all Muslim and that is what counts—in fact, that is all that needs to be retained and nothing else. For example, when talking about architecture in Muslim countries, it is always the mosques that are featured, and more "secular" buildings such as palaces, bridges, or national monuments and so on are ignored. This highlights for the children viewers that the single most important common denominator is religion/Islam. The same theme is also found in the *Muslim Scouts* series, which, as I noted earlier, features a group of American Muslim Boy Scouts who travel to Turkey, Egypt, and several countries in sub-Saharan Africa doing "good works" in the hope of earning the "ummah badge." In their travels, they meet other young Muslim boys from various countries, all speaking with different accents and possessing different physical characteristics. The films, however, repeatedly show these young boys engaging in communal prayer, where they become virtually indistinguishable from each other. Again the message is that we are all Muslims who believe in the same things. Indeed, a song of the series goes: "Muslims are never far apart / We are always together in the heart."

By portraying the American Muslim characters as part of a larger global ummah, these productions construct a Muslim identity that is internationally collectivized. This leads to the concerns of Muslims abroad becoming the concerns of Muslims at home, in America, illustrating the Prophetic saying that "the ummah is one body, if one part is ill the whole body feels it."[30] An interesting segment in an *Adam's World* episode entitled "Take Me to the Kaaba" shows a picture of Al-Aqsa mosque in occupied East Jerusalem being surrounded by Israeli soldiers. The narrator says: "We hope one day Muslims will be able to go there." Although he never explains why most Muslims are not able to go there now, the implied message is that the situation of Islamic holy sites in Jerusalem concerns all Muslims, not just Palestinian Muslims. Concern for the fate of all

Muslims collectively is also expressed in other productions. For example, in *Muslim Scouts,* one of the scouts says: "The ummah was once strong. Inshallah it will be strong again."

A Glorious Past

The glory of Islamic history and civilization is another dominant theme in Islamic media production. One animated film, *Sultan Muhammad II: Fatih,* is entirely devoted to this theme. The film tells the story of the Islamic conquest/liberation of Constantinople in 1453 by the Ottoman sultan Muhammad II. This event is important in both Muslim and Western popular imagination, with some Muslims viewing it as one of the crowning achievements of Muslim leaders and the West viewing it as an example of an Islamic menace seeking to subjugate Christendom.[31] The film stresses that while the Muslims were technologically superior to the Byzantines, the reason behind their successful conquest of Constantinople is not military might alone but also the fact that God was on their side. In a particularly dramatic scene, the Ottoman army is seen rushing to the gates of Constantinople to the cries of "Allahu Akbar" as the Qur'an is recited in the background. The film ends with the sultan renaming Constantinople "Islambul, city of Islam, where science, art, religion, and scholarship flourished."

Muslims often feel marginalized in the American educational curriculum, which in their opinion does not give enough (or even accurate) attention to Islamic history. In fact, "Muslim children in public schools across America are educated to believe they have no place in the scope of world history and that Islam has made no significant contributions to world history."[32] In the first volume of the *Muslim Scouts* series, the Muslim American Boy Scouts are given a tour of Al-Azhar University in Cairo and told about its role in producing some of the greatest scholars of history. The boys are astonished, and one of them sighs, "I wish I learned some Muslim history in school," underlining the feelings of Muslims about American education. In a way, these media productions are seeking to fill that gap by making animated films for children about Muslim history for educational consumption. This is intimately related to the role these media play in identity construction. By producing films that show historic Muslim "heroes" or by highlighting past Muslim scholarship, these media are giving Muslim children a valorized conception of the role their "ancestors" or fellow Muslims played in world history. This promotes a positive conception of the self by association. For example, in an episode of *Adam's World,* the narrator tells us: "Almost 1,000 years ago, Muslim scientists studied the fossils of sea creatures...so whenever you see an old animal, remember, Muslims studied them a long time ago." Yet another episode describes Muslim Spain (Andalusia) as "a leader in sciences, math, arts, hadith, and many other things." In a way, this is telling Muslim children to remember that Muslims are, well, smart too. The need to make such an assertion can be understood in light of modern-day scientific achievements of the West and the near monopoly on scientific innovation and knowledge production the West enjoys; its superiority in these areas puts Muslims on the defensive, causing them to assert that they too once contributed to knowledge production and that they still can.

Sacred Messages

God is very much a central and prominent actor in Islamic media productions for children. In fact, it would not be inaccurate to say that He is the unrepresented (and unrepresentable) ultimate hero of these productions. A useful way of analyzing the role God plays in these productions is to see which attributes of God are stressed and why. In *Salam's Journey*, an animated film inspired by *Surat Al Feel* in the Qur'an, a young Muslim boy, Salam, finds himself in several rather precarious situations. In each situation, he puts his faith in God, saying, "Ya Allah, please help," and God does not let him down. The story of Salam is juxtaposed against the story of the people of Mecca who put their faith in God to defeat the army of Abraha, an evil king bent on destroying the Kaaba. Clearly, the God of *Salam's Journey* is a Protector, a Being who will not let down His believing and faithful creatures. This film thus stresses the Islamic worldview in which man is in no way self-sufficient but, in fact, is in need of divine help to be successful. This worldview is also expressed in *Muslim Scouts*, where their motto is "put your trust in Allah and do your best." In one scene, one of the scouts saves another from the hands of poachers who were going to leave him in the jungle to be eaten by wild animals. The scout saved is not appropriately grateful, leading his savior to exclaim, "Doesn't he mean to say, 'Thank you for saving my life'?!" At this point, their Muslim mentor interrupts, admonishing firmly, "Don't say that! Only Allah saves!"

In two different episodes of *Adam's World*, "Happy to Be a Muslim" and "The Humble Muslim," the stress is on God the Creator. Children sing, "The world is so beautiful / Who could have made it except for Allah?" and, "Look around you and you will see all of the beautiful creatures / Nothing is greater than Allah, Lord of the Universe / That is why Muslims say, 'Allahu Akbar.'" These theological views are expressed while teaching children something about nature. Thus, while the viewers learn several important facts about, say, the ocean, what is ultimately stressed is how this is God's creation and a living testimony to His existence and wonder. For some Muslims this stress is imperative, given that, for them, "the most serious conflict between the secular and the Islamic curriculum is that the secular curriculum is not God centered...knowledge in the Islamic worldview is based on the realization that God created everything."[33] These media serve to contrast implicitly the God-centered Islamic worldview with the Man (or Self)-centered Western worldview through their constant allusions to the divine. For example, animated films/programs for children typically feature a hero who has to overcome some sort of obstacle and usually does so through a process of self-will and self-confidence, where the mantra is "I can do this if I believe in myself." In Muslim programs, however, the obstacle is overcome through the help/mercy of God, and the mantra is "I can do this if I believe God will help me."

The Prophet also figures prominently in Islamic media, and his Sunnah (praxis) is frequently alluded to. He is described in one *Adam's World* episode as "the most successful person in the world," and various behaviors are applauded by showing that they conform to the behavior of the Prophet. Adam the Muslim Muppet is far from being perfect. He has many faults, such as being forgetful, a procrastinator, and short-tempered. He always manages to correct these faults, however, by remembering the Prophet and asking himself whether or not the Prophet would approve of his behavior. Thus, when Adam talks about the need for people to have *sabr*, or patience, he does so by quoting a hadith (Prophetic saying) that shows that the Prophet valued patience. In this manner, it becomes evident that the real hero of the show is not Adam but, rather, the Prophet himself. Adam acts as the connection for children to the Prophet, a mechanism for making the Prophet relevant to their lives and eminently approachable as a role model.

In sum, Islamic media construct two essential aspects of Muslim identity: *taqwa* (God-consciousness) and a high regard for the Prophetic example. This fosters a sense of religiosity in Muslim children and makes religion *the* defining pillar of their identity, privileging it over and against other possible referents.

The Muslim Family

In all of the animated films and programs I viewed, without exception, either women play no role at all in them (meaning they are not physically present) or, if they are given a role, it is secondary and supporting. They are not the "heroes" who save the day. In fact, all of the protagonists of these films (from Adam the Muslim Muppet, to the Muslim Boy Scouts, to Salam, to Sultan Muhammad) are males.[34] Only one episode of *Adam's World* speaks explicitly of women, and it does so in the context of a Prophetic hadith, which says that "Paradise lies at the mother's feet." The episode then goes on to show various snapshots (or, in the popular jargon, "Kodak moments") of mothers with their children. By legitimating or allowing their presence only in their function as mothers and by giving them value and voice only in relation to that function, women are effectively marginalized and instrumentalized in these productions. This is indicative of the place of women within the traditional patriarchal family.

This carries over to the reality of some sections of the Muslim community, where women's roles are largely functionally defined in relation to men and within a familial context, meaning women are seen as mothers, sisters, or wives. This is especially true for the first generation of immigrants, who brought with them the conservative, parochial notions of their home countries regarding what it means to be a woman in society.[35] In this conceptualization, women are given the responsibility of upholding Islamic values through their upbringing of children according to "the straight path," thus collapsing the constructs of womanhood, religious piety, and child rearing. The domestic space becomes the space of woman par excellence. This sexual division of labor is perhaps best illustrated by recalling a scene from *Salam's Journey* that depicts Abu Salam working in the field while Umm Salam prepares his dinner. The closing credits of an episode of *Adam's World* recommend a work by Abou 'Alaa Maududi, the founder of Jamat-i-Islami, a Pakistani Islamic revivalist movement that has a strong following in the United States.[36] Maududi holds rather conservative views on the societal role of women. For example, he writes that "the real task of women is to look after the family."[37] This means first and foremost to "create an Islamic atmosphere in your homes in such a way that your children can see a living vision of Islam and assimilate it by direct experience...children should be acquainted with the message of Allah's unity and the meaning of prayer and their lives saturated by Islam."[38]

Within this discourse the "living vision of Islam" finds a manifestation in the hijab, or Muslim head scarf. When women (and most of the prepubescent girls) are shown in these productions they are portrayed wearing the hijab. There is a consensus among Muslim scholars (with a few important, mostly feminine, voices of dissent) that the hijab is not just permissible (and thus in the realm of personal choice) but obligatory.[39] However, while the majority of Muslim women would in fact agree with this consensus in principle, a substantial number of them still choose not to wear the hijab for various reasons.[40] These unveiled women have no place, however, in Islamic children's media. These productions construct an image of the Muslim woman that takes as a necessary ingredient that she be a *hijabi/mohajaba*.[41] This construction is idealized and artificial to the extent that it finds no problem in directly contradicting (or ignoring) reality. For example, in the first volume of the *Muslim Scouts* series, there is a scene on an EgyptAir flight that features a veiled air stewardess, even though EgyptAir does not employ veiled women to serve on board its carriers.

The veil has become a politically charged and symbolically loaded article of clothing in the West, regardless of the intention of its wearers. In the Western popular imaginary it is often seen as an instrument of male oppression and dominance and a potent symbol of the alleged antimodernism of Islam.[42] The hostile reactions of Westerners to the veil take it out of the domain of personal choice/belief and firmly place it in the domain of public opinion and therefore subject to public judgment/action. In this way, "taking off the headscarf was seen as a sign of integration, whereas wearing the scarf was a sign that integration was somehow being hampered."[43] However, for the Muslim producers of Islamic media, having the veil figure prominently in their productions could perhaps be legitimately construed as a sign of resistance to these pressures to integrate and a message to children to regard their veiled mothers, sisters, friends, and so on as embodying the "norm." Nevertheless, the multiple referents the veil represents for different Muslim women are not highlighted in these media, but the "meaning" of the veil is glossed over as an inherent part of a projected feminine Muslim identity that is limited to the (feminized) domestic sphere.[44]

This domestic sphere through its metonym the family is a recurring image in Islamic media production. Families (consisting usually of a mother, father, and one male child) are depicted doing "Muslim" things together like going to the mosque or praying at home.[45] The productions stress respect and obedience to parents as proper Islamic behavior. Indeed, for some Muslims "the strong assertion in the Oneness of God and His Worship is linked, as one of its inherent conditions, with respect for and good behavior towards one's parents...to obey one's parents, to be good to them, is the best way to be good with God."[46] This idea is underlined in an almost comical way in *Salam's Journey*. In one scene, the kidnapped Salam wants to leave to find his pet elephant, knowing that this will make his parents search to find him more difficult. However, an elderly Bedouin admonishes him that "your duty is to your parents first," not to your pet.

In addition, the productions stress parents as a source of wisdom and guidance for children. In *Salam's Journey*, Salam tells us that "my father taught me that Allah will look after me and I trust him." This is in keeping with the attitude prevalent or evident in the Muslim discussion of the vital role the family plays in forming loyalty and adherence to Islam among children, by leading through example, providing an "Islamic environment" at home, and socializing children into Islamic norms and values.[47] The family is consequently seen as the last bastion of hope for providing Muslim children with a firm grounding in Islamic teachings. On an Islamic Web page, a Muslim American writer makes the argument that "we as responsible parents need to ensure that our children do not absorb un-Islamic practices" through viewing television since "all children's programs produced by non-Muslims will contain elements which may not be acceptable to Islamic teachings."[48] By incorporating the family in its story lines, Muslim media productions for children are hoping to instill in children from an early age a respect for their parents and thus by extension a respect for the Muslim identity these parents represent and in some cases openly advocate.

Heroes and Villains

The declared aim of all of these productions is to teach children in a creative and engaging way "Islamic values" while promoting a positive image of Muslims.[49] It is therefore essential to take a closer look at what values are advanced by these programs, how they figure in the construction of a "positive" Muslim identity for children, and what they are contrasted against. The values preached on the animated films and shows could in fact be on any mainstream educational program such as Sesame Street. The admonishments to children to be clean, kind, patient, helpful, generous, and so forth are not original or specific to Islamic media. However, what is original is the fact that these admonishments are Islamized, where they are presented as being integral to being a "good Muslim," not just a "good kid." Values are rationalized Islamically. For example, in Muslim Scouts in Africa, children are told to not abuse nature and animals because "animals are Muslims too...let's watch what we do to the creation of Islam." The narrator goes on to say that a spider once helped the Prophet and Abu Bakr (the first caliph and companion of the Prophet) "be safe." This Islamization of values is essential to providing Muslim children with an Islamic, rather than secular, rationalization for why certain values/behaviors are good and others are not. The aim is to teach children values that emphasize their religious underpinnings, thereby consolidating a religious identity.

Intimately connected to the Islamization of values is the construction of a binary opposition between the Muslim Self and the non-Muslim Other in Islamic media productions as a way of creating a Muslim identity for children. The existence of an "Other" seems to be necessary in the process of self-identification, where, as Edward Said puts it, "the construction of identity... involves the construction of opposites."[50] While Said was concerned with representations and inventions of the "Orient" by Westerners, this discourse of "otherness" can also be applied to how the Muslim world (and even the Muslim community in the West) views the West. As Abubaker Al-Shingiety makes clear, "[T]he otherness of Islam and Muslims has two functions. It acts as a dynamic of identification, by default, for the American. At the same time it is appropriated by the Muslim as a form of self-identification."[51]

An interesting example of binary oppositions at work is found in *Sultan Muhammad II: Fatih*. The film paints two diametrically opposing images of the Muslims and the Byzantines/Christians. On one hand, we have the Byzantine emperor Constantine II and his minions portrayed as effeminate (the emperor sports earrings, is facially hairless, and is seen filing his nails), corrupt, and unjust. On the other hand, Sultan Muhammad is the epitome of masculinity (he possesses a muscular build, sports a thick beard, and is seen laying down stones to build a fortress) and has an uncompromising integrity and irreproachable sense of justice. These laudable qualities of the sultan are portrayed to stem directly from his faith in Islam and belief in God (in his own words: "our justice comes from our faith in Islam"). This "villainization" of non-Muslims is evident in other productions as well.

To take another example, the *Muslim Scouts* series features the American Muslim Boy Scouts combating various "evildoers," be they terrorists, thieves, or poachers. Aside from their engagement in illegal activities, what these bad guys all have in common is that they are not Muslim. Not only are they not Muslim, but their behavior is portrayed as being inherently un-Islamic. They engage in activities Muslims in this series simply would not do *because they are Muslim,* and indeed, Muslims actively try to stop them. By doing this, the Muslim scouts are following the Quranic injunction to "enjoin right conduct and forbid indecency."[52] This same idea is picked up in the *Adam's World* series, where the un-Islamic behavior practiced by non-Muslim gamblers, superstars, or unclean persons is explained by the various Muslim adult guests that appear on the show as being wrong and as therefore something Muslims would not/should not do. For example, the aptly named episode "The Humble Muslim" shows Adam becoming a little too arrogant when he thinks he has a fan club. In acting out his "delusions of grandeur" he sheds his skullcap and *jalabiya* in favor of a Beatles hairstyle and an Elvis-inspired shirt. In sum, when Adam stops acting like a Muslim (i.e., stops being humble), he stops looking like one too. Perhaps a quote from *Salam's Journey* best captures the very explicit normative meanings attached to being Muslim (being good) and being non-Muslim (being bad). Salam asks a stranger, "How do I know you won't hurt me [like the evil, non-Muslim pirates did]?" The man simply answers: "I believe in Allah."[53]

By presenting Islam as providing all the cures to the social problems engendered by Western culture and lifestyle, the role of Muslims in the West is valorized and imbued with new meaning/symbolism by these media.[54] Far from being mere economic migrants or a numerically insignificant minority, they are the new prophets of the West. As Al-Faruqi puts it, "[T]he Islamic vision provides the immigrant with the criterion with which to understand, judge and seek to transform the unfortunate realities of North America."[55] The Muslim immigrant or citizen need no longer look to the economically and technologically superior West for acceptance and approval but can instead stand in judgment of it. It is the Muslim who defines the West, not the reverse. In this there is much power—the power to name, define, judge, and ultimately enjoin specific actions; as Edward Said puts it, "[T]o have knowledge of such a thing is to dominate it, to have authority over it."[56] According to this discourse, then, Muslims in the West are refusing to "privatize" their religion by making it irrelevant to public life and relegating it to the ultimately rather confined parameters of the individual conscience. This would seem to be a counterexample to Cesari's assertion that "new forms of religiosity" are emerging among Western Muslims that are "characterized by individualism, secularism and privatization."[57]

Tensions between Overlapping Identities

It is clear that there are underlying tensions between Islamic identity and Western culture and between the different types of ethnic "Muslim" cultures in America. As one author attending a 1991 Islamic Society of North America meeting summarized: "One of the most frequently raised issues was that of ethnic divisions and their threat to Muslim unity and therefore to the mission of spreading Islam in North America. But an even greater fear was of assimilation into a non-Muslim melting pot and a consequent loss of identity and values. Muslims are asking how they are going to be able to retain their valued ethnic and cultural heritage, while developing a strong Muslim environment that will protect them from the perceived destructive and immoral aspects of the dominant secular culture of North American life."[58] These tensions illustrate the difficulty of constructing a coherent and universal Muslim identity in a context that is as pluralistic and complex as the United States. These tensions also reveal that Muslim identity in the West is a work in progress, a construction that has yet to be completed and is in a constant state of being and becoming. A central question in this dialectic is whether Muslims are "members of the *umma* whose orders they are completely bound by or rather true citizens of the state in which they live, bound, as all other citizens, by its constitution and laws? What are they first: Muslim or British, French, German or Spanish?"[59]

The responses of Muslims in the West to their minority status and their engagements with the majority culture have been varied and are in constant flux, making any neat categorizations an exercise in futility. For the sake of analysis, however, one can demarcate three idealized approaches. The first approach is that of complete assimilation by the Muslim minority into the dominant culture, whereby the two become virtually indistinguishable, leading to what Ramadan characterizes as a "European Muslim without Islam."[60] At the other extreme, one finds an isolationist approach, where contact with wider society is kept to a bare minimum in an effort to keep "authentic" identities "untainted." Muslims who follow this approach argue that developing deep ties to Western society will only serve to "pollute" their community with values and ideas that directly contradict their own sense of who they are (including culture and religion, of course).[61] Somewhere between these two approaches (or perhaps, more accurately, beyond them), there is a trend among Muslim communities that stresses the retention of a visibly Islamic identity while at the same time positioning that identity within a Western frame of reference. This approach presumably leads to an "original" Muslim identity that is neither a rejectionist reaction against its Western context nor an uncritically wholesale embracement of it.[62]

It is not unambiguously clear where Islamic media productions would place themselves, or should be located by others, within this continuum. At times, they seem closer to the isolationist position, in that they seek to develop an Islamic media "enclave" for children via communication technology in an effort to protect their Muslim identity from being influenced by "un-Islamic" Western values and culture. I would argue that the animated films *Salam's Journey* and *Sultan Muhammad II: Fatih* and even the *Adam's World* series are isolationist in outlook.[63] Nowhere in these films do we find a "synthesis" of Islamic and Western cultures. Rather, what we see is traditional, historical, and ritualistic Islam being simplified and presented to Muslim children born in America. The only Western aspect of this is the fact that the presentation is in English. In some cases, these productions take an explicit stance by highlighting the difficulty of being Muslim in a non-Muslim society. In the very first *Adam's World* episode, "Let's Pray," a segment is filmed in an Islamic school classroom of girls (all veiled, including the teacher) where the students express the difficulty of performing *salat* or prayer during school time. One of them complains: "I go to public school, so I have classes during Friday prayer; what should I do? I feel bad not being able to pray." One of her classmates readily responds: "You should go to Muslim school, where we can all pray." The teacher reinforces this comment authoritatively: "In a non-Muslim society, it is difficult for Muslim children to offer *jummah* [Friday] prayer." She adds that the child should ask the school administrators to allow her to pray during school time, reminding her that "we pray to please Allah, not people." Thus, these media would seem to agree with Maududi, who felt that "Westernization threatened the very identity, independence and way of life of Muslims."[64]

In other cases, however, Islamic media seem to adopt a more midway course, in that the Western background of the children is not ignored but, rather, incorporated into the media. The clearest example of this is the *Muslim Scouts* series, which takes a thoroughly American social institution for young boys, the Boy Scouts, and grafts it with an Islamic identity. It is an example of those Muslims "who want to maintain [their] group identity based on religion but also want to give full allegiance to society."[65] The first volume of *Muslim Scouts* features the Muslim American scouts away at camp with other Muslim scouts from different parts of the world. The boys sit in a circle and introduce themselves variously as Ahmed from Kuwait, Mohamed from Palestine, and so on. When it is the turn of the American Muslim scouts they introduce themselves as Zakaria Al-Kadi from Los Angeles, Faisal Mohieddin from Texas, and Jamal Abdullah from New York. Clearly the film aims to stress the American birthplaces of these young Muslims rather than their ethnic/national origin, which is never alluded to throughout the series. Later in the film, the scouts take a boat trip in the Sea of Marmara in Istanbul and are told by a Turkish guide about a campaign under way to "clean it up." Immediately one of the boys says, "We should do something like that and clean up Central Park." Thus, the boys are portrayed thinking about what they as Muslims can do to help *their* country, the United States. At the same time, while stressing the American context of the target audience, the series also attempts to draw linkages to the wider Islamic ummah by showing the boys traveling to different Muslim countries and working with scouts to "make a difference," as they put it. In a way such Islamic media are aiming to build safe, "sanitized" bridges between Islamic and Western cultures so that Muslim minority children are not assimilated or conversely alienated.

While differences between Muslims and non-Muslims are emphasized, differences *within* the Muslim community are de-emphasized in Islamic media. Muslims are very aware of the heterogeneity of their coreligionists in America and in some cases view it as a source of weakness. As one author writes, "[S]ome Muslims find the development of the ethnic mosque an objectionable and unhealthy development, part of the Americanization process which has historically divided the various immigrants into their constituent parts."[66] Muslim organizations such as the Islamic Society of North America and Islamic Circle of North America (ICNA) were formed in part to counter this ethnicization by seeking to "bring together much more ethnically diverse groups of Muslims for common action and mutual strengthening."[67] It is telling to note that ICNA is one of the main collaborators in Islamic media, helping to produce *Adam's World*. Its mission to bring together diverse Muslims is seen in the series, where ethnic affiliations are never explicitly mentioned (except in relation to Muslims *outside* of the United States) and where Muslims are presented as being just that—Muslims and nothing else. This is done primarily through an emphasis on the common *ibada*, worship of Muslims, the five pillars of Islam to which all Muslims universally adhere. In one episode Adam confides that he likes going to the mosque "because it makes me feel like a part of something so many others share." As Tariq Ramadan notes, "Islamic worship has a double dimension, individual and collective. In striving to attain excellence in the practise of their religion, Muslims are immediately called upon to face the community dimension of the Islamic way of life."[68] Other Islamic media productions also ignore ethnicity. The ethnicity of the four boys of *Muslim Scouts* is never discussed, and even Salam in *Salam's Journey* does not self-identify with any ethnicity.

The world of Adam the Muslim Muppet and others may seem to be an ethnic-free zone; however, the reality is not so uncomplicated. As one author puts it, "Muslims have always held up a unified *umma* as their ideal. But this is easier to do when individual Muslim societies stay put in their national and ethnic regions. When significant populations are set in motion, as is happening with large-scale migration, Muslims come face to face with their actual differences beneath the transcending levels of creed, cults and romantic myth."[69] Other Muslims, however, have expressed a more idealistic outlook, arguing that "American Islam is a purer form of Islam than is practiced in some Islamic countries, because of the absence of cultural amplifications."[70] Whatever the case may be, religion within this discourse emerges as the most salient marker of identity over and against the vast plurality of identities that a contemporary Muslim in America could potentially hold and choose from (for example, Punjabi, Pakistani, South Asian, or American as well as any combination of these together).

Conclusion

This chapter has attempted to highlight and interrogate a particular construction of Muslim American identity through Islamic children's media. Missing here is a plethora of identities constructed by other media that do not subscribe to this representation of Muslim Americans and might flatly and explicitly contradict it. Thus, the discursive identity presented in this study cannot be said to have achieved any degree of hegemony over Muslim American consciousness(es). Nevertheless, a close analysis of these productions is still important, in that it leads to insights into how these Islamic media privilege some components of this identity over others, some members of this identity over others, and some articulations of this identity over others. This leads to an exclusive representation and definition of what it means to be a Muslim. For while an individual in the modern world is capable of simultaneously possessing multiple identities and allegiances, at the same time the process of identity construction necessarily draws "boundaries," determining what constitutes a Muslim community and who is allowed to be a member of it.[71]

NOTES

1. The exact number of the Muslim population in both Europe and North America is not known. Most estimates put the number of Muslims living in America between four and six million. See Asma Hassan, *American Muslims* (New York: Continuum International Publishing Group, 2002), p. 183.

2. For a comprehensive discussion on the challenges faced by Muslims living in the West, see Yvonne Haddad, ed., *Muslims in the West: From Sojourners to Citizens* (New York: Oxford University Press, 2002).

3. Steven Vertovec, "Islamophobia and Muslim Recognition in Britain," in Haddad, *Muslims in the West*, p. 20.

4. Jessica Jacobson, *Islam in Transition: Religion and Identity among British Pakistani Youth* (London: Routledge, 1998), p. 104.

5. Haddad, *Muslims in the West*.

6. Karen Cerulo, "Identity Construction: New Issues, New Directions," *Annual Review of Sociology* 23 (1997), pp. 385–409. See p. 387.

7. For a recent excellent study of this in the British context, see Elizabeth Poole, *Reporting Islam: Media Representations of British Muslims* (London: I. B. Tauris, 2002). Orientalism is understood here as Edward Said defined it: "a style of thought based upon ontological and epistemological distinction made between 'the Orient' and (most of the time) 'the Occident.'" This style of thought reiterates several tropes about the Arab/Muslim world, for example, it is irrational, violent, etc. Edward Said, *Orientalism* (New York: Vintage, 1979), pp. 1, 3–5.

8. These media are thus "alternative" in a sense of "challenging, at least implicitly, actual concentrations of media power" (Nick Couldry and James Curran, "The Paradox of Media Power," in Nick Couldry and James Curran, eds., *Contesting Media Power: Alternative Media in a Networked World* [Oxford, UK: Rowman and Littlefield, 2003], p. 7). This context of power relations also applies to the construction of identity, of course.

9. In Poole, *Reporting Islam*, p. 88.

10. Linda Steet, *Veils and Daggers: A Century of* National Geographic's *Representation of the Arab World* (Philadelphia, PA: Temple University Press, 2000), p. 5; Norman Fairclough, *Media Discourse* (London: Edward Arnold, 1995), p. 104.

11. In some cases, these videos were pioneering attempts at producing original Islamic media in the English language. In other cases, the videos are English

readaptations of foreign media made in different Muslim countries. The videos I have chosen enjoy widespread popularity among certain segments of the Muslim community in America, judging by their relatively high sales and their serializing, as in the case of *Adam's World*. I selected videos that belong to different genres, specifically animated films that draw on historical and Quranic narratives and animated films that are more contemporary in focus as well as a puppet show series.

12. Sulayman Nyang, "Convergence and Divergence in an Emergent Community: A Study of Challenges Facing US Muslims," in Yvonne Haddad, ed., *The Muslims of America* (New York: Oxford University Press, 1991), p. 237.

13. See Carlos Cortes, *The Children Are Watching: How the Media Teach about Diversity* (New York: Teachers College Press, Columbia University, 2000). In a poll conducted by *U.S. News and World Report* in 1996, 81 percent of Americans surveyed felt that television contributes to the perceived decline in family values. Another poll undertaken by Gallup in 1991 showed that 62 percent of Americans believed that television does not represent their values. See Bill Johnson, "Pulling the Plug on Television Sex and Violence," www.nisbett.com/child-ent.htm, accessed November 27, 2002. Similar concerns are voiced in various cyber forums for Muslims living in America, including www.soundvision.com and www.altmuslim.com, accessed November 27, 2002.

14. Louay Safi, "The Transforming Experience of American Muslims: Islamic Education and Political Maturation," in Amber Haque, ed., *Muslims and Islamization in North America: Problems and Prospects* (Beltsville, MD: Amana Publications, 1999), p. 37.

15. Muslims of course are not the first faith community to adopt this strategy of creating alternative media worlds. Conservative Christian groups have been at the forefront of creating children's media that conforms to Christian values and ethics. For an excellent discussion, see Heather Hendershot, *Shaking the World for Jesus: Media and Conservative Evangelical Culture* (Chicago: University of Chicago Press, 2004).

16. As one author has noted: "Increased religiosity can also be attributed in part to the realization by second generation Muslims that their children were being assimilated by American Christians" (Emily Lovell, "Islam in the United States: Past and Present," in Earle Waugh, Baha Abu Laban, and Regula Qureshi, eds., *The Muslim Community in North America* [Edmonton: University of Alberta Press, 1983], p. 106).

17. Quoted in Sound Vision, "Up Close with Jawad Jafry: Adam's World's Asad," www.soundvision.com/Info/adam/jawad.asp, accessed November 27, 2002.

18. Jack Shaheen, *Arab and Muslim Stereotyping in American Popular Culture* (Washington, DC: Center for Muslim-Christian Understanding, 1997).

19. Ibid., p. 23.

20. Ibid., p. 15.

21. Cortes, *The Children Are Watching*, p. 21.

22. Patricia Greenfield, *Mind and Media: The Effects of Television, Video Games and Computers* (Cambridge, MA: Harvard University Press, 1984), p. 54.

23. Ibid., p. 55.

24. Ibid., p. 43.

25. Ibid., p. 42.

26. Everette Dennis and Edward Pease, eds., *Children and the Media* (New Brunswick, NJ: Transaction Publishers, 1996), pp. 65–66.

27. However, while it is important to look at what is visually/textually present, it is equally important to look at what is absent. There is a marked absence of "white" children in both the *Adam's World* series and other children's films about contemporary Muslims such as *Muslim Scouts*. We can only speculate as to the reason white children are not portrayed. Perhaps it is because the overwhelming majority of Muslims in America are *not* white and the images are therefore only striving to be faithful to demographic reality. In addition, it may be that the producers recognize that their primary consumers/buyers will not be the parents of white children but, rather, the parents of nonwhite children and are therefore trying to cater to consumer taste/demands.

Nevertheless, since these media take as their explicit aim the construction of a particular Muslim sense of self, rather than the reflection of "reality" or a concern for profit margins, the absence of Anglo-Saxon children can be examined as an instance of exclusion, of "othering," in drawing the boundaries of who is Muslim. As already discussed, these productions are made, to a large extent, to counteract the non-Islamic influences Muslim children are exposed to in daily life. These influences often come from non-Muslim peers, educators, and celebrities who come from the majoritarian white background. Thus, by leaving out the very people whom the Muslim child either directly or indirectly sees most, these productions are implicitly saying that these people are "different" from "us" and not to be emulated. This highlights the selectivity inherent in any mediated representations where decisions are made as to who/which groups should or should not be referenced in relation to the self.

28. For a comprehensive survey of the countries of origin of Muslim immigrants to America, see Sulayman S. Nyang, "Challenges Facing Christian-Muslim Dialogue in the United States," in Yvonne Haddad and Wadi Haddad, eds., *Christian-Muslim Encounters* (Gainesville: University of Florida Press, 1995), pp. 328–341.

29. Nyang, "Convergence and Divergence in an Emergent Community," p. 238.

30. Tariq Ramadan, *To Be a European Muslim* (Leicester, UK: Islamic Foundation, 1999), p. 158.

31. John Esposito, *Islamic Threat: Myth or Reality?* (Oxford: Oxford University Press, 1999), p. 41.

32. Freda Shamma, "The Curriculum Challenge for Islamic Schools in America," in Haque, *Muslims and Islamization in North America*, p. 275.

33. Ibid., p. 280.

34. There are some minor exceptions. In one episode of *Adam's World*, a woman appears as a teacher. In the first volume of *Muslim Scouts*, the first and only woman that appears is a veiled air hostess on an EgyptAir flight who does not utter one word. In the second volume, no women appear.

35. Jane I. Smith, "Introduction," in Haddad, *Muslims in the West*, p. 11.

36. Frederick Denny, "The *Umma* in North America: Muslims 'Melting Pot' or Ethnic 'Mosaic'?" in Haddad and Haddad, *Christian-Muslim Encounters*, p. 344.

37. Maulana Maududi, *Selected Speeches and Writings*, trans. S. Zakir Aijaz (Karachi: International Islamic Publishers, 1981), p. 136.

38. Ibid., p. 67.

39. See Fatima Mernissi, *Women in Islam: A Historical and Theological Enquiry* (Oxford, UK: Basil Blackwell, 1991); Amina Wadud, *Qur'an and Women: Rereading the Sacred Text from a Woman's Perspective* (New York: Oxford University Press, 1999); Asma Barlas, *Believing Women in Islam: Unreading Patriarchal Interpretations of the Qur'an* (Austin: University of Texas Press, 2002).

40. Forty-seven percent of immigrant Muslims disagree with the statement "Muslim women should not go out on the street unless their hair and arms are covered." Based on a study conducted by Haddad and Lummis, as quoted in Hassan, *American Muslims*, p. 41.

41. While usually the veil is not explicitly discussed or mentioned but serves more as a background, in one episode of *Adam's World*, a young girl tells her teacher, "I like your veil teacher Aisha," to which the teacher responds, "And yours is pretty too."

42. Jorgen Simonsen, "Globalization in Reverse and the Challenge of Integration: Muslims in Denmark," in Haddad, *Muslims in the West*, p. 127.

43. Thijl Sunier and Mira Van Kuijeren, "Islam in the Netherlands," in Haddad, *Muslims in the West*, p. 152.

44. The literature is vast, but see especially Fadwa El-Guindi, *Veil: Modesty, Privacy and Resistance* (New York: Berg, 1999). For a discussion of the practices and discourses of veiling in an American context, see Jen'Nan Ghazal Read and John P. Bartkowski, "To Veil or Not to Veil? A Case Study of Identity Negotiation among Muslim Women in Austin, Texas," *Gender and Society* 14, no. 3 (June 2000), pp. 395–417.

45. As Yvonne Haddad pointed out in a conversation with me: "This is a sign of Americanization as women do not go to the mosque with the rest of the family in the Muslim world." Personal communication, 2002.

46. Ramadan, *To Be a European Muslim*, p. 155.

47. Maududi, *Selected Speeches and Writings*, p. 66.

48. Aishah Ho, "Are TV/Video Programs for Children Safe to Watch?" http://homepages.ihug.com.au/~umm_pub/ChildrenProg.html, accessed November 17, 2002.

49. Blurb on the cover of a video for *Adam's World*.

50. Said, *Orientalism*, p. 332.

51. Abubaker Al-Shingiety, "The Muslim as the Other: Representations and Self-Image of the Muslims in North America," in Haddad, *Muslims of America*, p. 53.

52. Qur'an 3:114; the entire *ayat* reads: "They believe in Allah and the Last Day, enjoin right conduct and forbid indecency, and vie with another in good works. These are the righteous" (Pickthall, trans.). The Muslim scouts aptly (and perhaps intentionally?) fit this description.

53. Another example of the binary opposition setup and its implicit suggestions is seen in "The Humble Muslim," an episode of *Adam's World*. A song goes: "Always thank Allah when we are proud / we shouldn't be full of ourselves / we should be full of humility." As the song plays, a series of images is projected: a yacht, a stack of dollar

bills, a sports car, an American flag. The message given is that American society (as signified by these "symbols" of Americana) is too proud of itself and arrogant. The song continues: "We are all equal to one another / no one is better than anyone / the only thing that makes us different is the faith in our hearts."

54. John Esposito, "Ismail Al-Faruqi: Muslim Scholar-Activist," in Haddad, *Muslims of America*, p. 74.

55. Ismail Al-Faruqi, "Islamic Ideals in North America," in Waugh, Abu Laban, and Qureshi, *Muslim Community*, p. 269.

56. Said, *Orientalism*, p. 32.

57. Jocelyn Cesari, "Muslim Minorities in Europe: The Silent Revolution," in John Esposito and Francois Burgat, eds., *Modernizing Islam: Religion in the Public Sphere in Europe and the Middle East* (London: Hurst and Company, 2003), p. 259.

58. Denny, "The *Umma* in North America," p. 349.

59. Tariq Ramadan, "Islam and Muslims in Europe: A Silent Revolution towards Rediscovery," in Haddad, *Muslims in the West*, p. 162.

60. Ramadan, *To Be a European Muslim*, pp. 182, 184.

61. Simonsen, "Globalization in Reverse and the Challenge of Integration," p. 125.

62. Ramadan, *To Be a European Muslim*.

63. This isolationism is conscious and deliberate, as highlighted by a comment made by the director of *Adam's World*, Jawad Jafry, in an interview with Sound Vision: "Sometimes a really 'great' idea will come to mind, I'll start thinking about it feverishly and then it will occur to me, 'hey, didn't I see that in The Flintstones (or some other show)?' Those types of ideas get dropped quickly" (quoted in Sound Vision, "Up Close with Jawad Jafry").

64. Esposito, *Islamic Threat*, p. 131. I mentioned in the section on women that Maududi's name appears in the closing credits of an *Adam's World* episode, leading me to believe that the producers endorse his ideology.

65. Lovell, "Islam in the United States," p. 97.

66. Yvonne Haddad, "The Dynamics of Islamic Identity in North America," in John Esposito and Yvonne Haddad, eds., *Muslims on the Americanization Path?* (Oxford: Oxford University Press, 2000), p. 35.

67. Denny, "The *Umma* in North America," p. 335.

68. Ramadan, *To Be a European Muslim*, p. 156.

69. Denny, "The *Umma* in North America," p. 350.

70. Hassan, *American Muslims*, p. 56.

71. Michael King, "Muslims Identity in a Secular World," in Michael King, ed., *God's Law versus State Law* (London: Grey Seal Books, 1995), p. 92; Mohamed Muqtedar Khan, "Muslims and Identity Politics in America," in Esposito and Haddad, *Muslims on the Americanization Path?* p. 87.

8

The Search for Justice: Islamic Pedagogy and Inmate Rehabilitation

Anna Bowers

Islamic Programming and Inmate Rehabilitation

In the wake of 9/11, national security and the threat of terrorism became a prime concern for many U.S. government institutions, including the Department of Corrections, where Islamic conversion occurs at higher rates than it does on the street. Conversion to Islam is not a new phenomenon in American prisons, nor is the fear of its effects. Muslim conversions in U.S. prisons began with the Nation of Islam's conscientious objectors during World War II. In the United States today, Islam continues to be most popular among African Americans who are disproportionately represented in American prisons and urban ghettos. This chapter examines the appeal of Islam for inmates, the issues facing inmate converts while incarcerated and upon release, and the role of the Muslim chaplain, or imam, in providing rehabilitative services. This chapter focuses on male inmates, who are by far the majority of incarcerated persons in this country (93.3 percent).[1] Source material for this pilot study includes interviews with Islamic chaplains and former inmates as well as a review of relevant academic and policy literatures. Evidence indicates that despite the sizable Muslim population behind bars, Islamic programming and leadership in prisons remain underrepresented and underfunded. Furthermore, institutional biases that misrepresent Islam as a militant political movement make Islamic conversion and religious practice more difficult for inmates than forms of religious expressions deemed less threatening.

The cultivation of religious programming during the 20th century steered the course of modern corrections toward rebirth and rehabilitation. Though Christian converters dominated, the number of inmates converting to Islam in prison grew steadily despite persistent security concerns on the part of corrections officials and policy-makers. Today Christian programs thrive in America's prisons; most federal prisons utilize the services of a Christian minister, volunteer, or contractor. Support for similar Islamic programming falls short of need. In areas such as New York, the Upper Midwest including Cleveland, Chicago, and Detroit, and the West Coast including San Francisco and Los Angeles, the Muslim population nears 20 percent of the incarcerated, while Muslim representation in the general U.S. population is much lower (3–5 percent).[2] The research on recidivism supports the claim that any religious programming helps reduce repeat offenses. Programs such as the InnerChange Freedom Initiative have been shown to reduce reincarceration by up to 60 percent in a two-year follow-up period.[3] Religious programming provides inmates with morality, discipline, and the community connections they need to successfully reenter society as positively contributing members. For the criminal offender, Islamic pedagogy teaches self-discipline, responsibility, modesty, and a regard for worldly knowledge, values in stark contrast to those often proliferated in poor urban society.

According to the Department of Health and Human Services, American prisons are in a state of crisis; in 2002, the total number of adult persons under correctional supervision well exceeded six million, with another 600,000 prisoners being released into the community each year.[4] From 1973 to 2003, the U.S. prison population grew 900 percent; the United States leads the world as the nation with the highest percentage of its population behind bars.[5] Rates of recidivism paint a bleak picture: of those released on probation, over two-thirds are rearrested for a felony or serious misdemeanor within three years of their release. Expenditures on corrections increased from $9 billion in 1982 to $53 billion in 1999.[6] The reality of such high rates of incarceration and recidivism suggests that the punishment of "doing time" does not prevent crime and that these problems need to be addressed with rehabilitative and preventative measures.

Religious programming in prisons is considered among the most successful forms of rehabilitation, often providing not only spiritual guidance but many secular services for ex-inmates including housing, education, and employment assistance. Although today's economy has forced some states to reduce budgetary support for religious programming, nearly all states participate by hiring professionals or utilizing volunteers; nearly all state and federal facilities provide some support for Catholics, Protestants, Jews, and Muslims.[7]

When funding is available, the state or federal Bureau of Prisons (BOP) will hire a professional chaplain to hold services, counsel inmates, and act as mediator between inmates and prison officials. The Muslim chaplain or imam often takes on a nurturing paternal role while providing practical techniques for criminal rehabilitation. For Muslim inmates, the imam's leadership and expertise provide a safe space within prison walls to participate in prayer, daily lessons, and debates structured to address Islamic religiosity in the context of corrections. In addition to formal leadership, the sense of Muslim brotherhood provides the inmate with a supportive community committed to helping him make a positive change.

Whereas recent discourse on Muslims in prison has focused on the potential for radicalization, the counterargument—that Islamic programming in prisons adheres to orthodox, mainstream religious interpretations, which are nonviolent—is often dismissed. Muslim prison chaplains teach that Islam shuns the violence, racism, and the cowardice of terrorists that so many equate with Islam. Without an imam's guidance, incarcerated Muslim converts are more likely to be exposed to what Muslim chaplains have called "Prison Islam," politically radical forms of the religion sympathetic to marginal fringe groups like Al-Qaeda.[8] The critical shortage of Muslim chaplains in American correctional institutions is a greater threat to national security than the proliferation of Muslim inmates. Recent research also suggests that the Islamic pedagogy could be pivotal in reducing recidivism. The American corrections system must recognize the importance of Islamic leadership and religious education to its growing Muslim population. U.S. prisons need more qualified Islamic educators and local Islamic communities to make an investment in helping offenders transition back into society. By improving the quality of Islamic programming and leadership in prisons, the American corrections system would facilitate successful rehabilitation of individuals from a highly at-risk segment of the U.S. population, ultimately reducing the repeat offenses that burden families, communities, and society.

Islam behind Bars: The Controversy over Security

Prior to the 1960s, prison officials deemed Christianity the "standard" religion, with all other faiths designated "nontraditional." Administrators allowed Christians to possess a Bible, receive visitation by ministers, attend services, and display Christian medallions.[9] Research during this period on the rehabilitative effects of religious programming largely omitted mention of minority faiths, simultaneously ignoring their existence and legitimacy as religions.

Prior to the 1960s corrections officials operated prisons without interference by the courts.[10] This "hands-off" approach by the courts allowed wardens to assume authoritarian leadership, thereby silencing voices of opposition or dissent. The American public had little exposure to prison life except what was carefully disseminated by the administration.

During this period of willful ignorance and overt racism, African American Muslim communities formed with the intention of reverting "the so-called Negro" to his previous African faith. These movements—the most visible of which was the Nation of Islam (NOI)—exposed Christianity as a Eurocentric religion that preached the worship of a white man. The NOI rejected the inferior position of blacks in American society and worked toward establishing an independent nation of African Americans. Islamic jurisprudence designates God as the only authority over man—a belief directly at odds with American constitutional law, which regards religious law as secondary to the Constitution and subject to restriction by the U.S. government.

The Nation of Islam, as led by Elijah Muhammad, addressed racial inequalities and feelings of despair present in black communities. Instead of promising salvation through passivity, as the Christian rhetoric of "turn the other cheek" demanded, the NOI taught empowerment to its followers. Elijah Muhammad rejected allegiance to any nation other than the NOI. During World War II, NOI conscientious objectors brought Islam to the attention of correctional staff as a threat to prison security. In this period from the 1940s until the 1960s, prison administrators used tactics to deter potential converts, including "food deprivation, segregation from other inmates, denial of parole, and denial of religious practices."[11]

During the 1960s members of the Nation of Islam filed several court cases to establish Islam as a legitimate religion and thus deserving of First Amendment rights to practice. This step toward prison reform was the first instance of the courts becoming involved in corrections, and it opened the door for greater reforms to come. The successful challenges brought forward by Islamic inmates facilitated the awarding of First Amendment rights to religions formerly classified as nontraditional.[12] In her essay "Muslims in Prison: Claims to Constitutional Protection of Religious Liberty," Kathleen Moore notes the factors upon which successful Muslim litigation rested: "The responsiveness of the courts to Muslim inmates' claims for religious liberty has turned on a number of factors: the issue of equality of treatment of religious groups in prisons; the courts' reticence to reverse the decisions of prison officials; the degree to which the inmates' challenges would undermine the fundamental interests of the state (for example, prison security, administrative efficiency); and the showing that Islam is similar to the conventional Protestant, Catholic, and Jewish faiths."[13] More cases followed, each building off what had come before. Due to Muslim efforts in the 1960s, inmates were given the freedom to practice their religion of choice and the right to file suit against corrections officials. Once deemed "legitimate," Islamic customs of prayer, diet, dress, and identity gradually gained strength as Muslims challenged correctional institutions state by state. This period of prison reform is seen as a victory for Muslims. However, the exposure caused by these court cases and subsequent criticism of the Department of Corrections has in many cases increased tensions between Muslims and prison staff.

Since September 11, 2001, widespread fears about national security have led to a pervasive impugning of Muslim practices and beliefs as threatening. On June 24, 2002, in his *Wall Street Journal* editorial "Evangelizing Evil in Our Prisons," Chuck Colson warned of an "invasion" of radical fundamentalists into U.S. prisons and called for the BOP to increase scrutiny of Islamic chaplains to ensure that radical Islam would not take hold of American inmates. Colson, an evangelist preacher, founder of the Prison Fellowship Ministries and a former inmate, wrote his article in response to reports that "dirty bomber" Abdullah al-Muhajir (Jose Padilla) had done time in American prisons. Colson's representation of Islam fed off of the widespread American stereotypes of the religion as radical, oppressive, and dangerous. Colson omits any mention of successful, mainstream Islamic programs, to suggest that radicalization and terrorist recruitment are imminent. The general American population, whose understanding of Islamic doctrines tends to work backward by using the Al-Qaeda terrorist cell as a starting point or standard rather than beginning with the normative beliefs and practices of most Muslims, may too readily accept Colson's word as gospel. While many Muslims have publicly denounced the attacks, American public discourse continues to construct the religion primarily as a national threat. This oversimplification has more often led to a fear of Islam itself rather than an attempt to understand the implications of Islamic diversity and the positive possibilities it offers many Americans.

While Colson's assertion that terrorist groups recruit in American prisons appears logical, inmate conversion is overwhelmingly attributed to the desire for personal reformation, not to achieve radical political change or wage war. Islam has been shown to give men and women a renewed positive sense of purpose in life. Ex-inmate Mustafa Baker described his conversion experience this way: "I say that prison was actually a blessing for me. I would have to say that I actually became a man in prison, and it was due to the effects of Islam because that's exactly what Islam teaches: masculinity, it teaches you to be a man. It teaches you to take responsibility for the obligations that you have and to be a responsible man."[14]

Colson argues that radical Islam finds support among inmates because it espouses violence and vengeance on the society that oppresses them, saying: "Islam, certainly the radical variety, feeds on resentment and anger all too prevalent in our prisons."[15] As a prison chaplain himself, Colson describes having witnessed many inmates find God and engage in a rebirth of self that they hope will prevent them from returning to prison.

Extremism occurs in all religions, and the isolation of prison can allow deviant doctrines to develop independent of the rest of the religious community. A federal Muslim chaplain since 1987, Abu Ishaq Abdul-Hafiz described how a lack of structure or leadership can lead to radical views: "When there wasn't an imam in the prison system, the religion developed without any direction. Ideas become extremist and they adopted practices which were not accepted in the faith."[16] The majority of Muslim converts are new to Islam and unfamiliar with its doctrines. As a scholar of Islam, an imam can clarify and define orthodox Islam, the fundamental beliefs of all Muslims, as a preventative measure against radicalization. Imam Ashraf sees his expertise as an asset for imparting the true doctrines of Islam to new converts: "Muslims who are new to Islam will take their chaplain as the authority on Islam, not an inmate. So the chaplain has a big role to play as far as moderation is concerned and to explain the variants of Islam and what mainstream Islam is, and sometimes what is Islam and what is not Islam. Those issues become very murky and controversial."[17]

Without institutional support for this growing community, the voices of self-appointed leaders, whether moderate or radical, remain unchallenged. Furthermore, former inmates described experiencing better relations between incarcerated Muslims and the prison administration with a staff imam in residence. Simultaneously prison staff and inmate advocate, the imam often acts as liaison between the two parties, educating prison officials in Islam and working out compromises to ensure security and freedom to practice. Imam Ashraf pointed to a need for more, well-trained, professional imams, both to improve the quality of Islamic programming and to set a standard for Islamic practice behind bars.

Although the religious affiliations of inmates still reflect the society at large, with Christians being the majority, Islam has grown significantly and is considered the fastest-growing religion in the United States and its prisons.[18] In New York State, 20 percent of inmates are Muslims, and Islam has exceeded Catholicism as the religion of choice on Rikers Island, the largest prison population in the United States.[19] The popularity of Islam among inmates corresponds to larger sociological patterns. The majority of Muslim converts in America—in both the United States and its prisons—are African

Americans. Of the two million plus persons currently incarcerated, African Americans represent a disproportionately high percentage of the inmate population, between 50 and 80 percent of inmates in state prisons.[20] Nationally, 49 percent of prison inmates are African American, compared to their 13 percent share of the overall population.[21] The geographic distribution of the Muslim population in prison reflects the greater society, where the highest concentrations of Muslims occur in urban areas of the Northeast, the West Coast, and the Upper Midwest in places such as Chicago, Detroit, and Cleveland. The lowest percentages of conversion occur along the Southern Bible Belt, where Christianity dominates.[22] According to the 2002 Census, the distribution of African Americans across the country still favors the South (55 percent) and inner-city residences (51.5 percent), as compared to non-Hispanic whites, with 33.3 percent in the southern regions and only 21.1 percent living inside a central city. The geographic distribution of African Americans might be said to contribute to their higher rates of poverty (23 percent) than non-Hispanic whites (8 percent).[23]

The high percentage of African Americans in prison can be attributed to poverty, lack of education, and the institutional racism associated with the war on drugs. According to the U.S. Department of Justice, two-thirds of the prison population nationwide has less than a ninth grade education and in the year before their incarceration earned less than $2,000.[24] Blacks represent one-quarter of the U.S. population in poverty for 2001, which, in combination with a lack of education, is the leading factor in incarceration for African Americans.[25] However, one must also consider that sentencing policies most often favor whites with probation and community service, whereas blacks are given prison sentences. For example, in 1995, African Americans constituted 13 percent of all monthly drug users yet accounted for 35 percent of arrests for drug possession, 55 percent of all convictions, and 74 percent of all prison sentences.[26] The overrepresentation of African Americans in prison suggests that this community is in a state of crisis and that our approach to this crisis creates a self-perpetuating cycle of poverty, crime, and incarceration.

For many inmates, the socioeconomic disparities that lead to crime (drugs, poverty, broken families) are what defined their reality during childhood. While most convicts interviewed said they had always understood crime as negative and amoral behavior, most attributed their crimes to impulsivity and a lack of positive role models to follow. Saleem Wilder explained his choice to commit armed robbery as a lack of patience: "I was basically trying to improve my situation, but I was 20 years old and kinda immature, and I guess I just wanted fast money instead of taking the right route and taking my time like I was supposed to."[27]

Many former inmates described how, while growing up, "playing by the rules" was taken as a sign of weakness, signaling a blind respect for a white culture that exploits its underclass. Aside from the pressure to demonstrate one's revolt against the system, inmates, who are often first incarcerated in their youth and early adulthood, expressed that for them, committing crimes and "doing time" were nothing out of the ordinary. Ex-inmate Mustafa Baker described his understanding of why he became a drug dealer: "I was a product of my environment—I was around drug selling, I was around crime....I had a bad situation at home with my parents. I don't want to use the word *forced*, but I would say it was easier for me to choose that route than any other route. I feel that first time I did some crime or I did anything wrong it was basically out of necessity. We all have the ability to choose, and I chose to continue to do it, which is what landed me in prison. Now once being incarcerated, a person looks for something to fill that void with once you have been taken away from society. It may be recreation, it may be education, it may be certain things, and a lot of people choose spirituality."[28] That "void" is a loss of meaning in one's life. For many newly incarcerated inmates, prison is a time of self-reflection and reassessment of their values.

Sherman Jackson describes facets of Islam that appeal directly to blacks: the use of Arabic as an authentically African language, Islam's independence from white control and its foregrounding of people of color, Islam's deep fraternal spirit, its simple theology of "no god but God," and the lack of institutional hierarchy.[29] These characteristics of Islam establish the religion as an authentically African (or non-Western) alternative to the dominance of Christianity. Islamic doctrines address the needs of inmates by providing practical methods for developing discipline and humility, thereby making a more constructive use of one's "time." Saleem Wilder described how Islam changed his perspective on doing time from despair to optimism: "Your faith and your beliefs are so strong whatever happens to you, you understand that it's from God and you deal with the situation because who am I to question God? I always looked at it as a divine plan, this is what you wanted me to go through in life in order for me to change my ways. It was better because I had my religion to stand on, and I knew that God was on my side so I really didn't have no fears of never being returned home because I left everything in God's hands. I just woke up everyday and I was thankful for the little things in life that we take for granted like just waking up in the morning, being able to breathe, and being able to use my two feet."[30] After spending 12 years in prison, Wilder was married on the day of his release in August 2005. When I asked him how Islam helps him deal with the transition, he said he felt that the simple things are what help him stay motivated from day to day: "I love the concept of praying five times a day because as I grew older I understood that by me praying five times a day, it helps keep me focused because from one prayer to the next, see, I might have some thoughts or things that I shouldn't be doing and I go to pray and it helps me get back on track."[31]

In their study of African American mosques and programs for the formerly incarcerated, Lawrence Mamiya and Ihsan Bagby suggest that in addition to daily prayer, "communal worship, and fasting during the daylight hours...during the month of Ramadan also help incarcerated persons develop strong internal discipline, which provides the foundation for personal rehabilitation."[32] Muslims believe God tests the faith of believers by granting them free will and providing opportunities to choose different paths and holding them accountable for their choices. While serving a sentence, Islamic practice can help the inmate reflect on his actions and prepare himself for his second chance in society.

The fear of Islamic programming runs deep with historical context; the development of Islam in prisons as a black nationalist movement in conjunction with the American public's wariness of Muslims post-9/11 has led to institutional biases against these programs at the state and federal level. These claims against the programs are largely unfounded and speak more to the need for better programs rather than a restriction of existing ones. Imam Isma'il Abdul Aleem of Indiana State Corrections contended that the Muslim converts in prisons are mostly African American men with little understanding of, or interest in, international politics. Inmate converters, said Abdul Aleem, want a positive framework to live by in order to avoid the crime, which is characteristic of their communities:

> The issues of people in Egypt, Saudi Arabia, Afghanistan, those
> are their issues.... They got a saying that goes: "money, mackin',
> and mayhem." These young guys, that's what they talk about. It's
> referring to a lifestyle that they're living, and its what makes them
> authentic black men.... Because of the way they define themselves,
> prison becomes an occupational hazard, ultimately due to the
> lifestyle that they live and their definition of themselves is going to
> take them to the prison or to the cemetery. I think my responsibil-
> ity is to help them change how they define themselves—and this is
> what Islam does. Islam provides them with an authentic definition of
> self that is principled on justice, good behavior, temperance, sexual
> modesty, personal modesty. It provides them with that definition of
> self, and it's not a definition that makes them feel like they're less
> than a man. It has no problem with their masculinity.[33]

Muslim chaplains provide inmates with discipline, brotherhood outside of gang activity, and the hope of a better life. This redefinition of self allows an inmate to see his potential as a contributing member of his community, not as a voice of hatred and violence, as Colson suggests.

Critical Shortage: The Current State of Islamic Programming in U.S. Prisons

Though some prison administrators consider Muslim inmates suspect, many corrections officials believe that tight-knit Islamic communities behind bars actually help maintain prison security.[34] The concern remains, however, that Muslims will become radical and organize terrorist acts. Chuck Colson believes that inmates who are mostly poor and uneducated are "prime targets" for radical Islamists seeking to capitalize on the anger and resentment that this lifestyle breeds. According to Colson, radical Islamic groups try to infiltrate literature and leadership into the prisons. While subversive literature and inmates with radical beliefs are not uncommon, their existence points to a need for trained Muslim leadership rather than a restriction thereof. In the 2004 report by the Department of Justice, Muslim chaplains insist than any radical imam hoping to recruit for Al-Qaeda would find the prison environment too religiously pluralistic to produce committed suicide bombers. Instead, imams suggest that radicalization occurs when no Muslim authority exists to offer legitimate and moderate interpretations of Islamic law. Radicalization may occur, but BOP staff acknowledged that if a chaplain or volunteer were responsible, he or she would soon be discovered and removed from the position.[35]

Federal BOP Muslim chaplains described what they called "Prison Islam," which "results when inmates follow Islam without direction or analysis— inmates distort Islam to encompass prison values such as gangs and loyalty to other inmates."[36] Most often the radicalization of inmates comes in the form of pseudo-Islamic gangs, such as the Five Percenters, who appropriate Muslim identities without fully embracing Islamic doctrines. Prison imams are instrumental in making the critical distinction between these gangs and Sunni Muslims for inmates.

Although some inmates adopt Prison Islam to justify gang alliances, according to prison staff, most Muslims are seen as mediators who rarely become directly involved in physical conflict and more often opt to talk things out. With the support of a whole community, Muslim inmates have alternative venues to vent their frustrations. David Miller, the superintendent of the Eastern New York Correctional Facility, believes any religious practice among inmates improves prison security. Religion, says Miller, "create[s] a community within a community, which allows an old con to put an arm around a young con and tell him to cool down."[37] The sense of religious brotherhood has great power over its members, but its strength lies in the knowledge and abilities of its leadership. Professional Muslim chaplains with extensive Islamic education provide unparalleled guidance to the incarcerated community. Muslim chaplain Salahuddin Muhammad, who has worked in New York State's correctional system for 20 years, describes the role of the prison chaplain: "The Muslim Chaplain is a true liberator. His role is to free the captive believers through fostering proper growth and development in Islam. The Muslim Chaplain provides classes, worships, seminars, counseling sessions and some heart to heart talks to men and women who always needed to have a real friend, someone who truly cares about them."[38] The Muslim chaplain teaches proper Islamic knowledge; introduces converts to customs of washing, prayer, and diet; and is responsible for ensuring that inmates have the accommodations they need in order to practice. As an administrative official, the chaplain must oversee religious contractors, volunteers, and inmates who lead services for other faith groups. The chaplain also acts as an advocate for inmates by mediating between inmates and officials. Muhammad stresses that for an imam to be an effective advocate, he or she must be a role model in the institution. Earning the trust of both the officials and the incarcerated requires determination, consistency, and sincerity. While a professional chaplain provides superior religious pedagogy in the service of rehabilitation, he must also embody his teachings if he is to win the inmates' support. Imam Muhammad writes: "The Muslim Chaplain can only communicate this truth in an acceptable (palatable) way if he convinces the inmates that he is genuinely concerned about their welfare. The Chaplain has to be a good role model because he is under a microscope. The slightest imperfection or defect will cause him to lose credibility with those whom he wishes to guide."[39]

Most correctional institutions still lack residential imams for their Muslim population. Without a leader, inmates take on the role of imams, leading services, counseling, and often acting as liaison in times of conflict. Often inmate imams are older and serving longer sentences than their "brothers." Their leadership role provides them with the solace that they are helping those fortunate to have another chance to succeed in becoming successful and happy. Imam Mumina Kowalski, the first female Muslim chaplain in Pennsylvania, emphasizes to entering imams the importance of not alienating the Muslim community by rejecting the established routines and leadership: "I feel it is critically important to work with the inmate leaders who have established the Muslim program, especially inmates doing life or long sentences, and to act as mediator between inmates. Misconceptions and recalcitrant positions on controversial topics by Muslim inmates can be addressed gradually and through indirect methods."[40]

New imams may prefer to use a more democratized Socratic method to clear up confusion by using the works of Muslim scholars to debate given topics. Islam's lack of centralized authority makes the imam's role more like that of a teacher, father, or elder than a preacher. A significant amount of time is spent on religious instruction, or *ta'leem*, which includes Arabic lessons, Quranic study, and Islamic history. While the pillars of Islam, with regard to rules of diet, dress, and prayer, must immediately become a firmly established routine, the imam supports this discipline with an Islamic education. Ex-inmate Yahya Ali described his imam's Socratic four-step process that consults Allah, the Prophet Muhammad, Islamic texts, and human history when debating Islamic law: "Our imam wouldn't preach from himself. Learned men in Islam always invite the people they're speaking to to challenge what they're saying."[41] This pedagogical method helps the Muslim student make good choices as well as mediate and debate more effectively.

In some prisons, Muslims are given *masjid* space for worship, discussion, and study. Mamiya and Bagby describe the tranquility of the prison masjid: "This separate sacred space in a prison setting also allows for the development of a calm, quiet, and peaceful atmosphere. Everyone takes off their shoes before entering, a symbolic act that one has left the secular world [behind] and entered Islamic space. The peacefulness of the masjid area stands in stark contrast to the noise of the cellblocks."[42] Imams teach Islam as a way of life dictated by a set of morals. Good manners, Islamic law, and proper ritual show inmates how to live the Muslim lifestyle, while a curriculum structured on modern Islamic thought teaches inmates the doctrines they will need for life beyond prison. The philosophy of Islam requires as much attention as the practice of the religion; the two are not mutually exclusive. Doctrinal teachings help reorient thought processes that assist in making behavioral change, just as changing one's behavior helps a person accept a new perspective on life. When asked to describe a favorite teaching, Yahya Ali recited the Qur'an and explained what struck him about this passage:

> One of the doctrines that was promoted in my early learning says,
> "Say, your lord is one, he begets not, nor is he begotten, and there is
> none unlike to him." And when I had the honor of Islamic scholars
> teaching me the meaning of this, they explained to me that, even
> though we say Allah sees, his seeing is not with an eye...we have
> eyes because we need our eyes to see, he doesn't need eyes—he

created eyes. And he sees by his knowledge, he knows everything that will happen and everything that has happened, and he dictates everything that's going on right now. So he don't need an eye like you need an eye. I thought that was odd at first when he was explaining that to me, but the reason why this is so important is because we don't get into the concept of God being a man, he doesn't die. If God was born, it would sound ridiculous because he'd need his diaper changed, he'd need to be fed, he'd need to be protected. And nobody needs to protect God. I think that's one of the reasons that we don't have a formal clergy in Islam where we elevate people to positions of divinity...by this concept that everything in creation is incompatible to the nature of God. This is what struck me, and it kinda overwhelmed me at first.[43]

Ali articulates the value of Quranic study: it presents the notion of the divine plan through which inmates understand that prison is merely a test of faith, that life is a struggle, and that their conversion is their opportunity to better themselves.

Imams structure curricula based on the varied needs of inmates; for those serving long or life sentences an imam may stress the spiritual (Sufi) traditions or the need to help the younger generation; for those preparing for release, the imam conducts seminars on money management, family relations, and substance abuse. Imams hold daily study of the Qur'an, and many offer advanced discussion groups for those interested in debating the interpretation of Quranic text. Some prisons have sponsored an Islamic Therapeutic Program, which uses Islamic principles for dealing with drug and alcohol addiction.[44] Muslim chaplains say that one of the most important topics is marriage, which stresses the concept of man as provider/protector and the couple's respect for the marriage bond. These teachings prepare the inmate for release by presenting practical knowledge and skills that he finds within himself rather than depending on a rule book or a probation officer.

Islamic law or shari'ah instructs the Muslim on proper morality. By practicing the *din,* or the Islamic way of life, Muslim converts foreground the importance of diet, manners, cleanliness, respect for others, and the pursuit of knowledge. Islamic concern for justice is more relevant here than in any other setting: for the incarcerated person, a new moral code can be the key to avoiding run-ins with "the law." A Muslim inmate must accept responsibility for himself and his actions, and it is the job of the chaplain to emphasize this point.

In counseling inmates and conducting services, a chaplain must address the root causes of criminal behavior. Imam Muhammad uses William Glasser's psychiatric principles of "Reality Therapy" to help inmates understand what leads them to crime and violence and prevents them from changing. The individual desires a connection to people and respect from others that, when achieved, manifests as a positive self-concept, sense of self-worth or dignity, and self-confidence.[45] According to Glasser, an environment that teaches the individual to satisfy his or her needs with crime never achieves a basic level of satisfaction and instead perpetuates the cycle of destructive behavior. Despite his setting, an inmate who accepts Islam can redefine and reinvent himself in a positive way and gain the respect from his peers that will inspire self-confidence and dignity from within.

Imam Muhammad's application of psychiatric literature furthers the case for hiring a professional chaplain over any other contractor. The professional chaplain is best suited to Islamic leadership in prisons, as he or she understands Islamic doctrine, is trained on how to impart knowledge, understands the psychological needs of inmates, and as a civilian practicing Muslim, has a greater understanding of how Islam is practiced outside of prison.

The Offender's Path to Islam: The Search for the Self

Upon entering prison, the inmate experiences a loss of his or her individuality and personal freedoms while adopting the strictly regulated lifestyle. Many incoming inmates find that one facet of their previous identity persists in prison: their gang alliance. For many, the brotherhood of a gang provides easy protection, camaraderie, and purpose. Others, who seek redemption, look for a greater purpose to carry them through their sentence. Islamic teachings of righteous struggle help inmates to look beyond the prison wall to see the good they can do from inside, for themselves and their families. In some cases, inmates and chaplains describe Islam as an inmate's ticket out of the pervasive gang circuit. Imam Jawad Ashraf of Connecticut State Corrections explained that the generally high regard for Muslims among inmates is critical for the high rates of conversion to Islam: "Islam affords the [inmate fraternity], and many of those who don't want to go towards gangs turn to Islam as an alternative....A lot of times inmates will come into prison already affiliated with a gang and they want to get out. The Muslim population, since they're respected [by inmates], if you go to them most of the time the gangs will respect that. If you're a Muslim and you're true to what you say...you have actually changed your life, they have no problems with that, as far as I've seen."[46] Muslim inmates find that their religiosity separates them from prison culture and provides an inner strength to overcome incarceration. Imam Salahuddin A. Rashid expresses how Islam has rehabilitated him more than the concrete walls ever could: "I was happy to come to jail! I love it because Allah has chosen me to become a good person. How many guys got fifty-years-to-life and can smile and laugh every day? However long we've been in jail, adversity is a nourishment. We are physically slaves and Allah has made us winners."[47] Conversion to Islam is conceived as a rebirth; new Muslims often choose a new name, change their style of dress, and commence daily prayer and study. Notions of morality, of *halal* and *haram*, in regard to diet, dress, prayer, cleanliness, and sexuality, simultaneously separate the convert from his overseers and fellow inmates and link him to the *ummah*, or global Muslim community.

Inmates are often attracted to Islam because they meet other Muslim inmates whose character they admire. Mamiya and Bagby's survey of 100 Muslim inmates on Rikers Island found that the leading reason for conversion (or "reversion") to Islam was "social recruitment and attraction by Muslim role models; admired those who were Muslims; attracted by the unity of the Muslim community" (35 percent).[48] Men and women who embody Islamic ideals of patience, intelligence, and morality in an otherwise hollow existence are walking advertisements for the religion. Yahya Ali, who served over eight years in federal prison for money laundering and drug conspiracy, described the difference between his Muslim role models and the men he knew on the street:

> In Afro-American society I come from the guys are promoted to
> be masculine, but the masculinity is kinda twisted. They think
> that being masculine is only about being tough—so you can be as
> dumb as a box of bricks but if you're a tough guy, you're considered
> a man.... These guys, even though they were two different parts of
> the world, Africa and the Middle East, these two gentlemen—their
> attitudes, they were very masculine, they were tough, they was able to
> hold their own in the prison setting, but at the same time they were
> very intelligent. In our society, if you a man, and you're very smart
> you may be considered to be kinda soft, maybe probably can't handle
> yourself well. These guys had a lot of book smarts and academic
> sense but they had a lot of brawn too.... So they had masculinity,
> intelligence, and morality at the same time, and there wasn't any
> conflict in them.... That made me gravitate to these guys.[49]

In interviews, both inmates and prison imams expressed the appeal of Islamic masculinity for male prisoners. As Ali suggests above, Islamic masculinity asserts itself in contrast to traditional "gangster" masculinity in which the true characteristics of a man are taking responsibility for obligations to self and family, having patience, and being a role model for others. Ali described his imam's teachings as putting men in the role of a knight, protecting and providing for his kin, an ideal that many men at one time felt they could achieve only by selling drugs or by committing robbery. Another ex-inmate, Saleem Wilder, described the self-perpetuating image of machismo that leads to conflict and violence: "Where I come from, if a person may call out your name you would be quick to fight, your pride would get in the way, and it would seem like your manhood would be tested. But as I came into religion I understood what a man really does in a situation like that—I mean, I understood that the better man is the man who carries and conducts himself in an orderly fashion and does not act outrageous and lose his temper."[50] By transforming the individual's definition of manhood, Islam directly opposes the male ego and pride that often encourage men to "prove their manhood" through aggression. Islam's redefinition of masculinity also allows the inmate to regain self-respect through cultivating strong family ties. Ex-inmate Saleem Wilder, who served time for armed robbery, described how his conversion helped him redefine himself as a father: "I thought . . . that the more women you had, the more man you was. And I thought a man was being tough, and I thought that even when you wanted to cry or you hurt that you was weak if you cried or showed any feelings. Now I [teach] my son, 'I really don't condone you having sex until you're married and disrespecting women and disrespecting yourself and it's alright to cry, it's alright to be scared.' His manhood has just changed drastically. You know, I'm teaching him the total opposite of what I learned. . . . The decisions that you make will affect the ones you love. You can't be selfish in life. I get to tell him this, and he hears it coming from his father."[51] For inmates, the decision to change is often motivated by family relations and concern for one's children. Breaking the cycle of crime for one's offspring brings psychological satisfaction for the inmate but also carries a greater social potential for future generations.

In addition to this new notion of manhood, inmates alter mundane behaviors to place value on good manners and respect for others in everyday social interactions. Imam Jawad Ashraf saw these "little changes" as essential in the overall transformation of the criminal self: "That's one thing that Islam does is it habituates a person to do good things. This is what we should do, this becomes a habit of the mind and body to—every time you pass a person to—smile at him, that's counted as charity, it is to please Allah. If I give somebody charity, I get reward for that, but even a smile is charity. The first one who gives a greeting to the other, he gets the greater reward. And these things they take to heart, and these are just some minor things but by doing these habits it has a total personality change. You become that habit. This is the beauty of Islam."[52] Furthermore, inmates often associate Christianity with pacifism and are attracted to the spirit of justice in Islam, which permits fighting in self-defense. Loyal Muslim "brothers" in prison can offer protection from gang violence and homosexual rape. For many African Americans who grew up Christian, Islamic principles prove to be more practical than Christianity. For other converts, Islam is a way to reconnect with their African roots.

Ex-inmate Ali described an early experience with the Catholic Church:

> Our teacher, the priest, who was an excellent man, he did a great
> job with the boys, but it just baffled us, he was such a good person,
> I called him father, how come he can't have kids? He's the per-
> fect candidate to be somebody's dad, most of us had terrible dads
> at home.... So that was like a contradiction to us. So we felt, the
> people who was dictating this religion, they don't have more sense
> than what we have and we're ten, 11 years old. So we would think
> they really don't know what's good for us.... When I began to like
> girls, I couldn't go to him when I was teenager and I got somebody
> pregnant, I couldn't go to the father and talk to him about that, he's
> never been with a woman! What can he tell me? But in Islam it's the
> opposite.... In fact in Islam we say, marriage is half your religion.[53]

Many inmates interviewed described Islam's positive image of sexuality as a relief from their Christian upbringing. In addition, the choice to become a Muslim carries none of the ideological contradictions of Christianity, as the religion is devoid of ownership by white culture. Islam's authenticity as a black or at least nonwhite religion gives converts a new form of spiritual expression to exercise in hopes of bettering an oppressed community.

The values of Islam and the brotherhood it provides speak directly to inmates who hope to achieve personal change in an institution whose name does not reflect its purpose. Many men want to stop committing crimes but have no model for a positive lifestyle. Unfortunately, doing time most often exposes the offender to a cycle of crime and punishment. The true transformative power of Islam for the inmate exposes the failure of the correctional system to achieve its purported rehabilitative goal.

The Challenge of Reentry

The Muslim chaplain adds a voice of experience to his or her Islamic teachings; he or she is the connection between Muslim inmates and the outside world. For many inmates preparing for release, the imam's connection to the greater Muslim community is critical for the transition out of imprisonment. Inmates who convert or revert in prison only realize the demands of practicing Islam upon release. Formerly incarcerated Muslims say that after their release the difficulties of finding a job and housing make practicing Islam difficult, even for the most committed convert. Ex-inmate Mustafa Baker explained: "It doesn't make a difference how much you've learned, you have to make a choice, you have to choose to apply those principles."[54] As a felon, an ex-convict has diminished rights in American society; he may be denied housing, jobs, and social respect because of his past. Furthermore, his years in prison have removed him from the responsibilities of work and family—in many ways he must start from square one.

The months after release, said Imam Muhammad, are the true test of an inmate's rehabilitation: "We must remember that prison life is an artificial life. The inmate becomes totally dependent on the system for [his] life."[55] The dependency prison creates for the prisoner makes the transition to the street more complicated than just finding work and shelter. Without the support of the imam or the brotherhood, newly released inmates can get lost in their attempts to make a living as an ex-convict, which is what leads them back to crime. Imam Abdul Aleem attributed this phenomenon to a lack of continuity or guidance after release: "It's easy to practice Islam in jail because there's nothing else to do that's positive.... There's nothing else going on, none of the distractions that are going on in the outside world. Part of the problem of their definition of self is that this man is a slave—but he's afraid of freedom. He hates being in prison but he's afraid of freedom. And the only way that he can learn how to be free is if he can get with people who are free who can teach him how to be free.... There are a lot of people who do not want to go back to jail, they want to do the right thing, but they don't know how. They don't know how to be free people. In prison you learn life values that are useless in the real world."[56]

The challenges to reentry apply to all ex-prisoners; 62 percent of state prisoners are rearrested within three years of their release, and 41 percent of releases are returned to incarceration.[57] The cycle of reentry demonstrates the ineffectiveness of inmate rehabilitation in prison. According to a U.S. Department of Health and Human Services study, many inmates with longer sentences are finally being released back into society, making a record number of returning prisoners.[58] Reentry data suggest that returning prisoners are unprepared for life on the outside and that reintegration assistance is inadequate. The dangers of this ill preparedness are both physical and fiscal; ex-prisoners who commit crimes put our communities at risk and cost the taxpayers billions of dollars. An individual's one year spent in New York state prison costs $32,000.[59] Research suggests that religious programming—which is largely volunteer based—is inversely related to recidivism and operates at a lower cost than other treatment programs.[60] While little cross-comparison research has been done on the success of certain religions in rehabilitation, a 1997 study found the nationwide recidivism rate for Muslims to be just 8.21 percent, compared with 41.54 percent for all Protestants and 39.30 percent for Catholics.[61] More research needs to be done in this area to be certain of the consistency of these findings and to provide an explanation for this phenomenon.

Mamiya and Bagby suggest that the significant variable in determining reentry success is the extent of an ex-prisoner's participation in a local mosque.[62] Imam Muhammad adds to this point by explaining that in his experience, recidivism is more prevalent in inmates who are not married, are unemployed, and are not actively attached to an Islamic community.[63] Speaking to inmates one night at Fishkill Correctional Facility, Imam Muhammad reminded them: "Allah will return you to where you know Him best."[64] One must know Allah in the real world to avoid the pitfalls that lead to incarceration. Ex-inmate Wilder described how support from his imam and incarcerated brothers had helped him stay on track: "Imam [Muktar] Curtis gave me a list of mosques to go to, and some of the brothers they will call me and ask me how I'm doing, and I will call Imam Muktar and we will just talk. He would tell me to stay focused, and it's really good because you have so much love for these brothers that they want you to succeed so much that it makes you push stronger, it makes you push harder, because you would feel like you're letting them down. There's nothing like knowing that there's someone that has your back regardless, and the love is genuine.... You can never let somebody down who gave you a chance when others didn't."[65] Many inmates expressed how an imam's special attention helped build a sense of confidence and self-worth.

Muslim chaplains provide inmates with role models for successful reentry. To prepare inmates for the challenges of freedom, many imams hold seminars on release issues and have successful ex-convicts come to speak to share their experiences and difficulties. Imams also prepare inmates for the trials they will endure by encouraging connection to the local Muslim community. Recently released offender Mustafa Baker expressed his disillusionment with life after prison:

> [My imam] used to tell us that the hardest thing that we're going
> to have to deal with is having to be lonely; I'm pulling 15 hour
> days.... The brotherhood is not there anymore, and that is what
> tends to lead the individual back to crime again because he's not sur-
> rounded by brothers.... You have to be a very strong individual to go

back into those environments where you once lived, where you once
did your crime or whatever. That is very tempting because there's
nothing there.... There's only a network that's gonna bring you back
down, that's gonna take you back out there into the street and you're
lost, you're back to square one again.... So it's imperative that an
individual has a network of brothers, if its just one brother, that he
can go back to.[66]

Ex-felons, researchers, and chaplains uniformly agree that connection to
mosques and Islamic centers upon release improves an inmate's chances to
remain in the community. More research on this issue would shed light on the
effectiveness of these programs.

As of 2004, the Bureau of Prisons had hired only 12 federal Muslim
chaplains to service the needs of this community of approximately 350,000
inmates. In 2001, the ten BOP Muslim chaplains represented a little more
than 4 percent of all BOP chaplains.[67] The 2004 Justice Department review
of Muslim service providers states that the BOP is currently experiencing a
"critical shortage" of Muslim chaplains, defined as one chaplain serving 700
inmates of his or her faith. However, the shortage is beyond critical; each BOP
Muslim chaplain serves 900 inmates.[68] This is due in part to the BOP policy
of nondiscrimination of religion when hiring chaplains. BOP chaplains are expected to provide religious services to all inmates, and therefore the BOP considers denomination or religion irrelevant to performance. Muslims represent
20 percent of the inmate population, a greater proportion than in the general
U.S. population (~2 percent).[69] As many Muslim inmates first come to Islam
in prison they start out with little or no working knowledge of the faith. Islamic
practice in prison requires a depth of understanding of Islamic law; therefore,
more attention to the recruitment of Muslim chaplains by the BOP should not
be deemed discriminatory but, rather, a necessary reform to properly service
the needs of inmates.

When chaplains are not available to provide services, volunteers, contractors, or inmates conduct services to the best of their ability, but the chief of the
Chaplaincy Services stated that the BOP currently does not even have enough
contractors or volunteers to provide services where chaplains do not exist.[70]
Difficulty in the recruitment of Muslim contractors and volunteers, according
to BOP chaplains and officials, is related to (1) the remote locations of prisons,
(2) no BOP program or strategy for recruiting Muslim volunteers, (3) no time
allotted for BOP Muslim chaplains to utilize their connections to the Muslim
community in attempts to recruit, (4) no incentives for volunteers like compen-
sation for gasoline, (5) slowed recruitment due to Muslim fear of scrutiny by the

government since September 11, and (6) the lack of prison outreach programs sponsored by the Islamic community as compared to other religions.[71] While the Christian presence in prison requires no additional support from the BOP, Muslim leadership may need a more active recruitment policy in order to adequately represent the Muslim population behind bars.

Several studies on the prison outreach of mosques contradict the notion that Muslims do not have prison outreach programs: Mamiya and Bagby's nationwide survey of 130 predominantly African American mosques found that about 90 percent were involved in prison ministries and ministries for the formerly incarcerated, and a national study by the Council on American-Islamic Relations found that 81 percent of African American masjids take part in prisoner rehabilitation programs.[72] A more active dialogue with the Muslim community would encourage civilian involvement in Islamic prison programs.

Another obstacle that hinders Islamic programming from achieving its full potential is the institutional red tape created by biases against Muslims. Although many inmates and imams report good relations between Muslims and prison authorities, inmates describe corrections staff in some institutions deliberately ignoring imams' advice, and some report having witnessed verbal harassment of imams by prison staff, especially in the months after 9/11. In New York State, imams were restricted from discussing the events for fear that the inmates would become sympathetic. As the tensions waned, imams have asserted the need to discuss complicated issues. Imam Ashraf argued that skirting the issue lowers his effectiveness as a leader: "With the inmates the reason you have to say something about Iraq or why you even need to address these issues in an authentic way [is because] I can't hide from these issues here, because if you do the inmates sense that. My effectiveness as a chaplain depends a lot on my credibility with the inmates. They have to be able to confide in me, we have a chaplain-parishioner relationship; I keep things confidential unless it's a safety or security issue. They can only confide in me if they see me as somebody who is authentic."[73] Under the authority of the imam, discussions regarding Middle East conflict help inmates understand the state of the Islamic world of which they are a part.

Another way institutions have restricted imams is by using bureaucratic measures to hinder inmate exposure to Islam. This practice is not new, nor is it a secret. One imam, who wished to remain anonymous, said:

> One of the biggest problems we have is that a lot of these Christian ministers . . . do everything they can to prevent the number of people coming to the Islamic programs. When a Christian volunteer comes to the prison, they make a general announcement, "Christian

volunteer at the prison, who wants to go?" When it's time for a Muslim volunteer to come you have to go down to the chaplain, ask if you can be put on the list, and some of them will go as far as to look to see what you are listed as on your offender information sheet. If you're not listed as a Muslim they'll tell you that you can't go until you [convert]....I'm only saying about where I'm at and from talking to other people who do what I do, but this seems to be universal, these double standards, that Christianity and Catholicism are OK, but let us scrutinize these Muslims. It was like that before 9/11...they don't want us praying in groups...but if other religious groups can hold hands and praise God in the way that they do, then surely there should be some recognition of the fact that we practice our religion this way.[74]

Since Islam's early days in U.S. corrections, the religion has struggled to gain the legitimacy and respect Christianity has had since the first prison ministries. Religion has helped direct the course of modern corrections toward rehabilitation by providing spiritual guidance and support for prisoners. While the majority of inmates in this country are Christian, Muslims compose a larger percentage of the inmate population than they do of the general population. Islam has gained legal and institutional support since being legitimized as a religion by the courts, but prejudices against black militancy and the fear of Islamic fundamentalism continue to undermine the effectiveness of Islamic programming for prisoner rehabilitation.

Reentry poses perhaps the most difficult obstacle for an ex-inmate for a multitude of reasons. Laws that apply only to formerly incarcerated persons make finding employment and housing particularly challenging. For example, ex-offenders cannot live in federally funded housing projects; their only option for government-sponsored housing is the local homeless shelter.[75] Some states restrict formerly incarcerated persons from obtaining licenses to be plumbers, barbers, electricians, or real estate agents, as well as over a hundred other job categories.[76] Newly released inmates trying to "get back on their feet" are greatly disadvantaged by these laws. Restricted access to such necessities increases the chances that an ex-prisoner will revert back to crime. Though committing crimes is a choice the individual makes, for the ex-convict without viable options for shelter or employment, crime is the most efficient way to reintegrate oneself into one's community. Laws against formerly incarcerated persons coupled with social wariness of such individuals make support from the local mosque and Muslim community essential for successful reentry.

Recommendations for Policy-Makers and the Muslim Community

In an attempt to improve prisoner rehabilitation, recidivism rates, and national security, I offer a compilation of recommendations for the Federal Bureau of Prisons, researchers, lawmakers, and the Muslim community. Although American corrections has considerable work to do before realizing its goal of rehabilitation for all inmates, I hope to offer ways to improve Islamic programming to maximize its effectiveness and minimize the potential for radicalization:

1. *Create models for religious education for all BOP chaplains:* The current BOP chaplains and staff would greatly benefit from a general framework for appropriate religious programming. In addition to a generic model, an Islamic model with key terms and concepts would establish a starting point for new chaplains and would educate chaplains of other faiths who regularly counsel Muslim inmates. Establishing a teaching model and a set of ground rules that promote correct Islamic thought and practice will give religious contractors the freedom to educate and discuss topics of their choice without any confusion as to the appropriate teachings of Islamic doctrines for inmates.

2. *Educate the BOP staff on Islam:* The Department of Justice report recommends that the BOP educate its staff to improve security. McCloud and Thaufeer al-Deen's *A Question of Faith for Muslim Inmates* offers a concise review of Islam as it relates to the prison setting.[77] The more knowledgeable corrections officials are of Islamic beliefs and practices, the better equipped they will be in recognizing inappropriate religious behavior. Furthermore, conceptual understanding of Islam might alleviate staff distrust of, or bias against, Muslim chaplains and inmates. With increased knowledge of Islam, staff may feel more comfortable approaching imams with questions or concerns regarding an inmate, contractor, or volunteer.

3. *Recruit more Muslim chaplains, contractors, and volunteers:* The critical shortage of Muslim chaplains necessitates a more active recruitment policy on the part of the BOP. Professional chaplains are best suited to provide the Islamic education, which in some locations is currently being taught by volunteers and other inmates. The BOP should survey the religious population of its facilities to see where Muslim chaplains are most needed. As funding constraints may not support the hiring of enough Muslim chaplains, recruitment of other part-time Muslim

educators should be a high priority. With the help of the model established in recommendation #1, volunteers and contractors would better understand what is expected of them and how best to teach various Islamic concepts. Recruitment is of such a high priority that time should be allotted to current Muslim staff to utilize connections with the Muslim community to bring in qualified individuals to teach.

4. *Provide funding for outreach and reentry programming for inmates preparing for release and support groups for the recently released:* The high national rate of recidivism suggests that inmates are grossly unprepared for life outside of prison. Recidivism is a financial burden on taxpayers and a tragedy for the individuals who cannot break the cycle of crime and punishment. Mamiya and Bagby point out that "[e]ach person returning to prison eventually costs more than adequately funding programs that seek their successful reentry."[78] Prison outreach by the religious community provides the inmate with a future family that does not involve crime. Muslim inmates who connect with a local mosque while in prison are more likely to maintain that connection upon release and are less likely to be rearrested. The current influx of released prisoners into the community necessitates the improvement of prerelease programming. Topics include budgeting, marriage and family, employment, and education. Inmates expressed the lack of support in the community upon release and responded positively to the proposition of ex-offender support groups.[79] The responsibility for the improvement of reentry programming lies with both the BOP and the respective religious communities. Evidence suggests that diversity within the American Islamic community hinders outreach funding. Hopefully, the evidence presented in this chapter will motivate Muslim communities across the country to extend their support and pedagogical resources to the Muslim prison population.

5. *Encourage funding for further research on Islamic programming and recidivism, with a particular focus on the variable of involvement in the Muslim community as the key factor in determining the likelihood of recidivism:* More conclusive evidence that Islamic programming reduces recidivism would promote greater institutional and community support in the prisons. Isolating the connection to the mosque after release as a determinant of successful reentry would offer considerable encouragement for prison outreach by mosques. Further research would also increase public attention to this important issue.

6. *Consider reassessing punitive policies that prevent successful reentry:*
   Many of the laws established for previously incarcerated persons
   to protect the job market and public safety contribute to the high
   rate of recidivism. Without access to safe and affordable housing,
   formerly incarcerated persons are relegated to living in crime-ridden
   homeless shelters. State laws barring ex-inmates from using the skills
   they gained in prison to obtain certain minimum-wage jobs leave
   the ex-offenders few options for gainful employment. Preventing
   ex-offenders from obtaining driver's licenses denies them access
   to many jobs and support programs. Refusal to financial aid blocks
   ex-inmates from receiving the education that could provide them
   with a higher-paying job. The concept of paying one's debt to society
   carries no weight for the prisoner if he knows he will continue to pay
   off his debt indefinitely. Although releasing an inmate with a clean
   slate is not realistic for public safety, these punitive policies provide
   no support for inmate reentry; in fact, as one inmate put it, "they
   punish you for the rest of your life." Policies must enact measurable
   positive change to be considered legitimate, and these castigatory
   restrictions on ex-convicts must be assessed to determine whether
   they create anything positive for a society suffering from the crisis of
   mass incarceration.

Conclusion: Breaking the Cycle

> *A lot of people ask me if I would ever change anything in my life, and I
> always tell them no because it made me the person that I am today.... It
> could have been easily worse if I could have stayed on the street something
> else could have happened, something worse. It was decreed for me to go to
> prison, it was meant for me to go to prison to find Islam.... I'm not saying
> that I want people to go to jail and see the programs, but it's like, basically,
> you've got to see it for yourself.*
>
> —Habeeb Junius, phone interview with the author,
> November 26, 2005

Concern for national security since 9/11 has brought Islamic programming in
our nation's prisons into the public discourse. Historically, Muslim prisoners
broached topics relevant to the struggles of African Americans in gaining civil
rights, and today Islam speaks to the prevalent experience of poverty, drugs,
and crime in the black community. By giving inmates a new self-image that

is in contrast to the role models in urban society, Islam can transform former criminals into knowledge-seeking, patient, responsible, and humble men and women. The pillars of Islam speak directly to the experience of urban poverty and provide an alternative lifestyle predicated on discipline and respect for others. The lack of support for Islamic programming in prison is at odds with Islam's overwhelming rehabilitative success. Concern for national security and the lack of Islamic leadership in the Bureau of Prisons point to a need for correct Islamic knowledge to be present for inmates via Muslim chaplains, contractors, and volunteers. The high rate of recidivism among inmates points to a need for better reentry programming. Muslim chaplains provide reentry assistance by establishing programs that address the challenges of reentry and the importance of involvement in the Muslim community upon release. By providing more structure and support for the considerable Muslim population behind bars, the government and local communities would begin to move toward a more successful corrections system in the United States.

NOTES

1. Federal Bureau of Prisons, "Quick Facts," www.bop.gov/news/quick.jsp, accessed August 21, 2008.

2. Lawrence Mamiya and Ihsan Bagby, "Transitions from Prison to Community: African American Muslims and Programs for Formerly Incarcerated Persons" (unpublished report, Annie E. Casey Foundation, Baltimore, 2004), p. 37.

3. Jeanette M. Hercik, "Prisoner Reentry, Religion and Research" (Washington, DC: U.S. Department of Health and Human Services, 2004), p. 4.

4. Ibid., p. 2.

5. Mamiya and Bagby, "Transitions from Prison to Community," p. 1.

6. Ibid.

7. Ibid., p. 3.

8. U.S. Department of Justice, "A Review of the Federal Bureau of Prisons' Selection of Muslim Religious Service Providers" (Washington, DC: Office of the Inspector General, 2004), p. 8.

9. Aminah B. McCloud, *African American Islam* (New York: Routledge, 1995), p. 124.

10. Felecia Dix-Richardson and Billy R. Close, "Intersections of Race, Religion, and Inmate Culture: The Historical Development of Islam in American Corrections," *Journal of Offender Rehabilitation* 35, nos. 3/4 (2002), pp. 87–107. See p. 94.

11. Ibid.

12. Ibid., p. 89.

13. Kathleen Moore, "Muslims in Prison: Claims to Constitutional Protection of Religious Liberty," in Yvonne Haddad, ed., *The Muslims of America* (New York: Oxford University Press, 1991), p. 137.

14. Mustafa Baker, phone interview with the author, November 26, 2005.

15. Chuck Colson, "Evangelizing Evil in Our Prisons: Radical Islamists Seek to Turn Criminals into Terrorists," *Wall Street Journal*, June 24, 2002, opinionjournal.com/editorial/feature.html?id=110001885, accessed November 12, 2005.

16. Janet Rae-Dupree, "Sermons on the Island: Muslim Chaplain Gives Guidance to All Faiths at Prison," *Los Angeles Times*, December 13, 1991.

17. Jawad Ashraf, phone interview with the author, February 1, 2006.

18. John L. Esposito, "Introduction: Muslims in America or American Muslims?" in Yvonne Yazbeck Haddad and John L. Esposito, ed., *Muslims on the Americanization Path?* (New York: Oxford University Press, 2000), p. 3.

19. Mamiya and Bagby, "Transitions from Prison to Community," p. 3.

20. Ibid., p. 2.

21. Marc Mauer, "The Crisis of the Young African American Male and the Criminal Justice System" (Washington, DC: U.S. Commission on Civil Rights, 1999), p. 3; Jesse McKinnon, "The Black Population in the United States: March 2002" (Washington, DC: U.S. Census Bureau, 2003), p. 1.

22. Mamiya and Bagby, "Transitions from Prison to Community," p. 3.

23. McKinnon, "The Black Population in the United States," pp. 1–2, 6.

24. Mamiya and Bagby, "Transitions from Prison to Community," p. 2.

25. McKinnon, "The Black Population in the United States," p. 6.

26. Citizens United for the Rehabilitation of Errants, "The Prison Boom," users.bestweb.net/~cureny/prisons.htm, accessed December 7, 2005.

27. Saleem Wilder, phone interview with the author, January 10, 2006.

28. Baker, phone interview.

29. Sherman A. Jackson, *Islam and the Blackamerican: Looking toward the Third Resurrection* (New York: Oxford University Press, 2005), p. 44.

30. Wilder, phone interview.

31. Ibid.

32. Mamiya and Bagby, "Transitions from Prison to Community," p. 8.

33. Ishma'il Abdul Aleem, phone interview with the author, December 1, 2005.

34. Rachel Zoll, "Newfound Conviction; Inmate Conversion to Islam Spark Terror Concerns," *Washington Post*, June 5, 2005.

35. U.S. Department of Justice, "A Review of the Federal Bureau of Prisons' Selection of Muslim Religious Service Providers," pp. 7–9.

36. Ibid., p. 8.

37. Marek Fuchs, "After 9/11, Inmates Search for the True Nature of Islam," *New York Times*, September 21, 2002, query.nytimes.com/gst/fullpage.html?res=9504E 0DC1F30F932A1575AC0A9649C8B63&sec=&spon=&partner=permalink&exprod= permalink, accessed December 7, 2005.

38. Salahuddin Muhammad, "Chaplain Responsibilities" (unpublished memorandum, Fishkill Correctional Facility, 2005), p. 14.

39. Ibid.

40. Mumina Kowalski, interview by Saima Malik, n.d., macdonald.hartsem.edu/chaplaincy/profile2.html, accessed November 20, 2005.

41. Yahya Ali, phone interview with the author, November 28, 2005.

42. Mamiya and Bagby, "Transitions from Prison to Community," p. 8.

43. Ali, phone interview.

44. Mamiya and Bagby, "Transitions from Prison to Community," p. 8.

45. Muhammad, "Chaplain Responsibilities," p. 14.

46. Ashraf, phone interview.

47. In Robert Dannin, *Black Pilgrimage to Islam* (New York: Oxford University Press, 2002), p. 166.

48. Mamiya and Bagby, "Transitions from Prison to Community," p. 5.

49. Ali, phone interview.

50. Wilder, phone interview.

51. Ibid.

52. Ashraf, phone interview.

53. Ali, phone interview.

54. Baker, phone interview.

55. Salahuddin Muhammad, phone interview with the author, December 1, 2005.

56. Abdul Aleem, phone interview.

57. Hercik, "Prisoner Reentry, Religion and Research," p. 2.

58. Ibid., p. 3. (Approximately 600,000 in 2000 as compared to 423,800 in 1990.)

59. Mamiya and Bagby, "Transitions from Prison to Community," p. 35.

60. Hercik, "Prisoner Reentry, Religion and Research," p. 5.

61. Daryl Gale, "Islam Inside," June 27–July 3, 2002, www.citypaper.net/articles/2002-06-27/cover.shtml, accessed December 7, 2005.

62. Mamiya and Bagby, "Transitions from Prison to Community," p. 11.

63. Muhammed, "Chaplain Responsibilities," p. 4.

64. Salahuddin Muhammad, author's visit to Fishkill Correctional Facility, November 29, 2005.

65. Wilder, phone interview.

66. Baker, phone interview.

67. U.S. Department of Justice, "A Review of the Federal Bureau of Prisons' Selection of Muslim Religious Service Providers," p. 5.

68. Ibid.

69. Jen'nan Ghazal Read and Mustafa M. Dohadwala, "From the Inside Out: Coming Home from the Prison to the Islamic Faith" (Baltimore: Annie E. Casey Foundation, 2003), p. 13.

70. U.S. Department of Justice, "A Review of the Federal Bureau of Prisons' Selection of Muslim Religious Service Providers," p. 16.

71. Ibid.

72. Mamiya and Bagby, "Transitions from Prison to Community," p. 9; Read and Dohadwala, "From the Inside Out," p. 12.

73. Ashraf, phone interview.

74. Anonymous, interview with the author, December 1, 2005.

75. Mamiya and Bagby, "Transitions from Prison to Community," p. 35.

76. Ibid., p. 36.

77. Aminah McCloud and Frederick Thaurfeer al-Deen *A Question of Faith for Muslim Inmates* (Chicago: ABC International Group, 1999).

78. Mamiya and Bagby, "Transitional from Prison to Community," p. 34.

79. Ibid.

9

"I Didn't Want to Have That Outcast Belief about Alcohol": Muslim Women Encounter Drinking Cultures on Campus

Shabana Mir

When asked by a friend to sign a petition requesting that alcohol be permitted for a college event, Roshan, a Bangladeshi American sophomore, hesitated but assented. She wanted to refuse but felt that alcohol was integral to a "normal" American undergraduate persona, and if she placed herself on the outside of such a persona, she would be perceived as Other: "But I was put in this position where I didn't want to be like, 'No, I don't agree with it, I'm not going to sign it!' And they'd be like, '*Why?* What's your *problem?*' I just didn't want to be put in that position, so I was like, okay, whatever. I signed it. . . . I guess to be honest I didn't want to have that outcast— . . . that really foreign belief about alcohol." It seemed to Roshan that an undergraduate would *naturally* agree with such a petition. Refusal to sign the petition would be perceived as weird, excessively religious, boring, uptight, restrictive, oppressive, and foreign. At the same time, feeling that she was accountable to God to promote what Islam defines as good, she was shaken by her conformity: "See, it was such a minute thing to her, but it was such a huge thing to me. I didn't want to sign the petition because it's like I'm promoting alcohol. And to her, she'd be like, 'What's your problem? It's just alcohol!' . . . But I didn't want conflict or for her to be like, 'Dude, what's wrong with you?'"

Roshan's positioning was due to her fear of conflict, since Muslims are, especially post-9/11, identified as conflict prone. She wished to avoid being associated with disapproval of alcohol consumption and with strong religious opinions on a practice that is the measure of informality in majority American culture. She tried to "pass" as "ordinary" and associated herself with the image of average American youth—easygoing, laid-back, hip, and alcohol friendly—despite her cognitive dissonance. Since a "stigma is something that breaches the norms of day-to-day life," Roshan went about "covering stigma and [avoiding] social breaches" to "pass" as ordinary.[1] She believed her stance should be firmly principled against promoting alcohol but did not have the courage to face the stigma that this would bring upon her.

American Muslim women college students like Roshan live in American Muslim worlds. They are often stereotyped as members of a homogeneous, primarily religious, fanatical, and anti-Western religious community and as shy and withdrawn Muslim women without agency. Their identity work is constrained by Muslims and non-Muslims whose stereotyping they anticipate—correctly or incorrectly—stereotyping that traps them in cages of expectations, assumptions, difference, and fear. At such tender ages, when young people are intent on having fun, discovering themselves, and finding successful career paths, these Muslim women are engaged in identity work that entails multiple personal and collective risks—sometimes still unknown risks—in multiple (minority and majority) cultural fields. I refer to this work, following Homi Bhabha, as the construction of "third spaces."[2]

I conceptualized my research project prior to September 11, 2001. It was after 9/11 that a campaign of harassment and intimidation was let loose upon Muslims in the United States, through intelligence agencies, through physical and psychological attacks, and indirectly, through military campaigns replete with human rights violations of Muslim populations abroad. Hundreds of people were secretly arrested and incarcerated in the 9/11 investigation.[3] But even before these events, I believed that the identity work of American Muslim women was fraught with struggle and contradiction that merited examination.

I felt that American Muslim women students' experiences would help shed light on significant understudied aspects of American education. As members of a religious minority of diverse racial/ethnic composition, American Muslim women through their experiences help us puzzle out the ways in which gender, religion, race, history, and politics collude in the construction of marginality for minority groups in the United States today. I feel that it is important to make their voices heard, in the hope that these voices can articulate some of the gaps in American pluralism as it occurs in educational contexts.

Diversity, Marginality, and Religion on Campus

The ethnographic research for this chapter was conducted between July 2002 and June 2003. I employed a method of participant-observation and conducted open-ended "talking diary" interviews with my participants, American Muslim women of various ethnic backgrounds. I examined American Muslim under- graduate women's identity constructions, focusing on their encounters with dominant youth culture.

University campuses employ a great deal of official rhetoric about diver- sity, and university communities are often described as pluralistic commu- nities. Resources are provided and administrative offices are established to represent student diversity. Generally, even in the rhetoric, however, religion is conspicuously absent, so religious minority students become invisible in campus communities. Where minority students are visible, university officials do not generally formulate policies that are inclusive of their religious and cultural practices and norms. To some degree, university officials and even faculty tend to look the other way in matters such as alcohol consumption and the stereotyping of minority students. Generally, I find that in the experience of American Muslim undergraduate women, campus pluralism is a hollow pluralism. I argue that college campuses are cultures that do not facilitate "healthy" identity work for many minority students. In these cultures, domi- nant constructions are imposed on marginal groups and individuals, obliging them to engage these constructions in their identity work, to comply or resist them.

American Muslim women are not the only students who are marginalized by college cultures. The marginality specific to Muslims can be described by the two terms *Islamophobia* and *Orientalism* together. And as the white Muslim women in my sample demonstrated, Islam racialized identities in ways that members of other religious communities did not experience. Marginality of all kinds is, however, still marginality. And analysis of the marginality experienced by Muslim women, via the everyday rituals of campus life, sheds light on the "cultural center and margins" experienced by other students on campus.[4] But in other ways, their marginality is specific to them and is not experienced by other groups.

With current international and domestic political and cultural trends— including the Bush government's religious rhetoric and domestic and inter- national roles—it has become more important than ever for social scientists to focus on the relationship between (a) religious pluralism as it occurs in educational institutions and (b) religious students' identity construction work.

Ethnographic methods lend themselves best to the study of this relationship because they can bring out multiple, complex, and shifting identities, rather than essentialized notions of "who" communities are.

The Study

Research Sites

Georgetown and George Washington universities are both private universities located in affluent parts of Washington, D.C. These reputable universities have high tuition rates and attract many students from very wealthy to upper-middle-class families. They also have student aid packages, and though I did not probe my participants deeply on financial issues, many of my participants benefited from these packages, and some of them relied entirely on student aid. Both universities are undergraduate focused, as is the way with smaller universities, and had strong party cultures.

Muslim Students Association

The Muslim Students Association of the United States and Canada (also known as MSA National) turned 44 years old in 2007. This organization in turn gave birth to Islamic Society of North America, which became the major mainstream Muslim organization of North America. Its foci are religious growth, da'wah (educating Muslims and non-Muslims about Islam), intracommunity networking through educational programs, conferences, and distribution of materials. MSA National is the main organization, and local MSAs (at individual university campuses) tend to work quite independently. Both Georgetown and George Washington universities have active local MSA chapters which have earned recognition for service, and these organizations figure prominently in my fieldwork.

Alcohol in the Research

In the course of data analysis, it became clear to me that certain common practices and experiences on campus were significant to my participants. They became significant in how the women identified themselves and categorized themselves in reference to Muslim and non-Muslim others. Almost everyone brought up the issue of alcohol consumption, how they felt about it for themselves (whether they drank or not, whether they occupied spaces where alcohol consumption was a dominant activity), and how they felt about others who drank. So I selected alcohol as a salient "vehicle" in the data.

In this chapter, I explore the manner in which nondrinking renders Muslim students "not ordinary" as well as marginal to college culture. I use the consumption of alcohol to illustrate how my young participants walked a tightrope of identity construction during these important years of their lives. The ritual of drinking illustrates how Muslim college students work at being ordinary and normal—like everyone else—at the same time that they see themselves as different from others in terms of race, religion, and so on. They are poignantly aware of being seen as not ordinary and as representatives of a static stereotype. As my participants worked at being different *and* ordinary, they experienced pluralism on campus in ways that many other students did not. I selected alcohol as a key theme because it was mentioned most often as an obstacle in the quest for ordinariness and, as a sign of religiosity, an important indicator of difference.

College and Alcohol

The excessive consumption of alcohol by college students has not been adequately addressed by universities despite the scale of the damage being inflicted by this practice. Nearly half of college students report engaging in binge drinking. Nearly half of the students who abuse alcohol during the school year have five or more serious problems (e.g., missing class, physical injury, conflict with friends, and unprotected sex). Students who engage in excessive drinking are ten times more likely to drive after having consumed alcohol (automobile accidents are the major cause of youth deaths).[5] Over one million students per year are injured due to their own or other students' binge drinking, and almost 1,400 college students die annually due to binge drinking. Half of crime on campus is linked to alcohol, and 74 percent of campus perpetrators of sexual assault and 55 percent of sexual assault victims had been drinking.[6]

Though research on higher education has not taken religious development in students' lives seriously, research indicates that students who are religiously active are less likely to be involved in heavy drinking and other negative behaviors.[7] The image of students at Georgetown and George Washington, as portrayed in campus newspapers and student discourse, matches the normalizing message conveyed by the tour guide in Magolda's article—that students "work hard and play hard," that "normal" students are "interested in dating, . . . [and] prone to consuming alcohol."[8] This college culture represents a problem for many Muslim students because the overwhelming majority of religious opinion in Islam agrees that intoxicants (including beer, wine, and intoxicating drugs) are forbidden to Muslims. As Muslims practice or do not practice in a variety of ways, some drink and others do not.

At college campuses, dominant patterns of youth behavior, such as the consumption of alcohol, are the valued form of social capital. Drinking together at bars and clubs is assumed to be an important social ritual of college leisure life. A student's first legal visit to a bar is an important rite of passage. This ritual (drinking) excludes many Muslim students from the center of college culture—which is off campus. Muslim students are free to forego the evening activities of barhopping or to decline invitations to alcohol-oriented parties, but their refusal to participate relegates them to the margins of college life.

Most of my participants did not drink, though about four of them did and three had stopped recently. All were aware that they were categorized one way or another according to their choices.

Peer Pressure

High school communities in highly structured institutions are considered to be more oriented toward conformity to dominant norms than are colleges. However, some Muslim women felt that college gives students more freedom to experiment with drinking and other activities free from parental monitoring.

A relatively liberal nondrinking Muslim and a sociable Pakistani American freshman, Zareen was frustrated with the college social scene: "I think this is in general [the case] in college: the whole social scene is very much dominated by drinking. . . . But in high school it was very different because I was restricted by my parents from being in this kind of environment so that . . . I was dissociated from it, so it didn't really matter to me. . . . Here, it's like there's no restrictions, you're free to do whatever you want. . . . Like, I *hate* the parties on campus. . . . It's all just about drinking. . . . And especially if you're short, people like, run into you, their stuff is going to spill all over you. . . . I prefer going to clubs and stuff just because—I mean, yes, people are drinking, but people are there to dance." In high school, she said, drinking was a means to conformity for many people. But since Zareen was not allowed to attend drinking parties in school, the environment did not affect her. Freedom and the absence of parental restrictions, glorified in youth culture, can become a negative thing to some Muslim students. In college, Zareen found herself cornered by an inescapably alcohol-dominated social scene, where she could barely walk around in a party without having beer spilled on her. Alcohol, even beer or wine, is a form of impurity to Muslims, and if a certain quantity of alcohol is spilled on one's clothes, offering one's ritual prayers in the same clothes is religiously problematic. A social event that ends up interfering with one's daily prayers symbolically becomes an irreligious exercise. Conflict is therefore set up between one's religious identity and dominant-majority youth culture.

Nondrinkers like Zareen had perspectives on "fun" that were midway between those of their dominant-majority friends and those of their more conservative Muslim peers. Zareen liked nightclubs because the main shared activity was not drinking but dancing. In clubs, drinking was eclipsed in importance by dance.

Yasmin, a Pakistani American sophomore who drank, thought that drinking was part of youth culture promoted by vested interests: "It's pretty dumb what we do for enjoyment, but then everyone keeps telling you it's fun. And then you start believing it's fun. . . . And then you have a story to tell someone: 'I went to the club last night.' 'Oh, was it really fun?' 'Yeah, it was great!' Was it really? No-o. People dancing, you don't even know any of them. It's dark, it's smelly.— . . . College, I don't even know what it is. I feel like maybe it *is* something that's just marketed and packaged to us so we can consume large amounts of alcohol . . . and buy lots of cigarettes and things like that." Despite her alcohol-facilitated insider status, Yasmin perceived bars and clubs as places where college students in particular assume a certain lifestyle and conform to a certain image marketed to them by economic interests. But in Yasmin's analysis, these students generally buy into the image marketed by the media and the alcohol and tobacco industries and thus perpetuate this cultural practice until they leave college. Dominant youth culture in college reproduces the interests of corporate America.

Psychic Duality and the Orientalist Gaze

Many of my participants had a strong sense of being perceived as Muslim Other and observed by the non-Muslim Other. My participants felt that many of their peers associated Muslims with the stereotypes I have summarized in box 9.1. These stereotypes therefore constituted part of the consciousness of Muslim students and emerged from interview data. They were stereotypes that they were fighting, as well as strategically employing, or internalizing, in their own identity work.

Rymes and Pash contend that "a person is not simply 'ordinary' but is always working at achieving this identity."[9] My participants were working overtime at "being ordinary," aware that, as Muslims, they were by default often

BOX 9.1.   Stereotypes about Muslims versus desirable attributes.

Stereotypes	Desirable attributes
Weird	Normal, ordinary
Terrorist, pugnacious	Peaceful, friendly, "mainstream" activist
Boring, uptight	Easygoing, laid-back, fun
Purely religious, one-dimensional	Multidimensional, "interesting," not "just religious"
Restricted, oppressed	Free, independent, exercising choice
Foreign	(Diverse) American
"Extreme"	"Moderate"
Naive	Sophisticated, worldly

assumed to be *not* "ordinary" in white secular Christian-majority American society. The attributes in the right column of box 9.1 are attributes that Muslim women used in their identity work to oppose the stereotypes in the left column. The attributes on the right together make up an "ordinary" campus persona, while those on the left are "not ordinary." At the same time, the attributes on the right are static: many Muslims counter the stereotypes of the dominant majority with *their own* static notions of what Muslims are. They counter the "ahistoric essentialism" of the Orientalist gaze with their own ahistoric essentialism.[10] My participants were poignantly aware of being seen as not ordinary and were working at being ordinary. While they were working against Orientalist assumptions, they were contradictorily employing them as well.

Seen through the lens of alcohol, plurality of choice on campus gives Muslim women the choice to assimilate: dominant-majority peers socially embrace Muslim women by offering them alcohol. Thus Muslims have the choice of dissembling or becoming marginal and different. This happens within peer leisure spaces (bars and nightclubs) as well as academic spaces (department events etc.). Belonging and camaraderie are the prizes (dear to undergraduates) that are at stake here; passing as "ordinary" is key in this struggle. Pluralism therefore comprises a range of possible practices between cultural core (ordinary, white, Christian majority) and periphery (not ordinary, for example, Muslim) in college students' communities of practice. Overall, nondrinking emerges in my participants' perspectives as a strong indicator of religiosity and as a practice on the periphery of campus culture.

In campus leisure spaces, alcohol renders Muslim women either invisible as members of youth culture or hypervisible as Muslims. The necessity of positioning themselves vis-à-vis alcohol highlights their religious identity above other identities, especially in contrast to their peers' religious identities, which, in relative terms, operate in the shadows. At the same time, the inability of many Muslim women students to participate fully in the camaraderie of alcohol communities renders them invisible as friends and peers. Alcohol highlights Muslim difference from the majority norm and veils commonalities between the two.

Heather, a white convert and a senior, belonged to an honors club where she and two other Muslim students were the most active members. At a club meeting, a white non-Muslim board member suggested that the club hold a wine and cheese party for new members, who were freshmen and sophomores (i.e., underage): "And I'm very upset by this. . . . I was like, 'It's a freshman and sophomore honors society.' And she's like, 'Honestly though, I drink, we all drink.' And Razia and Mohamed and I were like, 'Uh-uh! [We don't.]' . . . No, I'm just going to be straight up with her. She doesn't know I'm Muslim, and quite honestly, I can sometimes get away with stuff when I don't say it—you know, when I don't say I'm Muslim, because . . . it can be a broader spectrum. . . . There's so many forums in which students already are marginalized if they're not part of that culture." Heather used her position as a white female on a majority white campus to lend racial and cultural power for a (Muslim) minority concern. Her (minority) opposition to alcohol as a Muslim blended almost completely into a ("culturally mainstream") opposition to underage drinking and concern for the health and social welfare of freshmen. Whiteness empowered her, but being Muslim disempowered her, so she employed her identities strategically. Even as she said she would be "straight up with" the woman, she used the invisibility of her own religious identity to wield her racial and cultural power ("quite honestly, I can sometimes get away with stuff when . . . I don't say I'm Muslim, because . . . it can be a broader spectrum"). Making "particularistic" arguments based on religious reasons was less likely to fly in her peer culture. She made a case based on a liberal concern for the marginalized (non-drinkers) in a hegemonic (drinking) campus culture. Yet Heather resisted the dominance of majority youth culture, even trying to rewrite culture by trying to change leisure norms.

Being white and apparently non-Muslim allowed Heather to "sometimes get away with stuff," whereas being a Muslim—even if one is white—means one can engage in a limited range of practices. As a non-Muslim, however, one can engage in behaviors on "a broader spectrum," as one is not immediately classified as belonging to a narrowly defined, stereotyped group. Instead, one has the advantage of belonging to a complex and uncategorized majority.

Heather framed her argument as a college student, not just as a Muslim: "I know, like, Mormons on this campus, Jews on this campus, Muslims on this campus, Catholics on this campus—who all are incredibly fun, fabulous, and great people but don't choose to drink on the weekends or during the week." Heather was unhappy with the marginalization, in social and certain academic contexts, of college students who chose not to drink. Repeatedly she argued that it was possible to be "a fun person" and to have fun without drinking and clubbing. Within campus culture it appears that being "a fun person" might make a nondrinker acceptable and ordinary. Heather represented herself and her friends as knowing how to have fun and "be cool with everyone." The fact that she did not drink obliged her to prove that she was ordinary and not "weird." She selected "ordinary" attributes such as being cool and fun and rejected drinking.

Zahida, a Pakistani American sophomore, had recently stopped drinking.

ZAHIDA: [I drank at college,] and then it lost its appeal to me in about a month. . . .

SHABANA: So why did you [drink]? . . .

ZAHIDA: . . . [I] just still felt like, all my friends in high school, I was really good friends with them, but there was this certain aspect that I couldn't click with them—just because they weren't from the Middle East, and I couldn't talk to them about certain things, you know?
And they always thought I was so interesting because I used to say all these things they'd never thought about. And I don't know, I just kind of thought I was missing something. . . . I was just so—so tired with everything being how it was; like, me not drinking at every party. I was tired of being the only person. . . . I wanted to be just another girl in high school that lived in [southwestern metropolis]. But especially when I went to boarding school, I realized that I have this total identity behind me that I didn't like, you know, trying to—when I was in the U.S.—keep it away and just focus on school and people I was friends with. . . . Yes, because it's so hard to—you know, especially when you're Muslim and you live with Americans, it's so hard to integrate both things. . . . [Now] I'll talk more about Islam and stuff. And especially here, I argue with people about Islam all the time.

Zahida felt that not drinking prevented her from being ordinary and offered her instead the exotic value of being "interesting." Being "interesting" made her feel alienated, and she felt that she was missing something while in boarding school. She continued to try to find a space for herself in college as well by drinking. When she came to college in Washington, D.C., it became easier for her to discuss matters related to her background. At this time, she stopped drinking and was able to build a third space: she remained comfortably a member of her peer culture, attending clubs and bars, but at the same time publicly acknowledging her background. Her public affiliation (talking about Islam) may have facilitated her decision to stop drinking.

Zareen found it reductive to always be defined by nondrinking and Islam: "[Being identified as 'Muslim' on campus] I think that's kind of like, putting me in a box. I mean, it's not like I don't want to be associated with being Muslim. But it's kind of like looking at any white girl and going, 'She's a Christian.' . . . So at Georgetown there's a lot of drinking . . . so there's a lot of 'Oh! [pause] You don't drink so you must be Muslim.' . . . Oh, 'the Muslim girl who's not drinking,' 'the Muslim girl who hasn't lost all her inhibitions and gone crazy.' . . . And they [friends] *want* you to come because they want you to be there—but I'm like, after some point they won't even remember you're there."

The centrality of alcohol in these parties made Zareen's religious identity hypervisible. Since being Christian is generally not a dominant-majority member's first identity (as another participant said), most of my participants— including the active MSA members—avoided making "Muslim" their first identifier. Aware that white women's religious identities are not primary, Zareen resisted bringing up her religious identity. In alcohol-centered parties, Muslim identity would tend to become simultaneously hypervisible, essentialized, and devalued (because it prevented full participation in the collective activity). Zareen's religious identity also became associated with other characteristics, such as not "being crazy" or not being a big partier. When partying was the central activity, this became another hypervisible characteristic.

Limited Pluralism and the Muslim Peer Group

Muslim women who did not drink said that they disliked occupying spaces such as bars because they felt uncomfortable about the pressure to drink. Roshan described how the MSA drew her into its fold and thereby rescued her from a social life of being a nondrinker always accompanying drinkers to clubs. As a freshman, her only social option—prior to involvement with the MSA crowd—was to socialize in clubs and bars. The alternative was what my participants mentioned as the worst disaster of college life—loneliness:

If [MSA members] didn't welcome—. Because I felt really lonely as a freshman. I would say I was stuck in two boats. Both of my legs [were] on two boats, and I couldn't get on one boat because I was just one thing and I had to agree with that, and I couldn't get on the other boat, but I was struggling not to fall in the river. Because I was stuck here not going out with my friends, and my non-Muslim friends would go out clubbing, they'd be drinking: they would be doing all these things. So I would hang out with them, but I wouldn't do everything they did. So I couldn't go on exactly their road. But at the same time, I was here with Islam, and I knew I shouldn't do those things. . . . But I couldn't go there completely because I felt so lonely.

Roshan vividly described the dilemma of a Muslim freshman who is "with Islam" inwardly, is trying to practice the religion, but is stuck between "the two boats" of complete Islamic practice and complete immersion in typical campus culture. She represented the two as incompatible. Roshan felt that living a typical college life resulted in failure to achieve an Islamic lifestyle and deprived her of camaraderie in her religious life. The social support of friends who used to take Roshan clubbing made their activities (dancing and drinking) tolerable; but she remained uncomfortable due to her inability to conform to all the activities associated with clubbing and due to her religious guilt (for attending bars and clubs). Active MSA members tried to bring students like her into their fold by providing them a protective climate to practice their religion, enabling them to "sail in one boat," as Roshan would put it. This social support helped set up a site of "formalised resistance" to college culture.[11] To Roshan, constructing a third space in terms of not drinking was not tenable within popular peer culture because it placed her in the uncertain space between an Islamic lifestyle and a full, enjoyable leisure life with her non-Muslim friends. Due to lack of integration in the dominant culture, Roshan felt that withdrawal into private spaces of the Muslim peer groups was necessary to commit fully to an Islamic lifestyle as well as to gain companionship.

Heather found herself faced with a choice: to be friends with "everyone" and to be trapped in social situations involving alcohol and sexual activity or to find different friends. This meant a choice between situations where she was ordinary and situations where she was not: "[In high school] I was pretty much friends with everyone in my class. That's the one I wanted to be, the one who knew everyone, who's like, friendly. . . . But . . . to be really knowing everyone and good friends with everyone, and not doing what most of them are doing— drinking, partying, hooking up randomly, etc.—it's sort of a challenge. . . . Friendships are based on commonalities. And you can't, no matter how cool or funny or outgoing you are . . . you can't be all the same friends with—if you're not drinking and partying and dating people like they are, simply because that's what their weekend plans are." Friendliness is, as Moffatt points out, "the central code of etiquette in student culture," and "to act friendly" (smiling, making casual physical contact, making friendly inquiries about the other person's well-being) is extremely important to students' lives.[12] As a Muslim, Heather was to some extent deprived of the status of a friendly person who was "friends with everyone." Even if one practiced important social skills such as being "cool or funny or outgoing," one could not continue to be friends with people whose weekend plans involved drinking simply because drinking/not drinking seemed to create a sharp division between students. Colleges are the scene of a great deal of rhetoric about diversity and the desirability of interracial and interreligious friendships. Most of my participants' closest friends tended to be Muslim. I found that a practical issue was often of far-reaching importance in preventing such friendships: weekend plans. These plans took many Muslim students into different physical spaces than their peers.

An African American convert, Charlise felt that sticking to the Muslim community could help her abstain from alcohol and other forbidden things.

CHARLISE: A lot of Muslim students separate themselves anyway. How many women in hijab do you see that are only with women in hijab? . . . I think a lot of it is, you want to be around people like *you!* . . . To a certain extent I can't really see anything wrong with it, as long as it's not actively excluding others. . . . It just makes it a little bit easier. . . .

SHABANA: What about the fear that if I have close friends who are non-Muslim—?

CHARLISE: In my case it's justified [laugh]. . . . I wasn't always Muslim. I've drunk before; I've been high before; it's a real struggle not to drink and not be high. . . . So I think that it is a valid fear. . . . Friends are influences, especially folks you like, who otherwise are like you in anything but religion. I often wish I lived in a community or a land where—like, I wonder what life would be like in Iraq where the *adhan* [Arabic, the Muslim call to prayer] is called all five times and you just got to do it and not be in the middle of class—that kind of thing . . . [sigh]. Friends are influences, and you definitely have to watch how you let yourself be influenced.

Charlise had a wide range of friends and was involved in a variety of extracurricular activities. She felt torn between religious practice and her friends' influence. I suspect that part of the reason Fatima, an Indian American, for example, felt more comfortable with her Muslim friends was because they shared immigrant cultural heritage. Charlise illustrated that this was probably true, since she had friends with whom she belonged in every respect except religion, and she was therefore wary of their influence.

Haseena, a Pakistani American sophomore, did not drink but loved dancing at clubs and was comfortable in the South Asian student community. Most of her friends were Muslim (though many were less religiously observant) and/or South Asian. The fact that she did not drink was important to her as an indicator of her religiosity, especially because she had a steady boyfriend. She acknowledged that some Muslims would consider her sexual behavior problematic, but she represented her nondrinking as evidence of her observing the "more important boundaries": "I do consider myself religious; I just don't consider myself conservative. . . . I go to parties and stuff, but I don't drink. . . . [T]hat's because I'm religious. . . . But a lot of conservative people wouldn't be at the party to begin with. I know the boundaries and all that, especially the important—the more important boundaries." Clearly, Haseena's "double consciousness" here was connected to her religious community and its perception of her as a young woman who attended drinking parties but who did not drink. I asked her why she did not have many white friends: "I think there's other factors, because I don't find as much in common with them, I think, sometimes? . . . I think it's a lot to do with alcohol really. Alcohol has a lot to do with being white and going out on a weekend here, and so like, if you're not—. . . . I feel like if you're not drugged, you're not having fun." Though Haseena indicated that alcohol was a barrier between her and friendship with white students, heavy drinking among South Asians did not disturb her much. She distinguished the white drinking culture from the South Asian one, which was, she claimed, more accepting of nondrinkers:

> HASEENA: And it's kind of true, South Asian people, they drink a lot! For some reason, with them, I feel like, more like it's okay that I don't drink. Because there's other South Asian friends that don't drink. Whereas it's really hard—. But [South Asians] understand more that you're not drunk, like, why you're not drinking. . . .
>
> SHABANA: If you're in a group of all white friends and they're all drinking, you'd feel weird?
>
> HASEENA: No, but—just not like as if I was joining in. Because—this is actually a really basic thing: but white people when they drink, they just kind of sit around and get drunk even if they're in a party. And the South Asian thing, dancing is a very big part of their social life, but like *they*

dance, and these [white] people don't. So I can just go and dance and have fun, whereas here, everyone just kind of sits around drunk, and that's just not fun!

Clearly, in Haseena's case, as in Zareen's, it was not drinking itself that alienated her but the particular ethnic leisure culture and the extent to which she felt she could belong to it. Drinking (in South Asian clubs) became more acceptable because of South Asians' relative acceptance of nondrinking. For many Muslim students, the ignorance regarding Islam they encounter in dominant-majority circles may be the source of alienation rather than drinking. It may be that for Muslim youth who end up finding camaraderie and cultural belonging in majority contexts, practices such as drinking will not be primary alienating factors. When Fatima, for example, described non-Muslim friendship circles as spaces of marginality for Muslims in a *religious* sense, it may be that she was essentializing Muslims as primarily religious, whereas at least some part of this marginality may be *cultural* difference. However, the key difference between Fatima and Heather, on the one hand, and Haseena and Zareen, on the other, is that the latter two enjoyed dancing in clubs, while the former two did not, so they had nothing to fall back on.

Constructing a Third Space

Some Muslim women construct third spaces for themselves by not drinking but socializing in bars and nightclubs. In doing so, they combine the Islamic discourse of da'wah (since they demonstrate exemplary Muslim practice by declining alcohol), the political discourse of pluralism and diversity, and the immigrant discourses of successful accommodation.

Amira and Haseena did not drink and visited nightclubs: such women felt that Roshan (who had stopped going to bars, clubs and many college parties) had constructed insularity and an unnecessary reification of difference. However, Amira and other participants—who constructed third spaces within dominant-majority spaces instead of occupying Muslim-only spaces—found that their peers still interrogated them for not conforming to stereotypical images of Muslims.

Amira was a member of an academic club where she was perhaps the only religiously observant Muslim woman. Her non-Muslim friends questioned her as to why she did not drink: "I guess at the [club] there's very few Muslim girls in there—or at least practicing Muslim girls. So people always are like, 'You don't *drink?* Oh! But you come to the parties anyway?!'" She constructed her third space, abstaining from alcohol but socializing with her friends in parties where alcohol flowed freely. But her third space became an issue for her non-Muslim friends who interrogated her about why she did *not* isolate herself from the parties: "My friends always joke around; they're like, 'Let's go, Amira, you and me, we'll get drunk!' And it's a joke, a big joke. . . . I'm sure the pressure is there. . . . But I just don't feed into it. I think because I've been in this environment where I'm always the minority but I'm just used to it!" Amira constructed her own agency as far more powerful than the pressure to drink, because she was "used to [being the minority]," as if this enabled her to not feel the pressure to conform anymore. However, her response to offers of alcohol was a careful one. As Heather hinted earlier, the range permitted a Muslim was rather narrow, and Amira was always conscious of her pedagogical role as exemplary cosmopolitan Muslim woman: "I don't act insulted, or [say] 'How dare you!' . . . And it shows to these people who probably have this perception that all Muslim girls cover their heads, all Muslim girls don't talk to people that are not Muslim, all Muslim girls are very intolerant or uncomfortable—it sends a message to these people that you can approach someone like me about it." Amira's representational work was integral to her social life. Both Amira and her peers had the default static Orientalist image of Muslim women, common in American popular culture, as socially withdrawn, intolerant, uptight, and veiled (not ordinary), so she made sure to behave in a comfortable, nonconfrontational manner, demonstrating the viability of Islamic religious practice. Her use of the word *uncomfortable* is illuminating: many of my participants made a strong effort to come across as confident and socially comfortable—self-consciously ordinary—around non-Muslims.

Complex Identities

Yasmin vacillated between drinking and not drinking, and some of her peers questioned why she did not have a fixed position. Though ambivalent about her decision to drink, she did not always feel free to express her ambivalence: "I mean, when people ask me if I drink, I'm always like, 'Um, I don't know.' They're like, 'What do you mean, you don't know?' That's the hardest thing to say." Yasmin was "in two boats," as Roshan would put it, but could not necessarily express this, because the "diversity" embodied in the social scene at college seemed to support black-and-white distinctions of identity, at least for minority groups such as Muslims. Most people could not comprehend shades of identity such as hers in minority personae. Muslim women were interrogated for not drinking but also for not being sure about their practice.

Yasmin considered the possibility of not drinking anymore when she started postgraduate studies in the future. However, even a postgraduate academic circle is not guaranteed to be free of alcohol. As an undergraduate, Yasmin found herself under pressure to drink, not just with students but with professors in a (mostly secular) Arab Studies Department. The effect of this social embrace (the invitation to drink) was hegemonic and homogenizing: "Sometimes I really feel like I'm going to stop. . . . [After college] it depends on what circle I fall into, honestly. Even if I fall into an academic circle, even if it's Muslim studies, plenty of those professors drink. After the [Arab Studies Department] conference, they had all this wine. Everyone was drinking. They're like, 'Why don't you drink? You did so well videotaping!' . . . So I had a glass of wine, because they're like, 'Oh, you deserve it.' . . . And the whole day was a conference about Iraq, and I was like, everything in the world is messed up!" Yasmin experienced the social pressure to drink as a negative thing, and it made her feel disoriented. Political and personal issues combined with her experience to make it feel as if "everything in the world is messed up." She was not entirely free to make choices. The professors tried to pigeonhole Yasmin into a "drinker" category—maybe because she appeared to "fit" (by dress and behavior) in a secular academic context:

YASMIN: [They're] like, "Do you drink?" And I was like [pause], "Y—eah." . . . Because you're on the spot, and you're like, "Do I? Do I not? Have I stopped?" . . .

SHABANA: But [you probably thought]: "You're a professor: can I say no?"

YASMIN: That's so true! . . . "Because . . . I know you drink, and everyone here is drinking." But—

SHABANA: Unless you're . . . used to saying, "I'm on the outside here."

YASMIN: [energetically] "I'm *different!*" [laughter].

She accepted the wine, more willing to conform than to articulate her reservations about drinking and unwilling to come across as a nondrinking Muslim in a secular academic context. Her laughter about broadcasting and flaunting her difference betrayed how difficult it can be to make religious difference public in secular academic spaces—even in a private religious university. For Yasmin, the construction of a third space was a minefield.

Conclusion

When we examine encounters with alcohol as they intersect with Muslim students' religious practice at college, we find that while choices related to alcohol consumption exist, and the rituals of alcohol consumption and drinking stories mark the center of college culture, the choice to not drink is at the margins. In terms of alcohol consumption, leisure culture may be far more powerful in its impact on the cultural production and identity work of college students than the official world of college policies. The rituals of peer culture powerfully define what "ordinary" is, what the campus community is, who belongs to this community, and who is marginal to this community. In this chapter, I show how nondrinking can render Muslim female students "outcast" and Other or marginal to campus culture. My participants—those who drank *and* those who did not—claimed that college leisure spaces were alcohol dominated and that drinking helped one fit in at college. My participants had a strong sense of the gaze of the Other, and the presence of alcohol on campus forced them to engage with their psychic duality in different ways, so that they encountered, resisted, and employed common stereotypes about Muslims and Muslim women.

Muslim women students were "being ordinary" and employing a variety of strategies to do so. Some disguised their religious identity in order to become ordinary enough to rewrite campus culture and fight their marginality. Others concealed their positioning on alcohol; they adopted "ordinary" characteristics (being free agents, fun, cool, etc.) as a counterweight to their lack of ordinariness as nondrinkers. Some drank in order to acquire ordinary status at college and to acquire full camaraderie in college leisure life, whereas others, with different personal circumstances, came to a point where they were able to become differently ordinary. In order to avoid being "weird," Muslim women often sought out Muslim-only spaces. Muslim Students Association spaces provided a site of "formalised resistance" to college culture.[13]

The pluralistic community in theory is an excellent idea, but the community that offers a reduced level of belonging to some of its members is not experienced as truly pluralistic. Muslim students and others are indeed free to refuse to drink—and to forego the relative advantage it offers in becoming part of a community. Many Muslim women are uncomfortable constantly declining drinks as they feel this is a denial of a social embrace, and probably for this reason, many avoid drinking situations altogether.[14] Many of my participants' peers urged them to drink, implying that they would achieve freedom by abandoning their foreign/minority behaviors and adopting dominant-majority behaviors (e.g., drinking). In other words, certain forms of social embrace are often experienced by Muslims as hegemonic.

Though some Muslim women who attend nightclubs and participate in dancing also claim to be "religious," none of the women I interviewed claimed to be religious if she drank. Not drinking was a powerful indicator of religiosity, capable of counterbalancing even having a boyfriend.

To some Muslim women, participation in "cultural" spaces such as South Asian and Arab organization activities is more pleasant, and perhaps more acceptable, than predominantly white nightclubs. This is partly because of the religious and cultural diversity in those cultural spaces and also because of different norms of drinking and dancing.

This also meant that Muslim students were often taken to be members of one of these categories. Religiously observant Muslim students often placed themselves in a (often essentialized) "purely Muslim" category. Some did this to avoid being categorized as, say, secular Arabs or Indians, but some probably also did this because they wished to avoid being identified in ethnic/cultural terms to the non-Muslim majority. Some Muslim students constructed for themselves a culture-free global-identity Islam (culture being immigrant culture).[15]

Some participants constructed third spaces within majority spaces by socializing with friends but declining alcohol. They contrasted their practice favorably with the impiety of Muslims who drank and the isolationism of those who avoided parties and bars. They constructed their strategy as powerful, overcoming dominant norms by disrupting them. They also represented themselves through such practices as "moderate Muslims" and higher-status assimilated cosmopolitans, in contrast with "intolerant" Muslims who do not/cannot socialize comfortably with drinkers.[16] To other Muslims (such as Heather), however, this strategy placed people in an untenable middle space and in uncomfortable and (spiritually and religiously) compromising spaces (e.g., bars).

Muslim women's identity construction incorporates uncertainty and conflict, but such identity construction is inhibited by the limited pluralism on campus. The central importance of alcohol in college culture serves as a vehicle for the limitations of campus pluralism. Peer culture and college spaces do not always permit Muslim women the freedom to construct third spaces; the categories of "drinker/nonobservant Muslim" and "nondrinker/observant Muslim" are easier for peers to understand than "doubtful Muslim/drinker and nondrinker." The dominant gaze seeks a monolithic persona—a persona consistent with popular images of Islam, Muslims, and ethnic persons and a persona whose various practices are seen as harmonious with each other. Minoritized individuals are constantly urged to produce minority personae in forms "digestible" for popular consumption.

American Muslim women college students' encounters with alcohol illustrate for us the limits of campus pluralism. They show us how Muslim students, though free to refuse or accept alcohol, must deal with consequences for these choices, consequences that most non-Muslim students do not face. Muslim women are, through their alcohol-related choices, relegated to the margins of college culture or to the margins of religious practice.

NOTES

This chapter is based on my doctoral dissertation, "Constructing Third Spaces: American Muslim Women's Hybrid Identity Construction." My dissertation examines the ways in which ethnically diverse American Muslim undergraduate women at two private universities in the Washington, D.C., area constructed their identities. I investigate the following questions: (a) What kinds of religious, ethnic, and cultural identities do American Muslim women undergraduates express? (b) What are the ways in which American Muslim women's subjectivities interact with campus climate and get produced in the spaces of higher education? and (c) Is their identity work facilitated and/or inhibited by structural and cultural factors in university contexts? How far, and in what ways, do campuses emerge as authentically pluralistic contexts in the experience of Muslim women undergraduates? In order to investigate these questions, I conducted an ethnography from summer 2002 to summer 2003 (excluding two weeks in August, as well as the months of December and January when I was abroad) at the two university campuses, with formal and informal observations and interviews. My dissertation is based on my analysis of that fieldwork. This chapter is based on part of that dissertation.

1. Betsy Rymes and Diana Pash, "Questioning Identity: The Case of One Second-Language Learner," *Anthropology and Education Quarterly* 32, no. 3 (2001): pp. 276–300 (see p. 279). The authors comment on how Goffman examines the elaborate ways people achieve this goal—covering stigma and passing as ordinary people. See Erving Goffman, *Stigma: Notes on the Management of Spoiled Identity* (Englewood Cliffs, NJ: Prentice Hall, 1993), p. xxi. They also cite Walter Goldschmidt, who says poignantly: "[I]n a measure, we are all passing, and we are all denying" ("Introduction," in Roy B. Edgerton, *The Cloak of Competence* [Berkeley: University of California Press, 1993], pp. i–xxii (see p. xxi).

2. Homi Bhabha, *The Location of Culture* (London: Routledge, 2004).

3. Human Rights Watch, "Human Rights after September 11," 2006, www.hrw.org/campaigns/september11/#Domestic, accessed August 10, 2008.

4. Peter M. Magolda, "The Campus Tour: Ritual and Community in Higher Education," *Anthropology and Education Quarterly* 31, no. 1 (2000): pp. 24–46; see p. 43 for quote.

5. National Commission against Drunk Driving, "Alcohol on Campus," 2005, www.ncadd.com/nyrc_campus.cfm, accessed January 6, 2006; E. R. Weitzman and Toben F. Nelson, "College Student Binge Drinking and the 'Prevention Paradox': Implications for Prevention and Harm Reduction," *Journal of Drug Education* 34, no. 3 (2004): pp. 247–266.

6. Henry Wechsler and Bernice Wuethrich, *Dying to Drink: Confronting Binge Drinking on College Campuses* (Emmaus, PA: Rodale Press, 2002).

7. Leah Temkin and Nancy Evans, "Religion on Campus: Suggestions for Cooperation between Student Affairs and Campus-Based Religious Organizations," *NASPA Journal* 36, no. 1 (fall 1998): pp. 61–69; B. G. Frankel and W. E. Hewitt, "Religion and Well-Being among Canadian University Students: The Role of Faith Groups on Campus," *Journal for the Scientific Study of Religion* 33 (1994): pp. 62–73.

8. Magolda, "The Campus Tour," p. 38.

9. Rymes and Pash, "Questioning Identity," p. 279.

10. Vered Kahani-Hopkins and Nick Hopkins, "'Representing' British Muslims: The Strategic Dimension to Identity Construction," *Ethnic and Racial Studies* 25, no. 2 (March 2002): p. 288.

11. Jasmin Zine, "Redefining Resistance: Towards an Islamic Sub-culture in Schools," *Race, Ethnicity and Education* 3, no. 3 (2000): pp. 293–316.

12. Michael Moffatt, "College Life: Undergraduate Culture and Higher Education," *Journal of Higher Education* 62, no. 1 (January–February 1991): pp. 53–54; see p. 53 for quote. Also see Michael Moffatt, *Coming of Age in New Jersey: College and American Culture* (Rutgers, NJ: Rutgers University Press) for an absorbing account of mainstream college student culture.

13. Zine, "Redefining Resistance," p. 293.

14. The situation would be similar to that of American Muslim women who do not shake hands with men. They are aware that most American men unfamiliar with common Islamic practices may take this as ill-mannered, cold and distant, and/or worse, an extremist expression of "infidel hating." I have observed that the refusal of Muslim men to shake hands with women is often interpreted darkly: their refusal to make friendly social contact with women is perceived as sexist and anti-feminist, as if they regarded women's bodies as an inherently polluting influence. Muslim women, being women—and subject to patriarchy like other women—are not perceived in this way for refusing physical contact, though the gesture is still commonly perceived as alienating.

15. Marcia K. Hermansen, "How to Put the Genie Back in the Bottle: Identity Islam and Muslim Youth Cultures in the United States," in Omid Safi, ed., *Progressive Muslims: On Pluralism, Gender and Justice* (Oxford, UK: Oneworld Publications, 2003), pp. 303–319.

16. Mahmood Mamdani, *Good Muslim, Bad Muslim: America, the Cold War and the Roots of Terror* (New York: Doubleday, 2004).

10

Authentic Interactions: Eliminating the Anonymity of Otherness

Barbara Sahli, Christina Safiya Tobias-Nahi, and Mona Abo-Zena

Thanks to the Internet and satellite TV, the world is being wired together technologically, but not socially, politically, or culturally. We are now seeing and hearing one another faster and better, but with no corresponding improvement in our ability to learn from, or understand, one another....As another writer recently noted in the *NY Times Magazine*, "In some ways, global satellite TV and Internet access have actually made the world a less understanding, less tolerant place."
— Thomas Friedman, *Longitudes and Attitudes: The World in the Age of Terrorism* (2003)

Ironically, in this high-speed global age, the more news we get about the rest of the world, the less we seem to understand one another. Muslims in America, especially post-9/11, know firsthand that instantaneous news access often contributes to the propagation of misinformation, invoking a heightened climate of intolerance. Even prior to 2001, learning about Islam and Muslims required an ability to distinguish myth from reality, and that distinction has become increasingly blurred as media coverage of world events and political discourse continue to link the religion of Islam with terrorism. As the late Edward Said noted, "Malicious generalizations about Islam have become the last acceptable form of denigration of foreign culture in the West; what is said about the Muslim mind, or character, or religion, or culture as a whole cannot now be said in mainstream discussion about Africans, Jews, other Orientals, or Asians."[1]

The current climate of Islamophobia prevails across America and beyond, and two 2006 attitudinal polls with adults confirm that almost half of Americans have a negative perception of Islam.[2] Lack of knowledge about Islam seems to contribute to these negative views; only 2 percent of respondents in a recent Council on American-Islamic Relations (CAIR) survey consider themselves "very knowledgeable" about the religion, while almost 60 percent call themselves "not very knowledgeable" or "not at all knowledgeable" about Islam, not even aware that Muslims worship the same God as Christians and Jews. According to Islamic studies professor Seyyed Hosein Nasr of George Washington University, "[T]oday the paradox of Islamophobia remains that many people that are afraid of Islam know very little about it."[3] Coupled with this lack of accurate knowledge, and perhaps contributing to it, is the significant finding that about 80 percent of respondents in the CAIR survey lack any personal contact with a Muslim.

Similarly, recent children's polls reflect the trend of worsening negative attitudes toward Muslims.[4] It is widely believed that children, lacking accurate knowledge about Islam, get their negative views from the media, the conversations they hear from adults, and the post-9/11 climate of fear about terrorism. Based on their key finding of the necessity to improve education and knowledge of other religions, researchers suggest a need to promote multiculturalism and narrow the chasm between Muslim students and their peers.[5]

Educators play a crucial role in narrowing this chasm, for they are mandated to promote accurate content knowledge while creating safe learning environments for all learners. Furthermore, the National Council for the Social Studies asserts that "knowledge about religions is not only characteristic of an educated person, but is also absolutely necessary for understanding and living in a world of diversity."[6] Yet, while teaching about religion is included in nearly all curricular standards documents, a preliminary policy study suggests that it "may be treated superficially overall, and is likely to be excluded from many areas of social studies where it would be relevant."[7] Particularly at elementary levels, teaching about religion is often confined to information about holidays and customs, with little about beliefs and everyday life.

In today's polarized sociopolitical climate, educators face growing challenges not only in meeting curricular standards about world religions but also in conveying sensitivity toward different belief systems and ways of living. Teachers themselves, who are rarely trained to teach about religion, often lack access to reliable information sources and may feel unqualified to teach about Islam or answer their students' difficult questions.[8] However, because information alone does not necessarily lead to changing attitudes, Muslim voices are needed to link accurate knowledge with greater personal understanding.[9] When teachers provide opportunities for connecting with the "other" through social group contact, students can experience authentic interactions, thereby increasing their understanding of Islam and Muslims and decreasing prejudicial attitudes.

The purpose of this study is to examine school visits that occurred between an Islamic school and two private independent schools and analyze their effects on students and teachers. The hypothesis states that authentic interactions between Muslim and non-Muslim students are vital in promoting both content knowledge and interpersonal understanding, which in combination can have a transformative effect on beliefs and attitudes. It is hoped that with a better understanding of how this process occurs, various effective interaction models can be designed and replicated. In *The Nature of Prejudice*, Gordon Allport states: "Most of the…methods in intercultural education call for active participation on the part of the student. He makes field trips into the neighborhoods where minorities live; he participates in festivals or community projects with them. He develops an acquaintance with minorities and not merely knowledge about them. Most investigators favor the participation method above all others."[10]

Background

For almost ten years, the Islamic Academy of New England (IANE), a full-time Islamic school in Massachusetts, has provided opportunities to bridge the gap separating Muslims and non-Muslims.[11] IANE hosts yearly educational encounters between its Muslim students and visiting students from several private schools, designed to provide the youth with firsthand experience interacting with their peers in an Islamic setting. The visits were originally initiated at the request of the visiting schools. Teachers at these schools were eager to supplement their intensive classroom study of Muslim history and culture with an opportunity for their students to interact with Muslim students, believing that a personal encounter would help their students recognize similarities, appreciate differences, and break down stereotypes. Likewise, IANE administrators and staff were eager to comply with the request. Working in an Islamic institution, they routinely accommodate both individuals and groups wishing to learn more about Islam. Moreover, as educators, they understand the difficult challenges non-Muslim teachers face in conveying a clear picture of Islam and Muslims to their students and are acutely aware of the deep misunderstandings that cloud the subject, often due to lack of contact with Muslims. IANE students do not have the same lack of knowledge and contact with other faiths: they learn about other religions in social studies as well as Islamic studies, which highlights the shared teachings of Judaism, Christianity, and Islam; they encounter people outside their faith in their neighborhoods and in everyday contexts; and they are regularly exposed to contemporary culture through the media. Yet they do lack contact with non-Muslim peers in an educational milieu. The desire to prepare their students for living, learning, and working in a diverse society encouraged IANE staff to offer their students that opportunity for interaction. The enthusiastic response of all participants after the first visit quickly made it clear that this "experiment" would become a treasured tradition.

The field trip is usually scheduled in the spring, as a key component of the visiting students' comprehensive unit of study on Islam. Both hosting students and visitors look forward to their meeting with excited anticipation. Upon their arrival, visitors explore an interactive museum-like display of artifacts brought in from home by the Muslim students. Traditional clothing, prayer rugs, Arabic calligraphy, and household objects are on view to illustrate the diversity and unity of the Muslim world. This display also functions as an icebreaker, for it allows the visiting students to adjust to the unfamiliar surroundings and gives the hosting students an opportunity to share their knowledge and personal stories about the items on display. Students are clearly distinguishable from each other based on their dress: visitors wear a variety of casual clothes, while IANE students are in school uniform; boys wear slacks and white shirts, and girls wear long-sleeved, ankle-length garments with white *hijabs* (head coverings worn by some Muslim females). Any pre-encounter apprehensions are quickly dispelled as students become engaged in the new experience. As one visiting student explains, "I went from awkward → normal" (*female, 7th grade*). Visitors also have their names written on index cards in Arabic by the hosts. Subsequently, students are seated on the floor of the prayer hall, girls on one side and boys on the other, as they listen to a presentation by the *imam* (religious leader) about the beliefs and practices of Islam, followed by an examination of common misconceptions.[12] Visitors are encouraged to ask any lingering questions during a question and answer period that wraps up the morning. Students have an opportunity to converse with each other over a buffet lunch of pizza and assorted ethnic delicacies provided by IANE parents. As the time for prayer approaches, visiting students observe the *wudu* (ritual washing), hear the *adhan* (call to worship), and witness the congregational *salat* (prayer). Weather permitting, there is an outdoor recess period, when students from each school form integrated teams and play impromptu and spirited games of kickball, soccer, or basketball. All too soon, the visit comes to an end, and students say their good-byes. One student recalls her departure, having spent about four hours at the Islamic school: "I felt extremely sad. We all had tearful goodbyes as we exchanged e-mails and gave each other hugs. It were as though we had known each other our whole entire lives and we were just old friends meeting up again" (*female, 10th grade*).

Despite the positive anecdotal feedback from students and staff at all the schools after nearly ten years of field trips, no formal study of the exchanges had ever been undertaken. Lacking baseline data and interested in evaluating the outcome of the visits in light of world events, our research team, comprised of three Muslim women educators, designed a retrospective two-page survey for several cohorts of students, with one version for visiting students and another for hosting students. A set of explorative questions focused around the following issues: In what ways can youth perceptions be changed when authentic interaction with the "other" occurs in a structured educational setting? Can students humanize the "other" and become more critical consumers of the media following such interactions? and Can such interactions create empathy with the "other" and change the dynamics for future cooperative interactions? The sets of questionnaires surveyed middle and high school students who had been involved in the one-day field trip to the Islamic school; a teacher version was also given but will not be fully interpreted at this time.

Methodology

Surveys were administered from late December 2005 through February 2006. The first survey, to Buckingham Browne & Nichols (BB&N; see the appendix), was sent out by the school on a listserv to current 8th through 12th graders (with an option to return it to us directly by e-mail or by postal mail). These students had visited as 6th graders, between the years of 2000 and 2004. The same survey, to Milton Academy (see the appendix), was distributed in school and collected by teachers. The respondents had all visited as 4th graders between the years 2001 and 2005 and ranged from 5th graders, whose experience was still fresh, having just visited the previous year, to 9th graders, who visited in 2001. A different survey was given to Muslim students currently in 6th through 12th grade who had participated one or more times while in 3rd through 8th grade at IANE (see the appendix). These students completed the surveys during class or study hall. In all cases, participation was voluntary, and anonymity was assured as no identifying information was requested beyond gender and grade.

Findings

Results of the survey were analyzed to determine the outcomes of coming face-to-face with the "other" and to explore the academic and social benefits for non-Muslim and Muslim students alike, both short term and long term.

Benefits to Visiting Students

TRANSMISSION OF KEY CURRICULAR KNOWLEDGE. For mainstream school students and teachers, collaboration with Muslims in learning about Islam helps transmit key curricular knowledge related to social studies standards. Encounters with Muslims can also provide the motivation or personal context to engage students, as opposed to mere reliance on materials available in the classroom. Students describe themselves as being "curious," "fascinated," "amazed," "intrigued," "eager to learn," and "enlightened" during the visit. As one student explains, "When I was going I was curious. When I came back, smarter" (*female, 6th grade*). Milton 4th grade teacher Carolyn Damp relies on the visit to emphasize and enhance what she has taught students beforehand. She shares, "I, too have learned a lot and know that I can show the students, first hand, what I have told them in class.... [T]he classroom readings and 'lectures' are not anywhere nearly as powerful or meaningful as first hand experience." In fact, 89 percent of respondents indicate that the visit increased their understanding of what they had learned about the religion in class. Student comments confirm their positive learning experience, citing the value of firsthand experience in reinforcing classroom learning: "We'd learned about the ritual prayers etc., but to hear about the rituals of the religion and to see them in action are two very different things" (*female, 12th grade*). Another student explains how the visit extended his knowledge: "Most of what I learned I didn't already know, but a lot of it built on what I already knew. (I liked that.)" (*male, 5th grade*). With solid academic preparation before the visit, students were ready to forge connections with prior knowledge and enrich their understanding of Islam beyond their classroom readings and discussions.

CLARIFICATION OF MISUNDERSTANDINGS ABOUT ISLAM. Given the significant confusion about the true beliefs and practices of Islam, interaction with Muslims can help clarify misunderstandings about the faith as well as identify other reliable information sources. Sixty percent of respondents confirm that the visit increased their personal understanding of Islam and Muslims, and one student relates: "It was after September 11th, so the visit cleared up some of the misunderstandings I had about some beliefs" (*male, 10th grade*). Coming face-to-face with a group of Muslim peers is a strong antidote to the powerful effect of current events replayed repeatedly through media images. As another student explains: "It allowed me to see Muslim life more closely than before. This was especially important in the modern world where society stereotypes Muslims so strongly" (*male, 9th grade*).

Lacking personal contact with ordinary Muslims, students are more susceptible to accepting stereotypes. One student admits that before the visit, "I was thinking that 'Ali' and 'Akhbar' were just names of characters, but now I've met kids with those names."[13] Another student affirms the power of casual conversation to dismantle stereotypes and highlight similarities.[14] Over lunch, a visiting student asks an IANE student if he and his family often eat at Middle Eastern restaurants. The student's unexpected reply, "I prefer Burger King!" instantly reveals how much these students have in common. The opportunity to interact with Muslim peers in an Islamic setting offers students a view they rarely, if ever, see in person. As Milton teacher Carolyn Damp relates, "Interacting with a Muslim of their own age takes away the mystery of how Muslims live and act. It is a hugely important event. The Milton students can see that a Muslim 10 year old is like a Christian or Jewish 10 year old...not a terrorist and not like what they are reading in the newspapers or seeing on television."

MORE CRITICAL MEDIA CONSUMPTION. Indeed, as non-Muslim students gain accurate knowledge about Islam after having made personal contacts, the students may be better able and more inclined to consume media and public images about Islam critically. Eighty-seven percent of respondents indicate that they were "much more critical" or "somewhat more critical" of media stereotypes following the visit. Confirming this finding, one student reports that he "intentionally avoid[s news] sources that I feel show tilted or ignorant views" (*male, 8th grade*). Another student relates: "One of the most disturbing things I've ever read was a report that a Congressman from Colorado said in a radio interview that he thought if there were another major terrorist attack on the U.S. we should respond by bombing Mecca. That to me demonstrated a great lack of understanding" (*male, 12th grade*). With a clearer picture of Islam, students are better equipped to critically evaluate public statements that may be based on flawed assumptions.

ALLIES IN THE DISSEMINATION OF KNOWLEDGE. Moreover, students and teachers with accurate information about Islam and Muslims can serve as allies who help disseminate their newly acquired knowledge and perspectives to others. Some responses provide evidence that many students needed to share the powerful impact of the visit with others. Entries by several students describe a strong desire to talk about their experience. One student states, "I couldn't wait to tell my parents about my day" (*female, 5th grade*), while another was "breathless going on and on about my day" (*female, 10th grade*). Several parents usually accompany the students on the field trip, and although they did not participate in this survey, feedback confirms the beneficial impact on them as well. One mother describes the visit as a "life-changing event," and another validates the importance of firsthand experience as the key to understanding, noting that the visit has "already made a significant difference for my family. Not only does [my 4th grader] have a better understanding, but also I have a far better one. This will lead our dinnertime discussions to a whole new level!" Parents, as well as students and teachers, can join the circle of allies.

Even long after the actual visit, effects can reverberate over time. Sixty-one percent of the respondents indicate that they have thought back on their visit, demonstrating the long-term implications of the interactions. Students report a variety of circumstances that stimulate their memories: visiting another place of worship such as a Japanese temple or a mosque in France, studying about Islam in medieval history or world religions classes, watching the news or seeing Islamic culture depicted on television, and even the sensory experience of trying a new food. Several responses indicate that sometimes hearing misinformation or pejorative comments about Islam triggers memories of their past visit. One student recalled the visit "when I heard someone being very offensive to Muslims" (*male, 10th grade*), while another reflected on his experience when "talking about issues in the Middle East, I was amazed by many people's misconceptions" (*male, 8th grade*). The firsthand immersion in an Islamic setting, even for only several hours, may be able to counterpoint misinformation that is encountered years later.

INCREASED SENSITIVITY TOWARD MUSLIMS. Thus, the combination of knowledge and personalization may prompt more sensitive thinking and attitudes by the students toward Muslims, fulfilling the social goals of education. Ninety-two percent of respondents state they would feel "very comfortable" encountering a Muslim as a neighbor, classmate, teammate, or coworker. One student retorts: "What is there to be uncomfortable about? Wouldn't it just be like working with anyone else really?" (*female, 11th grade*). Clearly, this response runs counter to widespread public expressions of suspicion, mistrust, and fear toward Muslims and is testimony to the positive attitudes that can stem from authentic interactions.

Many of the benefits to visiting students have indirect benefits to Muslim students, as well. Increasing accurate knowledge and clearing their minds of common misconceptions allow visiting students to become more critical consumers of media images and more sensitive in their feelings toward Muslims. When these altered perspectives are shared with others, Muslim students gain an expanded circle of allies beyond their immediate community.

Benefits to Muslim Students

VALIDATION OF IDENTITY. For Muslim students in mainstream classrooms who participate in the field trip, such educational encounters may validate their religious identity and provide an indirect way for their classmates to learn about their faith. One visiting student self-reports her mixed feelings during the visit: "I was sort of excited that people would know more about Islam, but sort of nervous since I was a Muslim myself and worried that people might say something" (*female, 8th grade*). After witnessing her classmates' positive reaction to the visit, however, she felt "happy and relieved." One teacher confirms that Muslim students in his class also benefit from the classroom study, discussions, and field trip to IANE, finding them to be "affirming."

FULFILLING A RELIGIOUS OBLIGATION. For Muslim students and teachers alike, collaborations with non-Muslims about Islam offer an opportunity to fulfill a religious obligation to clearly convey accurate information about their religion to others. Ninety-seven percent of respondents affirm the importance of hosting non-Muslims at their school, and most (94 percent) also feel it is important for Muslims in America to present Islam to others. Indeed, feeling maligned by the media, a number of IANE students are compelled to personally present a different picture of Islam. One student explains: "[M]any non-Muslims have the wrong picture of Islam and by seeing us behave and act they will see the true meaning of Islam" (*female, 8th grade*). Another student agrees. To counter prevailing stereotypes, he puts the responsibility on the shoulders of individual Muslims by saying: "If people recognize you as Muslim, it should be through your good character" (*male, 11th grade*). These students understand that Islamic beliefs must be linked with action and that the best way to clarify the true meaning of Islam is by reflecting its values in their own behavior.

CLEARING MISCONCEPTIONS ABOUT ISLAM. Responses by IANE students also indicate that authentic interactions provide an important opportunity to clear common misconceptions about Islam and Muslims, especially given the current sociopolitical context. Some students' motivations are personal: "so they'll know that we aren't terrorists" (*male, 9th grade*); "so they won't stare at us all the time" (*female, 7th grade*); so they will feel "more comfortable around a girl in hijab" (*female, 7th grade*). Other students recognize the far-reaching implications of sharing knowledge about their faith. As one student observes, "They learn from us about Islam and they can teach what they learned to others. And it also relieves tension between religions" (*female, 11th grade*). Muslim students express that their participation in interactive school visits could have an effect rippling beyond the visitors, which endows their role with a sense of importance.

In further probing the effects of the visit on Muslim students, one telling response is: "I felt I cleared the Muslim name" (*male, 11th grade*). This student's sense of responsibility to accurately portray his faith in the face of so much misunderstanding reveals the burden that even young Muslims carry. At the same time, many respondents indicate that they enjoyed the opportunity to teach others about Islam and felt "excited" and "happy" during the visit. One visiting student noticed the enthusiasm with which a Muslim student presented her religious practice: "When it was time to wash our hands and feet before prayer, [one girl from IANE] pulled me to the faucet and had me watch her. She was so energetic about sharing her culture with me. I will always remember that" (*female, 12th grade*). Muslim students' genuine desire to share the intricacies of their religion reflects their commitment to their faith and makes a striking impression on visiting students. This results in a sense of accomplishment for the Muslim students and a feeling of engagement for the visitors.

INCREASING CONFIDENCE. Engaging the wider community about the true beliefs of Islam transforms Muslim students from being victims of misinformation by the media to feeling increased confidence in themselves. As one student explains, "[In the media] we are portrayed as not human, we are portrayed as terrorists and nothing more" (*female, 12th grade*). In contrast to this negative portrayal, IANE students note that as a result of the interaction, visiting students gain "a very new perspective on Islam" and leave with "a good feeling about Islam" that will have "a lasting effect." Many students, recognizing the powerful impact on the visitors and the role they play in helping their non-Muslim peers to better understand Islam, come away from the experience feeling good about themselves. A hosting student reports that she "felt like I made a difference and I did something good in my life" (*female, 10th grade*). As another student explains, "[Now they know] we're not some really weird crowd, we're normal human beings like them" (*female, 11th grade*). One IANE student recognizes the connection between how others perceive him and how he feels about himself when he states, "They knew more about Islam; I felt confident" (*male, 11th grade*). In fact, 83 percent of respondents reveal that they are "much more" or "somewhat more" comfortable/confident talking to others about Islam as a result of the visits.

CREATING ACTIVISTS AND ALLIES. The structured experience of projecting their authentic voices to visiting students provides practice in presenting Islam and can activate Muslim students' leadership potential. By taking a proactive position, Muslims can become more empowered. Furthermore, such exchanges may also strengthen their ability to maintain a religious identity in the West while being active participants in the public arena.

The development of activism goes hand in hand with the cultivation of allies. Particularly when clear anti-Islamic sentiment abounds, it is significant when people outside the religion perceive Islamic values as positive and worthwhile, as opposed to parochial or outdated. In a thank-you note, a student writes: "I find it very interesting that [Muslim] women have to dress with a lot of clothing that covers most of your body including your hair. It is the inner beauty that counts. I think that it is real cool that your people respect you for who you are and for the inner beauty. People in America really should respect women for theirs too!" Several visiting students self-report that they left feeling "more respect" for Muslims and their lifestyle. One student reveals she was "surprised at how the Islam[ic] rules weren't as strict as I'd thought" (*female, 5th grade*). Another student realizes that Muslims "didn't seem so strange to me afterwards" (*female, 11th grade*). Through authentic interactions, individuals can gain sufficient accurate information to correct misperceptions, and this change clearly benefits Muslim students as well.

Benefits to Both Groups

HUMANIZING THE "OTHER." A tenet of multicultural scholarship eliminates the anonymity of otherness by enabling students to look through "mirrors" that reflect their own identity and "windows" that reveal the experiences of others, thereby providing "clarification of the known and illumination of the unknown."[15] The more we replace the anonymity of a faceless "other" with humanistic qualities that we are likely to share, the more likely we are to develop and respond with feelings of empathy. One concrete strategy for breaking barriers is to introduce a personal connection by authentic interactions. A personal voice, as opposed to a textbook or other traditional learning material, may convey the same information but may be able to "reach" students in a more direct manner. One visiting student recalls: "Studying it was one thing, but actually getting to experience what we had learned was helpful in my understanding of the culture and religion.... In many ways, it was just as if we had gone to another school of students our age, who although didn't at first appear to be like us, were in fact much like us" (*female, 11th grade*). A common thread running through both Muslim and non-Muslim surveys is the sense that students shared much in common beyond their visible differences. The effect of this momentous discovery is expressed by another visiting student: "I think it was refreshing and new to meet students our age practicing what we had spent so long learning about. It is truly a remarkable experience when you put a human face to seemingly abstract concepts.... This trip humanized Muslims for everyone" (*female, 12th grade*). This recognition was palpable to the Muslim students. In describing how she felt during the visit, one IANE student reveals, "I remember them realizing that we were actual human beings" (*female, 12th grade*). One can imagine the powerful impact on both sides: the enlightenment of suddenly seeing an "other's" humanity and the simultaneous validation and dignity the other feels when being seen not as an "other" but as a fellow human being. In fact, one of the most significant conclusions to be drawn from the survey analysis is the humanizing effect that is attained when students meet face-to-face and interact with each other. This is supported by Allport's statement that "contact must reach below the surface in order to be effective in altering prejudice. Only the type of contact that leads people to *do* things together is likely to result in changed attitudes."[16] One visiting student and another IANE student both self-report the same realization when, to their surprise, they noticed that getting along with the other group of students was actually not at all difficult. An IANE student notes, "It taught me of other religions and how much we have in common, not only religiously, but as normal people" (*female, 8th grade*).

Interactions that promote understanding and transform people or groups from being "others" to being similar fulfill two types of educational goals: they promote an increase in content knowledge and the development of social skills. Furthermore, getting to know an "other" as a unique individual is a tool for preventing the broad generalizations that can lead to stereotypes. Describing the profound and lasting impact that the visit had on her, one student explains: "It was a different experience from anything I had done before. As I grew up, went to summer camp, middle school, and eventually high school, I kept the memories from that visit as a kind of reference in my mind. It wasn't exactly what I learned, but the entire experience of being outside my comfort zone that gave me a new kind of confidence and opened my mind to other people. Muslims weren't such a 'mystery' to me, an 11 year old white student at BB&N, anymore. Now, of course, I know several Muslims and am mature enough to realize that different cultures aren't necessarily 'mysteries,' but at that age [6th grade] I think the experience was essential" (*female, 12th grade*). A number of students report that the visit opened their eyes to people with different backgrounds and beliefs and affected them at an impressionable age when identity development is awakening.

ACTIVATING PERSONAL CONNECTIONS. When multiple perspectives are valued, it allows validation of both the self and others. As educator Emily Style recognizes, "The delightful truth is that sometimes when we hear another out, glancing through the window of their humanity, we can see our own image reflected in the glass of their window. The window becomes a mirror!"[17] The current survey results demonstrate that conversations about religion and efforts to understand others trigger connections to one's own life experience and the societies in which we live. From a visiting student we hear: "In 4th grade, I hadn't thought too deeply about different religions, until I went there [IANE]" (*male, 8th grade*). Annette Raphel, former Lower School principal at Milton Academy, observes this effect on her students following the visit to IANE: "I think they begin to understand the values that are shaping their own lives in a way that they could not if they had nothing to compare them with—after all, our upbringings, if they are the only way we know, do not encourage reflective thought. I also think that this age [4th grade] is a perfect age—children are not constrained by being politically correct which can lead to some insensitivity but also to honest questions and exploration." Similarly, BB&N 6th grade teacher Dean Spencer recognizes that visiting students better understand the Muslims' religious practices by relating the unfamiliar beliefs to their own religious explorations: "Many of our students are preparing for bar or bat mitzvahs or first communion. Their minds are engaged with these issues. In the end, I think they tended to come away from the [IANE] experience with an enhanced appreciation of their own beliefs."[18] One of his students recalls how some of her classmates activated their own religious connections during the visit to IANE: "It was fun because my school has a large Jewish population, and so many of my classmates wrote the names of the students of your school in Hebrew, too [after having their names written in Arabic]" (*female, 11th grade*). Learning how other people, especially those outside the dominant group, experience religion may be an indirect source of support for other religious-minority students and a validation of their own process of religious identity development.

THE POWER OF FRIENDSHIP. Inquiry and human contact seem to stimulate more inquiry and the desire for more contact. In an effort to refine understanding of *how* contact among members of different groups can have a transformative effect on individual members of groups, one researcher, Thomas Pettigrew, notes that intergroup contact will result in improved group relations if there is sufficient friendship potential: "the contact situation must provide the participants with the opportunity to become friends."[19]

Both visiting and Muslim students recognize the friendship potential that characterizes authentic interactions. Many students' remarks clearly reveal that they enjoyed each other's company, got along well together, and had fun interacting with each other. Furthermore, when asked how they felt when it was time to depart, numerous students indicate that they felt sad to leave and wanted to stay longer or come back again. One student announces, "I would take any opportunity to revisit them" (*male, 5th grade*). Nearly one-quarter (24 percent) of all students volunteered the information that they wanted to continue contact. Both educational and social reasons were cited: some students wanted to learn more, others wanted to keep playing, and many just wanted to spend more time together. "I liked being with those kids," a visiting female 5th grader reports. A number of students felt they had made some friends and wanted to get to know each other better. The striking scene at the end of each visit, as students swarm around each other, exchanging e-mail addresses and bittersweet good-byes, does indeed resemble a parting of old friends.

PREPARING FOR A DIVERSE SOCIETY. The resounding reply of 96 percent of respondents from all schools is that it is "very important" to get along with people from diverse backgrounds, beliefs, and cultures, and most recognize realistically that they will need to deal with people from diverse backgrounds in college, in the workplace, and in an increasingly global society. An IANE student realizes, "It's better for us to all be comfortable with each other, because we all live here" (*female, 12th grade*), while a younger visiting student considers the negative domino effect of failing to accept others who are different: "They are people and if we don't get along, we are then enemies—what then? War, discrimination, slavery, torture.... Bad stuff" (*female, 5th grade*). Moreover, many students note that accepting diversity benefits both themselves and others. Another visitor explains: "'Getting along' leads to a greater understanding of each other and inevitably ourselves.... A lack of understanding leaves people sheltered in their little boxes that, although they seem perfectly stable and comfortable, are truly confining and useless. There is much to gain from collective understanding and appreciation and much to lose from intolerance and ignorance" (*female, 12th grade*).

In fact, a fundamental reason that the visiting schools in this study bring their students year after year to the Islamic Academy is to help them learn to appreciate differences rather than fear them. Principal Annette Raphel tells us: "We think that primary experiences help break down stereotypes and that children who fundamentally understand the similarities of other children will have a more open mind to the world as they grow older.... The best way to counter prejudice is through personal relationships and experience." Teacher Dean Spencer agrees. Providing an opportunity for human interaction is the major reason he brings his students to IANE, and he reports decisively, "The primary goal of seeing Muslim students as students much like themselves has been accomplished with almost all children [who have participated over the years]." This result is consistent with the overall approach to diversity at his school, with the goal that students "learn to understand and appreciate that the world includes people who have many different beliefs, experiences, and traditions—all of them with value."

Muslim students report that being in an Islamic school helps prepare them to live in a diverse society because "it teaches me what's right and what's wrong" (*male, 9th grade*), while another student adds, "[W]e learn how to present Islam in a good view and we can keep our values" (*female, 11th grade*). By understanding, strengthening, and internalizing their core religious values, these students feel better equipped to participate in a diverse world while maintaining their own identity. Bolstering their own religious knowledge and practice is a way to relieve the tension of being exposed to conflicting value systems.[20] Moreover, understanding not only one's own value system but also those of others reflects the multiple perspectives that coexist in a pluralistic society. In a study of racial and ethnic diversity and educational outcomes, the Civil Rights Project at Harvard University finds, "One basic theory concerning the educational impact of diversity is that interaction with peers from diverse…backgrounds—both in the classroom and informally—has major educational importance, particularly when the interaction is done in positive ways. By exposing students to multiple perspectives, students learn to think more critically and to understand more complex issues."[21] As one visiting teacher remarks, "I always feel encouraged about the world after spending a day with our children interacting with one another."

PROMOTING POSITIVE RELATIONS BETWEEN DOMINANT AND NONDOMINANT GROUPS. In an interdependent society, cooperative efforts between participating parties demonstrate that the product of collaboration is greater than the sum of its parts. In his research relating to community organization and action primarily within the black community, Charles Willie developed a hypothesis describing the interdependence between dominant and subdominant groups. Although his work focuses on black families and school desegregation, it can be applied in a Western setting to the relationship between the Muslim community and the broader society. According to the hypothesis, "an effectively functioning society encourages minority and majority groups to interact as complementary populations with one group doing for the other what the other group cannot do for itself."[22] The interaction between Islamic schools and mainstream schools illustrates the multiple benefits of collaborative partnerships, for the Muslim students and their educators as well as for their mainstream counterparts. For both groups, the interaction promotes personal understanding and positive relations rather than tension. Some of the positive changes include assuaging the individual's fear or misunderstanding of the "other" and potentially informing how the individual interacts with others and consumes media images, ultimately becoming an ally for sharing the newly developed ideas with others. In this way, collaborative partnerships between dominant and nondominant groups allow both groups to assume complementary roles, each completing for the other what it cannot attain independently.

Multicultural education that promotes social justice requires a diverse and vast social network to challenge stereotypes and other negative internalized images. While nondominant groups must strive to portray themselves accurately, it is crucial to build alliances with other groups. In order to correct prevailing stereotypes, it is even more important that other members of the society are willing to receive the "corrected" image, thereby becoming allies with reliable information about Islam that can be shared with others. After gaining knowledge about Islam through authentic interactions, non-Muslim students join the circle of allies of a misunderstood group. Principal Annette Raphel recounts in her teacher survey: "As a result of these personal connections, for example, I believe that our children [at Milton Academy] experienced September 11th differently than many others—their concern for the wellbeing of their country was shared with their very real concern about the prejudice being shown to people who looked [like] they came from the Middle East and some of our families connected with their buddies' families [at IANE] to see how they were doing. Our children also wrote notes to the [Islamic] school and read editorials and news with a more critical eye toward stereotypical judgments. These are important fundamental understandings which have enormous potential to make the world a better place." In fact, in the days following 9/11, a parent of one of the students who had visited the previous spring drove out to IANE to hand deliver a gift and notes from the students. The profound effect of a sincere act of human kindness is reflected in one IANE student's journal entry, which records her grateful reaction to the many expressions of support and concern at that troubling time: "We are so thankful to the people who are coming to our school from different churches and organizations to make us feel safe. They are bringing beautiful flowers every day. I want people to respect each other this way. The Muslims respect every religion. We thank the people who have been giving us these gifts for respecting us, too" (*female, 5th grade*).[23] This vignette illustrates the ripple effect of personal understanding and positive relations that may result from collaboration between dominant and nondominant groups.

Discussion

The findings illustrate that interactive visits have multiple academic and social benefits for all participants, yet as a preliminary study, it has certain limitations. First of all, the respondents were in various grade levels at the time of interaction, some in elementary school and others in middle school; however, data have not been analyzed according to the age of participants, nor was there any comparative analysis done of the different curriculum content covered by the two visiting schools or of differences in teaching style. Second, this is a retrospective study that queries participants from nine months to five years after the interaction; not only are some memories of the event diminished, but also there was no baseline pre-visit questioning of knowledge and attitudes with which to compare and correlate results. Furthermore, while our research demonstrates the effectiveness of a single visit, it is difficult to determine how much of the positive effect is the result of interactive influential factors, such as the tolerant mission of the visiting schools and their comprehensive units on Islam.

Recommendations for Further Research

In considering future collaborations, a number of research areas need further exploration in order to optimize interactions, including the best ages for the visit and how the content of the visit may be modified based on students' age. Program developers should evaluate different interaction designs, including a series of visits or interactions and joint service-learning projects, particularly for diverse school groups that may not have invested as much preparatory efforts as the schools that participated in this research project. Additional research should also explore the optimal method and timing to measure the impact of such visits. Ideally, there may be a series of surveys or evaluations at different time intervals to explore the short- and long-term effects of the interactions on all participants.

This study has also shown that further research is needed on children's attitudes toward Muslims in the American context. As part of this undertaking, it is vitally critical to include an in-depth literature review of children's exposure to media and a pre- and post-visit study correlating television viewing with children's attitudes. However, it remains that parental input is a primary influence in children's attitudes.[24] For this reason, we emphasize the importance of parental involvement in the school contacts, either as participants in the field trip itself or through special programs that introduce religious pluralism, again with authentic voices. Another strong recommendation is that the schools involved continue to collaborate and plan for additional contacts between the grade cohorts to allow a space for friendships to blossom. For example, Milton Academy reciprocates by inviting IANE students to its annual Middle Eastern bazaar, where students can reconnect after their initial encounter. It has been shown that contacts both competitive (such as sports) and cooperative (such as service projects) can be beneficial, as long as the guidelines for the structured activities continue to foster understanding and positive relations as the ultimate goal.[25]

Both Muslim and non-Muslim students report that the interaction made them "feel better" about each other, and to this end it is recommended that further research explore designing replicable models for this process to occur. New research on *allophilia* (favorable attitudes toward out-groups) conducted by Todd Pittinsky of Harvard University may offer suggestions on how to foster positive intergroup relations that extend beyond mere "tolerance," which is only a midpoint between negative prejudice and positive feelings.[26] In addition, social psychologist Elliot Aronson's "jigsaw" technique should be examined in relation to developing classroom programs to support the numerous Muslim students in public schools who may be facing the negative effects of exclusion.[27] We could also look to Richard Lerner et al.'s study on the diminution of hate, which discusses the role of adults, families, schools, and other community institutions in providing opportunities for youth to develop into thriving participants in a just society.[28] Developing joint service projects for Muslim and non-Muslim students could allow an opportunity to cooperate with the "other" in a community effort while also serving the educational goals of developing civic participation and encouraging leadership development. Most importantly, such projects would allow a forum for exploration of the bigger philosophical questions around poverty and other social issues and expose a diversity of views that will benefit youth as they move into college or the workforce. It would be hoped that by continuing to activate personal connections, the ultimate result will be fostering affinities between individuals. These are the true authentic interactions.

Conclusions

If education is the key to combating Islamophobia and improving perceptions of Islam, then it is essential that Muslims and their institutions participate in those educational efforts to narrow the chasm between Muslims and non-Muslims. The present study illustrates the transformative power of collaboration between Muslim school communities and their mainstream counterparts. Such collaborations promote accurate and engaging representations of Islam to help fulfill the curricular requirements of teaching about the religion. On a more human level, the collaborations increase knowledge and facilitate personal interactions that often affect attitudes. The program described in this study could be replicated at other Islamic schools or youth organizations, particularly those interested in promoting their institutions as community resources, training their youth in presenting Islam, and reaching out to the broader community with the ripple effect of positive relations.

Even with the extensive classroom coverage of the subject prior to the visit, the students in this study overwhelmingly report an increase in their understanding as a result of firsthand experience, echoing Allport's theory that accurate information alone is not enough to change attitudes. The key to altering perceptions about Islam is the crucial element of human contact gained by authentic interaction with Muslims. The experience of spending several hours together made a strong impact on visitors and hosts alike. A Muslim student notes, "It was a great learning experience for *all*" (*female, 12th grade*), and at the end of one survey, a visiting student proclaims: "I believe that every child should have the experience that I did!" (*female, 5th grade*). The results of this study suggest that even greater benefits are possible if longer-term interactions have friendship potential. Expanding the authentic interaction opportunity to one that allows repeated contact could benefit not only the participants but also the wider community.

The survey results indicate that those with more knowledge actually do have better opinions of Muslims, and they also seem to support the conclusion reached by Waleed Aly, a member of the Islamic Council of Victoria, that "the only way you can combat this kind of prejudice is on a personal level. It's much harder to hate people when you know someone in that social group."[29] Coming face-to-face with Muslim peers enables visiting students to dismantle stereotypes, recognize commonalities, and not feel threatened by differences. Perhaps a student sums it up best: "Even though the kids at the Muslim School learned and lived under very different circumstances from us, we still all wanted to play kickball after. We found a common ground where kids are kids, regardless of outside factors. It is so important to find this common ground so that we can all live together happily some day, and rather sooner than later" (*female, 12th grade*). If the ultimate goal of education is that students gain a range of academic and social skills in order to be able to navigate and flourish in an increasingly diverse world, then one approach is to "narrow the gap between differing cultures and political traditions so we can share this shrinking planet.

You can't do this on-line. You can't download understanding. You have to upload it, the old-fashioned way—with exchange programs, outreach, diplomacy, real communication, and one-on-one education."[30] Providing opportunities for students to connect with the "other" through authentic interactions is a vital key to that goal.

APPENDIX

The following are shortened mission/vision statements of participating schools as taken from institutional Web sites:

- *The Islamic Academy of New England* provides a fertile environment for the maximum social, emotional, physical and academic development of each child according to the values of Islam and challenges students to reach their maximum human potential. The academy guides the children to lead decent contemporary lives, enrich their families, serve their community, tolerate differences, think critically, promote collaboration and respect others. School activities help the children develop individual talent, self-esteem and leadership characteristics and offer an outlet for demonstrating creativity. The entire school community provides high learning and practice standards preparing the students to live in a complex, technological and multi-cultural society as proud practicing Muslims.
- *Buckingham Browne & Nichols* fosters intellectual curiosity, critical thinking and a deep concern and respect for others. Our educational program, coordinated from Beginners through grade twelve, provides a rigorous core curriculum, taught in flexible and innovative ways. Students acquire the skills and discipline necessary for academic accomplishment and learn to reflect, take risks and to discover. The curriculum is strengthened by our commitment to a comprehensive program in the arts and athletics. In all of our experiences, both those within the school and those which use our urban location, we encourage self-reliance, knowledge of oneself and a capacity for leadership.
- *Milton Academy* cultivates in its students a passion for learning and respect for others. Embracing diversity and the pursuit of excellence, we create a community in which individuals develop competence, confidence, and character. Our active learning environment, in and out of the classroom, develops creative and critical thinkers, unafraid to express their ideas, prepared to seek meaningful lifetime success and to live by our motto, "Dare to be true."

NOTES

1. Edward W. Said, *How the Media and the Experts Determine How We See the Rest of the World* (New York: Vintage Books, 1997), p. xii.

2. A survey on American public opinion about Islam conducted by the Council on American-Islamic Relations (www.cair.com) shows that one-fourth (23–27 percent) of Americans consistently believe stereotypes such as "Muslims value life less than other people" and "The Muslim religion teaches violence and hatred." Results also show that only 6 percent of Americans have a positive first impression of Islam and Muslims and indicate that *education is the key to improving public perceptions of Islam*. A similar poll released in March 2006 by the *Washington Post* and ABC News also finds that one in four Americans "admitted to harboring prejudice toward Muslims." That survey indicates that 46 percent of Americans have a negative view of Islam, a 7 percent jump since the months following the 9/11 terror attacks, and also shows that the number of Americans who believe that Islam promotes violence has more than doubled since 2002. Experts quoted in the *Post*'s report say that negative attitudes about Islam are "fueled in part by political statements and media reports that focus almost solely on the actions of Muslim extremists." Claudia and Deane and Darryl Fears, "Negative Perception of Islam Increasing," www.washingtonpost.com/wpdyn/content/article/2006/03/08/AR2006030802221.html, accessed February 1, 2007.

3. Steven Malik Shelton, "Islamophobia," *American Muslim*, April/May 2005: p. 17.

4. A 2005 study of 1,500 British students aged 13 to 24 demonstrated that overall, the attitudes of 43 percent of participants toward Muslims were worse or much worse since 9/11: "The younger pupils were more likely to exhibit extreme views and Islamophobia than older students" (see Maxine Frith, "Fear and Hatred of Muslims on Increase in Young Generation," www.independent.co.uk/news/uk/this-britain/fear-and-hatred-of-muslims-on-increase-in-young-generation-530799.html, accessed March 20, 2006). Researchers plan to determine if a correlation exists between more knowledge and better opinions of Muslims; see John von Radowitz, "Racism Simmering in British Schools Survey," *Press Association*, April 1, 2005, retrieved from the LexisNexis database. Further, a study released in 2006 of 551 Australian 10- and 11-year-old students indicated that 45 percent of respondents had negative attitudes toward Muslims. More than half of the schoolchildren viewed Muslims as terrorists, and two out of five agreed that Muslims "are unclean." See Chee C. Leung, "Schoolchildren Cast Judgements on Muslims," www.smh.com.au/news/national/schoolchildren-cast-judgements-on-muslims/2006/02/05/1139074109950.html, accessed February 6, 2006.

5. Radowitz, "Racism Simmering in British Schools Survey."

6. National Council for the Social Studies, *A Teacher's Guide to Religion in the Public Schools* (Arlington, VA: First Amendment Center, 1999), p. 2.

7. Susan Douglass in collaboration with the First Amendment Center, *Teaching about Religion in National and State Social Studies Standards* (Nashville, TN: Council on Islamic Education and the First Amendment Center, 2000), p. 21.

8. Bob Brustman, "Training Teachers to Teach about Religion," *Harvard Gazette Archives*, February 16, 2006.

9. Gordon W. Allport, *The Nature of Prejudice* (Reading, MA: Perseus Books, 1979), p. 268. Allport notes that prejudice is "reflected both in *beliefs* and *attitudes*." He writes that it is highly probable that increased knowledge of a minority group would

lead directly to a truer set of beliefs about others but that it does not follow that *attitudes* will change proportionately.

10. Ibid., p. 488.

11. For a comprehensive profile of this school, see Christina Tobias-Nahi and Eliza Garfield, "An Islamic School Responds to September 11," in Sue Books, ed., *Invisible Children in the Society and the Schools* (Mahwah, NJ: Lawrence Erlbaum Associates, 2007), pp. 81–102.

12. Throughout the day, students are separated by gender. Clear explanations are given to visiting students about the reasons for minimizing contact between males and females, linking it to the Islamic principle of modesty, which applies to both genders, without any implications of superiority of one gender over another.

13. Cited in "Sixth Grade Visits New England Islamic Academy," in *BBQNotebook*, June/July 2000: p. 27.

14. Ibid.

15. Emily Style, with Peggy McIntosh, "Curriculum as Window and Mirror," in Emily Style, ed., *Listening for All Voices* (Summit, NJ: Oak Knoll School, 1988), p. 11.

16. Allport, *The Nature of Prejudice*, p. 276.

17. Style, "Curriculum as Window and Mirror," p. 9.

18. Cited in "Sixth Grade Visits New England Islamic Academy," p. 27.

19. Thomas F. Pettigrew, "Intergroup Contact Theory," *Annual Review of Psychology* 49 (February 1998): p. 76.

20. Yvonne Y. Haddad and Adair Lummis, *Islamic Values in the United States: A Comparative Study* (New York: Oxford University Press, 1987), p. 168.

21. *The Impact of Racial and Ethnic Diversity on Educational Outcomes: Cambridge, MA School District* (Cambridge, MA: Civil Rights Project, Harvard University, 2002), p. 3.

22. Charles V. Willie, *Theories of Human Social Action* (New York: General Hall, Inc., 1994), p. 48.

23. Tobias-Nahi and Garfield,, "An Islamic School Responds to September 11," p. 93.

24. Allport, *The Nature of Prejudice*.

25. Ibid., pp. 262–263. Allport discusses the factors of contact affecting outcome such as, but not limited to, frequency, duration, number of participants, status roles, social atmosphere, and encouragement by authority figures significant to the individuals participating in the contact.

26. Ashley Pettus, "The Law of Dissimilars," *Harvard Magazine*, January–February 2006, www.harvardmagazine.com/on-line/010671.html, accessed February 1, 2007.

27. Elliot Aronson, "History of the Jigsaw," www.jigsaw.org/history.htm, accessed February 1, 2007.

28. R. M. Lerner, A. B. Balsano, R. Banik, and S. Naudeau, "The Diminution of Hate through the Promotion of Positive Individual ← → Context Relations," in R. J. Sternberg, ed., *The Psychology of Hate* (Washington, DC: American Psychological Association, 2005), pp. 103–120.

29. Leung, "Schoolchildren Cast Judgements on Muslims."

30. Thomas Friedman, *Longitudes and Attitudes: The World in the Age of Terrorism* (2003), pp. 391–392.

11

The Outlook for Islamic Education in America

Farid Senzai

This volume has explored key issues and debates regarding Islamic education in North America generally and the United States in particular. It has covered a wide range of topics from full-time Islamic schools and homeschooling to Muslims in public schools, universities, and prisons. Contributors have examined conceptual notions of education, including related issues of identity, integration, preserving culture, civic engagement, creating safe havens, and ghettoization.

This initial effort at assessing the education of Muslims in North America has only scratched the surface, and more questions have been raised than answered. There is clearly much more to be done. But this will always be the case when a venture is still in its infancy. Our hope has been to spark the interest of scholars in the fields of anthropology, sociology, political science, religious studies, and other related disciplines. We hope that such studies will add to our understanding of an emerging community and contribute positively to the religious pluralism we all cherish.

Current Research

It is clear that very little statistical information and few reliable baseline data are available about Islamic education generally or Islamic schools more specifically. Consequently there is much confusion about the identity, practices, and governance of schools as well as their impact on the collective identity of the Muslim community in the United States. The primary reason is that there has yet to be a comprehensive national study of full-time Islamic schools in this country that can provide empirical data.

The first significant qualitative study of Islamic schools was conducted in 1989 by the Education Department of the Islamic Society of North America. The findings of that first study were presented at the Islamic Education Symposium in Indianapolis, Indiana, on October 13–15, 1989. This study noted that at the time only 49 full-time Islamic schools were in existence and that none of these had a principal with a degree in educational administration.[1] Since 1991, several new organizations have been established to study Islamic schools in the United States, including the Center for Islamic Education in North America, the Council of Islamic Schools in North America, the Universal Institute of Islamic Education, and the Council on Islamic Education, among others.[2]

A very small number of dissertations and reports have been written addressing Islamic education broadly and Islamic schools more specifically.[3] The recurrent theme is the need for empirical data that can inform researchers and eliminate recurrent questions and duplication of efforts. One of these studies, by Fatma Al-Lawati, entitled "Exploring Gifted Education Programs, Services and Practices in Islamic Schools in the United States," found that schools were not effectively addressing student needs and teacher preparation for gifted students.[4] A second study, "Identity, Acculturation and Adjustment of High School Muslim Students in Islamic Schools in the U.S.A." by Mohammad Adnan Alghorani, found that students in Muslim schools demonstrated high levels of success in fostering Muslim identity but had a low level of acculturation into the larger society, while the reverse was true among those who attended public schools, with high acculturation and low Muslim identity.[5]

Finally, in one of the first comparative studies of Islamic schools in three countries—the United States, the Netherlands, and Belgium—Michael Merry and Geert Driessen situate Islamic schools within the broader context of educational policy and practice.[6] In particular, the authors examine the mechanisms for funding, choice, and control, which for reasons specific to each context—monitoring by either the state or accrediting agencies—pose both challenges and opportunities for Islamic schools.

Mapping the Landscape

The growth of the Muslim community in the United States and its experience have put increasing priority on establishing Islamic schools for Muslim children. This is especially evident in states with significant Muslim settlement such as California, Florida, Illinois, New York, New Jersey, Michigan, and Texas, where new schools are popping up every year.

Some of these schools are small, consisting of one or two rooms in a building. Other schools may be significantly larger, serving hundreds of K–8 students with a community center, gym, and computer and science labs, such as the Granada Islamic School, which is affiliated with the Muslim Community Association in Santa Clara, California.[7] Regardless of size, as noted in the previous chapters, Islamic schools are fulfilling an increasing demand for spiritual education and Islamic learning in this country. While Muslim children are learning about math, science, and biology, they are also taking lessons in morality, Islamic history, and the recitation and interpretation of the Qur'an.

The essays in this volume have highlighted the growing demand for Islamic education generally and full-time schools and homeschooling more specifically. It is estimated that approximately ten new Islamic schools are established every year, and the demand for them continues to be very high.[8] This is quite ironic, considering the fact that many of the immigrant Muslims come from countries that either ban or water down Islamic studies in their own public schools. "The Islamic schools in the U.S. are hardly perfect educational environments, yet they provide what is often missing in other schools," says educator Yahya Emerick: "Mainly, they tend to have smaller teacher-student ratios, more discipline, a spiritual orientation and an environment conducive to learning."[9]

The demand for Islamic schools is increasing so fast that the current institutions struggle as a result of lack of funds and lack of space. For example, as Susan Sachs reported in the *New York Times,* the Al Noor School in Brooklyn has had to turn down some 400 students due to lack of space.[10] The establishment of Islamic schools, she said, can be seen as part of a wider effort to create an American Muslim identity that can counter the negative image of Islam that is often portrayed in the media and reinforced by politicians. Sachs notes that identity is also being molded through national organizations, lobbying groups, voter-registration campaigns, and outreach programs. For Sachs, "[t]he challenge for Islamic educators is to create a spiritual educational experience for young Muslims that is also relevant to their lives in a secular society," and "establishing Islamic schools has been a process of trial and error, ad-libbing and self-discovery."[11]

Most Islamic schools appear not to have formulated a long-term strategic plan but, rather, have evolved through a kind of organic process as the needs of parents grew beyond their small immediate circles. In discussing the legal issues facing Islamic educational institutions, attorney Safaa Zarzour points out that most Islamic schools start out as a "labor of love," in which a few dedicated people provide their children with Islamic education at any cost. These schools have small beginnings with only a few families. Problems and differences are resolved within this tight-knit community. Ultimately, these schools grow larger, requiring a more streamlined structure of governance and operation. Zarzour attempts to present a legal structure for establishing Islamic schools in the country in order to avoid liabilities.[12]

The Key Challenges

According to Hamed Ghazali, the principal of an Islamic school of Greater Kansas City, Islamic schools must go through three stages of development, which he identifies as the challenge stage, the stability stage, and the professional stage.[13] The first stage is wrought with financial challenges and is characterized by attempts to find qualified instructors. Many, but not all, Muslim schools in the United States are currently passing through this initial stage of challenge, which could take years to overcome. Despite these difficulties Muslim parents are satisfied with seeing that their children are learning religious texts and principles that are often forgotten at home. To them, this alone makes the efforts worthwhile. During the second stage, the school stabilizes and school functions improve, including teacher quality and curriculum. However, financial difficulties remain a problem. Ghazali recommends developing four-year plans, certifying teachers, providing professional development for teachers, planning to improve facilities, and hiring an assistant principal. The third and more professional stage is described as a time when salaries are competitive, the offices are well maintained, teacher and student attendance is assured, a nurse is hired with a nursing room, the school has different departments, all labs are complete, and the school has a gym and a physical education teacher, among other things.[14]

In a June 2000 issue of *Islamic Horizons*, Ibrahim B. Syed, a clinical professor of medicine in Louisville, Kentucky, and president of the Islamic Research Foundation International, analyzes the advantages and disadvantages of various school systems, including private, Islamic, and public school systems.[15] In his view many of the problems often associated with public schools including drugs, violence, and sexual abuse exist to a far lesser extent within Islamic schools. Yet he acknowledges that Islamic schools are not without a long list of their own, including smoking, profanity, unqualified teachers, lack of textbooks, lack of female representation, and high costs. The "moral degradation" of American society, says Syed, is manifested in the school system.

Islamic schools are not necessarily immune to these behavioral problems that plague public learning institutions. He cites a list of problems that have been cropping up in Islamic schools, including (1) no *adaab* or Islamic etiquette or behavior, (2) students have girlfriends and boyfriends, (3) smoking, (4) spoken and written profanity, (5) rough behavior, and (6) discipline.[16] In general such behavior is no different from that in the public schools, but because Islamic schools claim to have higher standards of education and spiritual learning they must be held to higher standards.[17] Therefore, these and other behavioral problems should be viewed as the extreme and not the norm in an Islamic environment.

During the early stages of a school it is often difficult to convince Muslim families to enroll their children, yet parents who want their children to receive Islamic education take a major risk by sending them to faith-based schools. Once an Islamic school has established itself and gains a reputation for providing a wholesome and holistic education, the high cost of sending children to these schools becomes prohibitive to many families. The challenges faced by Islamic schools can be seen as falling into five general categories.

Financial Difficulties

Many new religious schools have strong affiliations with local mosques or Islamic community centers. Because such institutions do not receive federal support, budgets are naturally low. Thus, the quality of services provided, in the beginning, will likely not even match the public school system, which receives public funding. As fund-raising becomes more common within the community, competition for limited resources often results in reduced revenue for schools. These financial problems have the tendency to spiral out of control.

Local Resistance

Finding a school location and dealing with local community resistance have become a daunting task in post-9/11 America. Many Muslims are running into fierce opposition when it becomes known that they are trying to establish a mosque or a school in the area. Islamophobia in America has increased since 9/11 despite sustained efforts by Muslims, nationally, regionally, and locally, to build bridges with other local and faith communities.[18] The constant barrage of negative media images portraying violence in the Iraq War, terrorist attempts in Western countries, and the rising and falling threat levels in the United States, as well as high-profile terror cases, have all contributed to create an atmosphere of fear and suspicion toward Muslims.

The anti-Muslim sentiment and ongoing attacks have required the Muslim community to take more time and effort to prepare, raise funds, and plan for future steps so that their efforts are not in vain, as is the case at the Khalil Gibran International Academy, based in Brooklyn, New York.[19] Muslim communities have become frustrated with having to spend years negotiating, planning, and applying for permits to build schools and mosques only to be rejected by neighbors and community leaders.

In the Houston area the Katy Islamic Association met strong opposition to its plans to build a new mosque on an 11-acre site that would include a community center offering after-school activities, housing for senior citizens, a fitness center, and an Islamic school.[20] Knowing Muslims' prohibition against eating pork, Craig Baker, who lives on the edge of the property that the Islamic association wanted to buy, began racing pigs on his land every Friday in an attempt to pressure the Muslims not to buy the land. Baker's efforts drew national attention, even becoming a joke story on the popular satire news show *The Daily Show with Jon Stewart*.[21] While this is an extreme case of anti-Muslim sentiment, other Muslim communities are also facing opposition in town hall and city council meetings when they attempt to purchase land to build mosques, rezone property already held, and establish schools.

Quality of Teachers

Islamic schools continue to be criticized for the poor quality and inadequacy of the teachers. Many Islamic schools cannot afford to hire experienced and accredited teachers due to lack of funds. In some schools, the wives of community activists or sheikhs, many of whom may be immigrants, often end up taking on the role of teacher or administrator—not because they are necessarily capable but because they are dedicated to the cause of providing an Islamic education. Though the intentions are good, more often than not these instructors are not experienced or sufficiently knowledgeable in transmitting information or relating to the problems that face American Muslim students. Immigrant instructors are likely to bring with them cultural norms and values from the home country that may not apply to the United States.

Another problem is the lack of oversight or accountability from a higher authority, which allows school administrations to operate on a needs basis rather than providing a wholesome education. This trend has the unfortunate effect of limiting the quality of education that Muslim students receive at these schools. Thus, the benefit of having smaller class sizes—namely, enhanced quality of education through greater attention and care from teachers—is lost due to the inadequate number of qualified teachers.

The Curriculum

There is much debate in American Muslim communities about how to teach the faith to future generations. One of the first questions that must be answered is whether schools should provide Islamic instruction in a special class or throughout the entire curriculum. Does the "Islamization of knowledge," where everything taught is related back to the Qur'an and Sunnah, make the learning process easier or harder for students? This debate has been ongoing, even in many Islamic countries where Qur'an and Sunnah are taught within the context of a single class while other subjects, such as math and science, are taught separately. Some educators have promoted the Islamization of the curriculum.

According to Freda Shamma, the director at the Foundation for the Advancement and Development of Education and Learning and an expert in Islamic curriculum development, many Islamic schools currently teach Islam in one class for practical and logistical reasons. However, Shamma argues that Islamic schools should integrate Islamic teachings in all subjects taught at schools, from math to biology to history.[22] In other words, Islamic principles and teachings should be infused into the teachers' lesson plans and textbooks. She argues that this will help reinforce religious principles in children's minds. She also writes that students often become bored with one Islamic class because the lessons, stories, and materials are usually repeated year after year. Shamma recommends that schools adopt the curricula developed by the Tarbiyah Project.[23] This project, designed to teach Islamic values and creative approaches to Islamic teaching and learning conceptually, has been a significant effort but is experiencing enormous operational problems with parents and teachers, says its founder, Dawud Tauhidi. This raises further questions as to the availability of adequate textbooks and whether the religious information will overwhelm the subject matter.

Another issue often raised is: What version of Islam is being taught at these institutions? The lack of a template for Islamic education in America means that much of the teaching about Islam comes through improvisation. At times the curriculum is cobbled together from various readily available sources. How can schools guarantee parents as well as critics what kind of Islam will be taught in these schools? Salafi Islam? Shiite or Sunni Islam? How do administrations evaluate teachers' knowledge of Islam? Are teachers required to take tests on the religion? Do they follow an already prepared lesson plan? These questions have posed problems for potential students and their parents.

Occasionally problems arise at Islamic schools that might have been avoided if a specific and approved curriculum were in place. For example, in Canada, the Abrar Islamic school was forced to suspend two of its teachers after students wrote a violent story about martyrdom and killing Jews. The teachers were accused of encouraging and praising the student's "hateful words."[24] At the Masjid As-Saffat in Trenton, New Jersey, the imam began applying strict rules of worship and prayer, in stark contrast to past practice of religious diversity. Last year, the imam closed down the school, alleging that it was not sufficiently Islamic. Many worshippers claimed that he began preaching Salafi ideology. A group of Muslims who disagreed with the imam came together and sued him, calling for his removal from the board and a turning over of all accounting books.[25]

No Guidance or Standards

Many of these Islamic schools, established with low budgets, low quality of education, and low standards, operate with almost no accountability. They function independently from one another with little incentive to improve. Thus, poor policies and procedures are not only repeated but exacerbated with increased demand. The lack of uniform standards of Islamic education leaves schools to independently decide how to teach Islam in a modernized, secular school system. This problem is not unique to North America but is one faced by Muslim societies throughout the world.

The seminal First World Conference on Muslim Education, which met in Mecca in 1977, brought together Muslim scholars and educators from throughout the world, in the hope of creating an educational system based on Islamic principles that at the same time would be accountable to the modernizing needs of contemporary society. "The conference was a landmark in Islamic education, for it was the 'first attempt of its kind to remove the dichotomy of religious and secular education' from the current educational systems of Islamic countries."[26] Despite three decades of efforts since that time, however, educators have yet to come up with an adequate framework or model for teaching Islam. Muslim communities in the United States are only beginning to tackle many of the issues that have been dealt with on the international level.

Recommendations

National Organization

A strong national, umbrella organization should be formed in order to bring together efforts of local Muslim communities. Perhaps current national organizations, such as the Council of Islamic Schools in North America (CISNA), could also be supported and expanded to take on a wider mandate. CISNA, which was established in 1990, marked a new beginning for private Islamic schools in the United States.[27] It provides an accreditation process for Islamic schools and "acts in the capacity of an organizational witness (*shaheed*) of the credibility of the preschool, elementary, and secondary schools by voluntary peer recognition based on accepted and published standards of excellence."[28] But CISNA leaves somewhat ambiguous the exact nature of those standards. Further, this organization does not have the enforcement capability to ensure that the nation's Islamic schools are up to par and remain so year after year.

The more information is exchanged and shared, the more the various communities that are engaged in Islamic education in America will be empowered and hopefully will be able to prevent the same mistakes from being repeated. There must be a strong platform for a national dialogue among Islamic school administrators, teachers, and mosque boards. Such an organization would also serve as a clearinghouse for Islamic school accreditation similar to the Bureau of Jewish Educators for Jewish schools. The organization not only would be given the nominal task of coordinating efforts but would also establish standards of excellence and best practices for schools to follow. In doing so, it could hold annual conferences for school administrators to network and share experiences. As an institute of accreditation, it would be given the enforcement capacity to penalize schools for noncompliance and to offer incentives for exceeding goals and objectives. Ultimately, this organization would provide the necessary oversight and accountability that are currently lacking in our nation's Islamic schools.

Qualified and Accredited Teachers

Better-educated teachers will lead to better-educated students. Islamic schools must hire qualified and adequately trained and accredited teachers to fill teaching vacancies. Schools must maintain high standards and require teachers to meet certain benchmarks of education. This may mean that school administrations would need to readjust their budgets to allow for more competitive salaries to help boost teacher retention, a difficult task given the current financial struggles that burden many Islamic schools.[29]

Also, schools may need to reconsider their policies (if they exist) on hiring non-Muslim teachers. In such cases non-Muslim teachers could teach secular subjects unrelated to Qur'an or Sunnah, with the fundamentals of the faith taught in a separate class by a Muslim. This would widen the pool of available and capable teachers, strengthening the academic capacities of the school.

The American Institute on Islamic Education has worked with the University of California, Irvine, to develop a Teaching Certificate in Islamic Education for Muslim Teachers in Islamic Schools. The aim of this program is to address Islamic education as pedagogy, specifically, the philosophy, principles, and practice of Islamic education from the sources of Qur'an and the Sunnah.[30] This program might well serve as an important template for certifying teachers in Islamic education.

Professional Leadership

As a school develops and advances, it may be necessary to shed the skin of its old leadership. At many schools, administrators do not have the experience or expertise necessary for good management and operation. They tend rather to be leading elders of the community with a determination to provide an Islamic educational environment for their children. If the head of the Islamic school or the school board is performing poorly, this performance inevitably will be reflected in the overall operation of the school, in the curriculum, and in student test scores. When problems accumulate in relation to a school's performance, divisions within the community may begin to arise, making it even more difficult to provide an adequate academic environment. The question for many schools is how to change their foundation leadership, particularly if they are well-intentioned and well-respected members of the community, without causing acrimony and division (*fitna*) within the local community.

Clear Bylaws

Operating within established bylaws can prevent divisions and avoid discord. If a school does not have bylaws, such laws should be developed, reviewed, and updated in coordination with the latest professional standards. These bylaws provide a clear manual on how the school functions, especially financially and operationally. They must allow for the opinions of the stakeholder, (board members, students, and parents) to be heard and their concerns to be aired and addressed.

Long-Term Financial Planning

One of the major challenges faced by private schools, regardless of religious affiliation, is earning the revenue needed to maintain sustainability. Schools must plan ahead for their future. One major source of funding is the school's tuition. High tuitions also prevent many Muslims from placing their children in Islamic schools. Schools must create an appropriate balance between establishing investment opportunities that provide sustained revenue and charging high tuition costs.

Schools also rely on contributions from generous donors. But such revenue is intermittent and cannot be guaranteed from one year to the next. In an effort to save time and money, a school's administration may be left to one or two dedicated—but not necessarily capable—individuals, considering that highly qualified professionals are simply not willing to work for low pay. In such cases the governance of the school remains in a poor state, and administrators end up planning on how to stay financially afloat from year to year rather than planning and implementing long-term growth strategies.

Administrations must set five-year goals for development and growth. This may require hiring outside financial consultants and investment advisers to help the school find creative ways to address financial challenges. Despite the upfront, short-term cost of hiring such consultants, in the long term, such a move may be essential for the sustainability and survival of the school. The long-term benefits make such a move well worth the cost.

Outreach

Muslim communities that want to establish or have already established schools must make efforts to reach out to local non-Muslim and interfaith communities. Building bridges with neighbors will help to set strong foundations for future generations of Muslim leaders and students. For example, there may come a time when an Islamic school may need to present its case for expansion before a local city school board. Having support from other local associations, religious groups, and schools will help to advance the Muslim community's case. Such interaction and support help to educate the greater community about Islam and Muslims—breaking down stereotypes and allaying unfounded fears.

Since 9/11 there have been numerous institutions established to educate about Islam and Muslims, including the One Nation For All project sponsored by multimillionaire George Russell.[31] Though many of these efforts are relatively new and at times reactionary, there are others that have a long proven track record. One of the most notable is the Islamic Networks Group (ING) based in the San Francisco Bay Area. ING is a national educational organization with affiliates and partners in 20 states, Canada, and most recently, the United Kingdom. ING promotes education about Islam and Muslims by delivering thousands of face-to-face presentations in schools, universities, law enforcement agencies, corporations, health care facilities, and community centers.[32] The organization reaches hundreds of groups and tens of thousands of individuals a year at the local as well as national level.

Although many of these organizations are not explicitly religious, they often acknowledge that part of their motivation is religious. The motivations for an organization such as ING and others are to put a positive face on Islam, to counteract negative images of Muslims, and to "reach out" to non-Muslims. In most cases, leaders of these educational organizations articulate their explicit rejection of proselytizing while expressly endorsing the idea that they and their organizations are "representing Islam" and providing a highly visible witness by example to "what Islam is all about."

Future Research

It is clear that there is a pressing need for further research. In-depth case studies would be a worthwhile place to start. A comprehensive empirical study will strengthen the efforts of Muslim educators by providing the essential baseline data required to effectively analyze, plan, and develop policies that will significantly affect future generations of Muslims in America regarding issues of education and the pedagogy of Islamic schools.

Questions to consider for future studies include the following: What is an Islamic school? What are the models existing in the American environment? What are the educational practices employed? How do the various models affect Muslim identity, the Muslim community, and the larger community? It is essential, therefore, to determine *what exists* (beyond one's local school), the effect *what exists* is having, the direction *what exits* is heading, and the potential consequences *what exists* encounters as it moves on its designated course. Of additional interest is to identify and distinguish between schools affiliated with and dependent on mosques and those that remain independent.

In addition, possible research questions include the following:

1. What is the demographic makeup of students attending Islamic schools?
2. What are the actual and preferred professional qualifications for teachers and principals?
3. What kinds of curricula are used in religious and academic instruction?
4. What kinds of services exist for exceptional children (e.g., students with special needs, gifted and talented children)?
5. What kinds of counseling services exist for students?
6. Where do Muslim graduates go (from public schools, private schools, homeschooling, Muslim schools, other)?
7. What are the major challenges facing Islamic schools in America?
8. How competitive are students that graduate from Islamic schools?

Future researchers are encouraged to replicate and expand the preliminary work in this volume. Comparative case studies across religious schools within other communities might also provide helpful insight and suggest ways in which to build on the more established traditions of Christian and Jewish schools. This could also include comparative studies conducted at the middle and high school levels. Longitudinal studies over time will help identify trends and help educators plan for the future and will also help leaders to provide more strategic and tailored educational programs to meet the real needs of Muslim children.

Future researchers also might choose to examine staff development and teacher retention. A review of training offered at university, district, and school levels would provide insight for leaders. Embedded job training might be compared with traditional staff development opportunities. Such a study may stimulate innovative thinking and planning for assisting teachers and other educators.

Conclusion

The United States is one of the most religiously and ethnically diverse countries in the world, with members of religious communities from across the globe having settled and established their roots here. This pluralism has allowed Christians, Jews, Hindus, Sikhs, Buddhists, and others to come and establish their faith communities and religious schools. Muslim Americans are the most recent manifestation of this integrating community.[33]

The mass migration of Muslims in the past three decades and the growth of the indigenous Muslim community in the United States are certain to affect the broader American society. Louay Safi, the executive director of the Islamic Society of North America Leadership Development Center, an organization that attempts to train and develop future Islamic leaders and educators, suggests that if the Islamic school project is to succeed in achieving the goal of graduating well-rounded human beings, the creative energy and financial resources of the community must be channeled to the task. This includes a concerted effort by educators to produce a school curriculum capable of integrating knowledge and consciousness, so that students graduate from Islamic schools with (1) clear awareness of their purpose in life and responsibilities to their family, community, and humanity at large; (2) sharp vision as to what has to be accomplished for the betterment of human life; and (3) methodical thinking and substantive knowledge of the social and natural environments.[34] All indications are that the Muslim community is realizing the gravity of the task and is stepping up to the challenge.

NOTES

1. For the full report, see "In-Depth Study of Full-Time Islamic Schools in North America" (Plainfield, IN: Islamic Society of North America, 1991). To understand the proliferation of full-time schools, see Zakiyyah Muhammad, "A History of Islamic Education in America" and "Islamic Schools in the United States: Perspectives of Identity, Relevance and Governance" (prepared for the Woodrow Wilson Center of International Scholars Symposium on Muslims in the United States, Woodrow Wilson Center, Washington, DC, 1998).

2. For more information on the Center for Islamic Education in North America, visit www.ciena-usa.com (accessed November 15, 2007). For more information on the Council of Islamic Schools in North America, visit www.posttool.com/cisna/ (accessed November 15, 2007). For more information on the Universal Institute of Islamic Education, visit www2.islamicity.com/uiie//default.htm (accessed November 15, 2007). For more information on the Council on Islamic Education, visit www.cie.org (accessed November 15, 2007).

3. Nimat Hafez Barazangi, "Perceptions of the Islamic Belief System: The Muslims in North America" (Ph.D. dissertation, Cornell University, Ithaca, NY, 1988); Freda Shamma, "Designing an Islamic Multi-cultural Social Studies Course of Study" (Ph.D. dissertation, University of Cincinnati, 1980); Omar Mahmoud Ezzeldine, "Factors at Religious Schools that Affect Teacher Retention" (Ph.D. dissertation, University of California, Los Angeles, 2004); Vincent F. Biondo III, "Integration vs. Isolation: The Challenge of Islamic Education in Southern California" (Ph.D. dissertation, University of California, Santa Barbara, 2004); Fatma Al-Lawati, "Exploring Gifted Education Programs, Services and Practices in Islamic Schools in the United States" (Ph.D. dissertation, Utah State University, Logan, 2003); Mohammad Adnan Alghorani, "Identity, Acculturation and Adjustment of High School Muslim Students in Islamic Schools in the U.S.A." (Ph.D. dissertation, University of Texas at Austin, 2003).

4. Al-Lawati, "Exploring Gifted Education Programs, Services and Practices in Islamic Schools in the United States."

5. Alghorani, "Identity, Acculturation and Adjustment of High School Muslim Students in Islamic Schools in the U.S.A."

6. Michael S. Merry and Geert Driessen, "Islamic Schools in Three Western Countries: Policy and Procedure," *Comparative Education* 41, no. 4 (November 2005): pp. 411–432.

7. For more information on the Granada Islamic School, visit www.granadaschool.org (accessed November 17, 2007).

8. Yahya Emerick, "Working in Muslim Schools," www.islamfortoday.com/emerick14.htm, accessed November 8, 2007.

9. Ibid.

10. Susan Sachs, "Muslim Schools in the U.S., a Voice for Identity," *New York Times,* November 10, 1998, p. A1.

11. Ibid.

12. For more detail, visit Safaa Zarzour, "Legal Issues Facing Islamic Education," www.isna.net/Resources/articles/education/Legal-Issues-Facing-Islamic-Education.aspx (accessed August 15, 2008).

13. Hamed Ghazali, "Islamic Schools: Where Are We? And Where Are We Going," *The American Muslim*, April 2000. For more detail, visit www.iberr.org/islschools.htm (accessed November 12, 2007).

14. Ibid.

15. Ibrahim B. Syed, "Education of Muslim Children: Challenges and Opportunities," *Islamic Horizons*, May/June 2000, www.islamfortoday.com/syed07.htm, accessed October 28, 2007. Also see Nimat Hafez Barazangi, "The Education of North American Muslim Parents and Children: Conceptual Changes as a Contribution to Islamization of Education," *American Journal of Islamic Social Sciences* 7, no. 3 (1990): pp. 385–402.

16. For complete lists and further discussion, see Syed, "Education of Muslim Children."

17. Ibid.; Nimat Hafez Barazangi, "Islamic Education in the United States and Canada: Conception and Practice of the Islamic Belief System," in Yvonne Haddad, ed. *The Muslims of America* (New York: Oxford University Press, 1993): pp. 157–176.

18. For statistics on anti-Muslim incidents, see "The Status of Muslim Civil Rights in the United States, 2007" (Washington, DC: Council on Islamic-American Relations, 2007). This report, along with previous reports since 1996, is available at www.cair.com/CivilRights/CivilRightsReports.aspx (accessed November 20, 2007).

19. For further discussion about the Khalil Gibran International Academy, see Julie Bosman, "Plan for Arabic School in Brooklyn Spurs Protests," *New York Times*, May 4, 2007, www.nytimes.com/2007/05/04/nyregion/04school.html?n=Top/Reference/Times, accessed November 8, 2007. The ongoing campaign against the school can be found at www.danielpipes.org/blog/731 (accessed November 10, 2007).

20. Rasha Madkour, "Plans to Build Mosque Sparks Dispute in Houston Suburb," *Associated Press*, December 8, 2006, *New York Sun* Web site, www.nysun.com/article/44815, accessed November 20, 2007.

21. Nick Georgandis, "Baker Rd. Pig Races Go 'Daily,'" *Katy Times Online*, February 8, 2007, http://katytimes.com/articles/2007/02/08/news/01news.txt/, accessed November 23, 2007.

22. For more detail, visit www.4islamicschools.org/admin_curr.htm (accessed October 15, 2007).

23. For more information on the Tarbiyah Project, visit www.tarbiyah.org (accessed November 20, 2007).

24. "Teachers Suspended, Students at an Islamic School Show," *The National*, March 24, 2005.

25. Lisa Miller, "Islam in America," *Newsweek*, July 30, 2007, p. 24.

26. Syed M. Naguib Al-Attas, *Aims and Objectives of Islamic Education* (London: Hodder and Stroughton, 1979), p. v as quoted in Bradley J. Cook, "Islamic Versus Western Conceptions of Education: Reflections of Egypt," *International Review of Education* 45(3/4): p. 342.

27. Merry and Driessen, "Islamic Schools in Three Western Countries."

28. See Council of Islamic Schools in North America, "Private School Accreditation: Its Meaning and Purpose for Islamic Schools in North America," www.posttool.com/cisna/ (accessed on November 12, 2007).

29. For a closer examination of teacher retention in Islamic schools, see Omar Ezzeldine, "Teacher Retention in Religious Schools as Primer for Teacher Retention

in Public Schools," Policy Brief #17 (Clinton, MI: Institute for Social Policy and Understanding, October 2006), www.ispu.org/files/PDFs/untitled-2.pdf, accessed November 22, 2007.

30. Institute for Social Policy and Understanding, "Islamic Education in America," April 6, 2006, www.ispu.us/reports/articledetailpb-11.html, accessed October 21, 2007.

31. For more information on the One Nation For All effort, visit www.onenationforall. org (accessed November 20, 2007).

32. For more information on the Islamic Networks Group, visit www.ing.org (accessed November 20, 2007).

33. Pew Report, "Muslim Americans: Middle Class and Mostly Mainstream" (Washington, DC: Pew Research Center, May 22, 2007).

34. Ibid.

Index